The Antique Buyer's
Handbook

The Antique Buyer's Handbook

Peter Cook

MULBERRY EDITIONS

Published in the United Kingdom 1993 by
Parragon Book Service Ltd Bristol, England

By arrangement with Reed,
a division of William Heinemann Australia Ltd, Australia

© Peter Cook 1993

ISBN 1 85813 059 X

Printed in Hong Kong

Contents

CONTENTS

Ceramics

Introduction

Learning about antiques takes time. This book is planned to help in the learning and to be a useful reference. The four major sections of the book cover glass, silver, ceramics and furniture. In each section, style, material and manufacturing techniques are examined, and people and events that influenced and changed taste are looked at in historical perspective. As you read you will come to understand that many small things affect desirability and value.

The evolution of antiques is international, however, most of those available are of British origin because, prior to the middle of last century, Britain had a middle-upper class population very much larger than that of other countries. It was this class that had the leisure and money to indulge the aesthetics of taste.

Throughout the centuries the style of home furnishings whatever their origin has changed with each generation. One aim of this book is to show how to date antiques within a period of about thirty years. I have therefore tried to avoid defensive, vague terms and show the high period of fashion. For example, fiddle pattern spoons were popular from 1805, although examples exist from 1780. The reader should think of dates as part of a period rather than as isolated years.

The appendix includes a section on valuation, where items sold at auction are shown with prices. Readers might like to put their judgement to the test, since another aim of this book is to help you avoid the pitfalls Oscar Wilde observed in his phrase about 'A man who knows the price of everything and the value of nothing'.

The glossary is a reference to the terms used in the book, and also includes terms which readers may see elsewhere. The glossary words are set in italic the first time they appear in each section of the book. (The small numbers that occur frequently in the text refer to picture numbers.)

Collecting antiques is a delightful hobby, and I trust that this book will help both the beginner and experienced collector to more fully explore its pleasures.

Glass

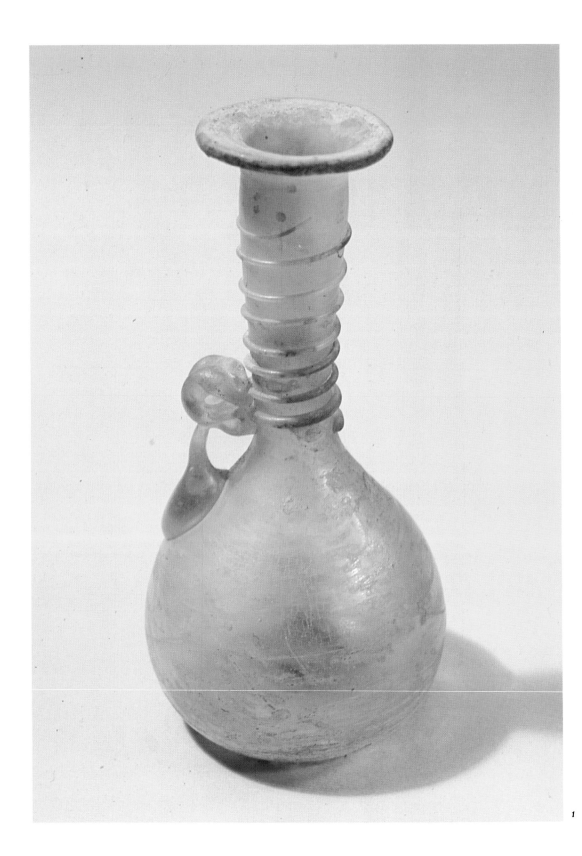

The beginning and Roman glass

Although the Romans introduced glass manufacturing to Europe, glass was first made before 2000 BC in eastern Mediterranean countries.

Glass is made by the high-temperature fusion of silica (such as sand, quartz or flint). There is a story that it was discovered accidentally by sand melting beneath a camp fire. But such a fire would give a temperature of about 600°C, less than half that required to fuse silica. For fusion at lower temperatures an alkali *flux*, either soda or potash, must be added. Soda glass is significantly thinner in body and lighter in weight than potash glass. It also solidifies more slowly, so may be used for trailing decoration and for shaping.

Mediterranean glass-makers used soda as a flux because it was readily available from marine deposits. Glass-makers in Germany (from about 1000 AD) and England (from the end of the 17th century) used potash, which was obtained from wood ash and so was well supplied by the large forests in these countries. France, particularly during the 14th century, produced a potash glass from burnt ferns. Calcium, as limestone or crushed sea shells, was added to increase stability.

From the 3rd millennium BC, beads were the first articles to be made of glass. After about 1500 BC, glass vessels were used and became relatively common in western Asia by 300 BC. The first bottles were formed by trailing molten glass around a clay core, which was removed after the glass had set to leave a hollow bottle. Glass bowls and similar articles were made in moulds. *Cutting* was sometimes used to make vessels or to complete those made by other methods. The art of glass blowing was discovered, probably in Syria, just prior to the Christian era.

From the 1st century AD, the Romans spread glass-making techniques throughout their empire. Glass was more generally used in Roman days than at any time prior to the 19th century. Although different areas produced articles with local characteristics, it is not always possible to discriminate accurately between these various forms of *Roman glass* until the division of the empire in about 400 AD. Glass made after this time is known by its area of manufacture, such as Syrian or *Frankish.*

With the wider spread of Christianity throughout Europe from c. 700, glass vessels were no longer buried with the deceased. For this reason European glass made between 700–1400 is very rare.

1 Small-handled Roman jug with cylindrical neck, 4th century AD. This thin, lightweight soda glass has the iridescence of glass that has been buried. Height 10 cm. (The Grafton Galleries, Sydney)

Italics indicate glossary entry.

9

Islamic glass

After the fall of the Roman empire, glass making in Europe made no further advances until the 11th century, but in the Middle East, particularly in Syria, the industry remained active. The emergence of the Islamic empire in the 7th century led to the development of an Islamic style that varied very little across the empire (2). The leading glass-making centres were Syria, Egypt, Mesopotamia (modern Iraq) and Persia (modern Iran).

Engraved and *cut* decoration was used in the 8th and 9th centuries. Later, the characteristic Islamic glass—decorated (frequently with painted inscriptions) in red, blue and opaque-white *enamels*—appeared during the 13th and 14th centuries.

With the fall of Islam and the sacking of Damascus in 1400, glass making declined. By the second half of the 15th century, the Sultans of Egypt were importing glass from Murano near Venice.

Venetian glass

Venice was a great trading state, a focal point between western Europe and the Middle East. A glass industry began there in the 10th century with the aid of Byzantine and Syrian artisans. Venetian glass soon developed a distinctive character and the industry was flourishing by the 13th century. At the end of that century the glass industry was nationalised and moved to the nearby island of Murano, because the increasing numbers of glass furnaces were a fire hazard to the densely populated city. Also it became easier to prevent artisans leaving the area and passing on glass-making techniques to outsiders—death was the penalty for any Venetian found guilty of breaching security.

Early Venetian glass was thin, lightweight *soda glass*. Initially soda was obtained from burnt seaweed, but later it was imported from Spain and Egypt. *Silica* was available locally from the quartz pebbles of Italian river beds, and calcium was obtained from sea shells or marble.

Since the days of Marco Polo (about 1350) trade had been maintained between China and Venice. The Syrian ports, terminals of this old 'silk road', had an important influence on Venetian glass. The techniques of glass enamelling, which began in Syria in the 13th century, were used to decorate some 15th-century and early 16th-century Venetian glass with bands of white or coloured dots.

Enamelling became less popular in the middle of the 16th century, when the clearer and thinner *cristallo* glass was developed, so named because of its resemblance to *rock crystal*. Glass with green tints from impurities such as iron, was clarified by the addition of manganese as a decoloriser. Clarity, shape and fineness were important.

The technique of *diamond-point engraving* was developed in the mid-16th century. However, it soon became a more popular technique in other glass-making centres, because thin Venetian glass was unsuitable for engraving. The characteristic Venetian decoration, *latticino,* was used from about 1550 until the 18th century. The practice was revived in the mid-19th century. Threads of opaque-white glass, in simple or interlaced patterns, were embedded in clear glass. The term *filigrana* (literally meaning 'thread-grained') could be used for all thread glass, and certainly for glass with coloured threads.

Despite state control from the first half of the 16th century, Venetian glass-makers managed to make their way into other countries. Venetian glass-making techniques thus were spread to northern Europe. Other influences came from artisans of the small Italian glass-making town of L'Altare, near Genoa, who were free to travel throughout Europe.

The style of glass making used in Venice (known as *façon de Venise*) was used elsewhere in Europe during the 17th century. The product was almost indistinguishable from Venetian glass *(3)*. By the end of the 17th century, Venice had diminishing influence in the European economy. Other European glass-houses had been established, and Venetian glass declined in importance.

2 Islamic beaker decorated with coloured enamel. Made in Syria, mid-13th Century. This is the beginning of enamelled glass. Height 15.7 cm. (Victoria and Albert Museum, London)

3 Goblet made in the façon de Venise. This fine clear cristallo glass was developed in Venice in the 16th century, and was soon made in other European countries, particularly the Netherlands. Note the trailed decoration on the stem, which illustrates the more slowly solidifying characteristics of soda glass. (Miss Sheila Knott, Sydney)

The beginning of European glass

During the 16th and 17th centuries the glass industry in Europe was no longer entirely dominated by Venice.

ITALY Glass-houses had been established by the end of the 16th century in most of the large Italian States such as Bologna, Verona and Genoa.

NETHERLANDS From the early 17th century in the Netherlands, glass-makers from Venice and L'Altare had developed a product that was almost indistinguishable from Venetian glass. Prior to this, the local type of *Waldglas* or 'forest glass' was unimportant. The greatest Dutch contributions to glass were engraving and cutting, established during the 17th century and at a peak of quality in the 18th century (*4*).

FRANCE In Roman times, the French artisans had produced fine glass. This was followed by a *potash glass, verre de fougère* ('fern glass'), which was particularly characteristic of the 14th century. However, French glass was relatively unimportant until the 19th century, except for the production of large mirrors in the 17th and 18th centuries.

5

4

SPAIN Like the French, the Spanish had begun glass making in Roman times. Again, little of importance was made during the 16th and 17th centuries. Poor-quality soda glass with enamel decoration was typical of the period up until the mid-18th century. Later that century, some *lead glass* was produced.

RUSSIA Some production began in the mid-17th century with Venetian assistance. During the 18th century lead-glass chandeliers, candelabra, *lustres* and *girondoles* were made in the English style. During the peak years 1775–1825, coloured and cut glass of high quality was made.

GERMANY The German contribution to glass development was important. Frankish glass (about 400–700) was made principally in Belgium and the Rhineland—this was soda glass; from around 1000, German glass was mainly potash glass. During the late Middle Ages there was a distinct German influence on glass in Europe, from the Baltic in the north to the Venetian borders in the south. This was seen in the making of coloured glass for church windows, and of *Waldglas*. Later the Germans produced fine cut, engraved enamelled, and coloured glass.

4 Newcastle glass, c. 1745. This was wheel-engraved in Holland and bears the arms of Amsterdam. (Sothebys, London)

5 German Roemer, late 16th century. The ovoid bowl is decorated with enamel, and the strawberry prunts can be seen on the cylindrical stem. The ring of white enamel dots to the lip is of Venetian inspiration. (The Grafton Galleries, Sydney)

A typical German *Waldglas* drinking vessel was the *Roemer* (5), which was as popular in the 15th century as it is today. This glass had an ovoid bowl (shaped rather like an orange with the top removed) and a hollow spun-glass stem which was decorated with raspberry *prunts* or blobs that provided a grip. The glass was usually a green or brown colour due to impurities, and had a swirly bubbly appearance. *Roemers* were also made in the Netherlands and France.

Enamelled decoration was applied to glass in Germany after the mid-16th century. Wheel-engraving and cutting were developed in Germany from the *rock crystal* industry, which flourished there in the 15th and 16th centuries. This technique was first used for German glass in the early 17th century. A famous glass wheel-engraving school developed in Nuremberg at this time and remained important until the 18th century.

Coloured glass, particularly ruby and blue, was made at Nuremberg and Potsdam during the 17th century. Colour, cutting and enamelling were the three specialities that gave German glass its superiority in the first half of the 19th century.

Towards the end of the 18th century, the Germans were the first to use hydrofluoric acid to *etch* glass.

The beginning of English glass— Verzelini and Ravenscroft

By the time of Henry VIII in 1530, imported Venetian glass was very popular among the European royal families. Apart from *'forest glass'* the first English product was window glass.

Jean Carré, a French immigrant, arrived in 1567 with a team of European glass makers and opened glass houses. He died in 1572 but by 1575 his enterprise was well established under the leadership of one of his artisans, the Venetian Verzelini. Although opposed by local glass importers, who were supposed to have burned the factory down, Verzelini was granted a monopolistic manufacturing patent in 1575 and Venetian imports were banned. By 1590 he was employing about 150 people and drawing licence fees from at least fifteen other manufacturers of *cristallo* glass.

Verzelini based the design of his goblets on earlier silver shapes. Each goblet was made in three pieces: bowl, stem and foot. Sometimes diamond-point engraving was used. The goblets were similar to, but simpler than, those made in Venice at that time *(6)*.

Verzelini retired in 1592 and sold his business to Sir Jerome Bowes, a financier and former ambassador to Russia. The new owner retained the

6

7

6 Wine glass attributed to the Verzelini glass-house. Diamond-engraved and dated 1580. Height 13 cm. (Victoria and Albert Museum, London)

7 English decanter jug (crizzled, c. 1680. Wheel-engraved, probably in the Netherlands. (Victoria and Albert Museum, London)

monopoly for a further twelve years and was granted an additional clause to the patent that gave him exclusive right to import Venetian glass. Bowes was not sufficiently interested in glass manufacture, but more in the sale of glass, so his product deteriorated as skilled artisans left the factory.

By 1624 Venetian imports had been stopped again. A Vice-Admiral, Sir Robert Mansell, held the licence and employed 4000 people in glass factories throughout England, as far apart as London, Newcastle, Stourbridge and Kings Lynn. Mansell was forced out of business in 1649 when Cromwell put a stop to such monopolies.

After the Restoration in 1660, the industry resumed its pre-Cromwellian character: it was controlled by financiers who owned monopolies, and glass manufacturing remained neglected.

In 1664 the Worshipful Company of Glass Sellers was incorporated with a charter to experiment and improve English glass. There was no important result until 1676, when Ravenscroft, almost exactly a hundred years after Verzelini's experiments, produced lead glass.

RAVENSCROFT LEAD GLASS Although small quantities of lead had been added to glass in earlier times, George Ravenscroft first realised its significance late in the 17th century.

8

Ravenscroft was a shipping agent trading with Venice, which may have initiated his interest in glass. He opened his London Savoy Glass House in 1673, when he was 56. His interest was more scientific than commercial, and his early experiments were concerned with the composition of glass and the prevention of 'crizzling' (a series of small surface cracks) (7). In 1674, he used silica in the form of calcined flint imported from Italy, and added refined potash as the alkali flux. This glass still had a crizzled surface which he eradicated in 1676 by the addition of lead oxide. It had a ringing tone, was heavier and had better reflective qualities than Venetian glass. Although lead glass was more suitable for cutting than earlier products, it was not cut in England until 1709. Ravenscroft was rewarded with a three-year patent, given guaranteed sales of his first three years' production, and granted a raven's head seal. He died in 1683 shortly after the expiration of the patent in 1681.

8 English goblet and cover, c. 1690. This clarity, compared with the crizzling of the illustrated decanter jug, was the aim of Ravenscroft's experiments. (Victoria and Albert Museum, London)

Other English glass-makers then began the manufacture of lead glass, in London, Newcastle, Bristol, Stourbridge and other centres. The new technique reached the rest of Europe by 1690.

Cut and engraved glass

Glass may be engraved by several processes, including wheel-engraving. Wheel-cutting has been used since Roman days, and uses the same principle as wheel-engraving: the item is pressed against a rapidly rotating wheel. For engraving, small wheels (often less than 2 centimetres in diameter) are used which are usually made of copper; fifty different wheels may be needed for one design. For cutting and shaping, very much larger wheels of iron or stone are required.

Islamic glass was expertly cut during the 8th and 9th centuries. German artisans also produced fine cut glass in the 17th century, aided by their experience in rock crystal cutting.

WHEEL-ENGRAVING began in England in about 1709 and was well established by about 1740. Popular *rococo* motifs during the mid-18th century were sprays of flowers, and, on ale glasses, hops and barley. Commemorative themes were used for the launching of ships and to mark military or political events. '*Williamite*' glasses were first made in about 1720, and were most popular as '*Jacobite*' glasses in about 1745, a time of hostility between England and Scotland. These glasses were decorated with roses for England and thistles for Scotland.

Formal geometric cutting was fashionable from the middle of the 18th century. Until 1790 a smooth flat cutting known as faceting was used, often only on the stems of wine glasses. In the years 1760 to 1770, faceting was more popular, sometimes being used to decorate the entire surface of decanters.

The style during the period 1790–1810 favoured broad and narrow *flutes* and thumb flutes. In the early 19th century steam-driven machines began to replace the treadle, and cutting was deep and sharp. The original glass thickness was often double that of the finished article.

The period 1810–1825 was characterised by heavy cutting over the entire article. Step-cutting, as illustrated on the Irish decanters (*10*), was typical. Diamonds, rosettes and strawberry-cutting (large diamonds divided into smaller diamonds) were used together with narrow flutes.

During the second quarter of the 19th century there was a return to simple broad flutes. Geometric cutting went out of fashion between 1850 and 1885. However, during the period 1865–1885, Scottish and English glass-houses used wheel-cutting to decorate decanters, drinking glasses and claret jugs with ferns and flowing foliage. From about 1885 there was a return to the earlier

9 Wheel-engraved flashed amber Bohemian decanter, c. 1840. This shows a monkey climbing a vine and is typical of this romantic age. Ruins, stag hunts, waterfalls and forests were favourite decorative themes. (The Grafton Galleries, Sydney)

geometric diamond, and similar cut designs.

DIAMOND-POINT ENGRAVING *(11)* was employed from the middle of the 16th century. The surface was scratched by a splinter of diamond fixed to a holder. Because of the cutting method some designs have a scratched amateurish appearance. Excellent diamond-point engraving was done by Dutch artisans.

STIPPLE ENGRAVING created a finer more accurate effect by using a diamond-point to scratch minute dots rather than lines on a glass surface. By varying the density of the dots, shades of light and dark were produced *(12)*. This technique was prominent in Holland during the 18th century. English glass was usually

10

10 Pair of Irish step-cut decanters, c. 1820. (The Grafton Galleries, Sydney)

11 Diamond-point engraved lead glass bowl, attributed to the London Savoy glass-house of George Ravenscroft, c. 1676. The arms are those of Butler, Buggin and his wife Winifred Burnett, who were married on July 16, 1676. (Victoria and Albert Museum, London)

11

required, because it was more suitable for engraving than the lighter Dutch glass. The best decorators were Frans Greenwood (1680–1761) *(13)*, Aert Schouman (1710–1792) and David Wolff (1732–1798).

ACID-ETCHING originated in Germany with the discovery of hydrofluoric acid, which attacks glass. This technique was discovered by a German chemist, Karl Wilhelm Scheele, in 1771. Most acid-etched glass was made in the 19th and 20th

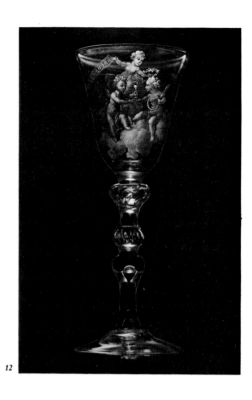

12

12 Stipple-engraved Newcastle glass, by Dutchman David Wolff, c. 1775. Stipple-engraving was such a detailed time-consuming procedure that it was more a labour of love than a commercial proposition. (Geoffrey Wills, Cornwall)

14 Acid-etched decanter, c. 1860. (Geoffrey Wills, Cornwall)

centuries. The glass piece was coated with wax and a steel point was used to draw the design. This exposed the glass only along the lines of the design. The piece was immersed in acid, then washed and the wax coating removed (*14*). Acid-engraving was very popular at the end of the 19th century for classical decorative borders. When used pictorially, as was popular in about 1820, the result was often photographic in appearance.

Acid-etching was also used in the Art Nouveau period by Gallé and others.

Irish glass

Irish glass making had begun before the introduction of lead glass, but only became famous after the Ravenscroft era. Captain Philip Roche opened a glass-house in Dublin in 1690, and manufactured lead glass or flint glass by the Ravenscroft method. Later, in the 18th century, Irish table wares were nearly all of the London style.

The production of late 18th-century Irish glass was boosted by two Acts of the English Parliament. Firstly, in 1777 a new English Excise Act doubled the excise duty payable on all glass produced in England. Secondly, in 1780 Ireland

13

13 Stipple-engraved goblet by Frans Greenwood, signed and dated 1742. Height 28.5 cm. (Geoffrey Wills, Cornwall)

was granted free trade and, accordingly, Irish glass was available both duty-free and excise-free to the English consumer.

During the period 1783–1851 a glass factory flourished in the Irish town of Waterford. This began under an English manager and English methods were used, so that unless Irish glass was marked (which was rare) it could not be distinguished from English glass made in the same period. The Irish produced heavy lead glass that was very suitable for deep cut decoration. Late 18th-century English glass pieces have sometimes been classified as Waterford, because the glass was a greyish colour. However, most English and Irish glass of that period has this discoloration, due to impurities in the glass.

An important glass-house was opened at Cork in the same year (1783) as the Waterford factory, but this closed in 1818. Two other factories operated at Cork until the middle of the 19th century. Belfast and Dublin were also glass-making centres. Although fine Irish glass continues to be made, its main period was 1783–1825.

In 1825 an Irish glass excise act restricted Irish production. Most Irish glass-houses had closed by about 1840, but the Waterford factory continued production until 1851. The Waterford factory was re-opened in 1951, exactly one hundred years after its closure, and is operating today.

Bristol and Nailsea coloured glass

The high quality of clear table glass probably contributed to the small demand for coloured glass in the 18th century. Fine coloured glass was made in Bristol, particularly during the period 1760–1840. Bristol glass was usually blue, but green, amethyst *(15)* and amber glass was also made. Red glass was

17

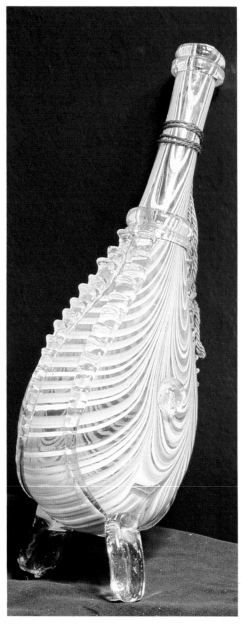

15

very rare until the 19th century. An *opaque white glass* **(16)**, to compete with the new porcelain, was popular in 1760–1800. Blue glass and opaque white glass was painted by the famous decorators James Giles of London and Michael Ekins of Bristol. Bristol was also an important manufacturer of clear flint glass during the 18th century.

Bristol became a major source of blue glass for two reasons: firstly, the cobalt oxide pigment for blue glass was easily imported from Germany into the busy port of Bristol; and secondly, cobalt imports ceased during European wars and a local substitute was available near Bristol.

Popular items were blue decanters with disc stoppers, frequently marked in gilt—Rum, Brandy, Hollands (gin) or Shrub (spirit, fruit juice and sugar). Finger-bowls and *wine-glass coolers* were popular in 1770–1840. The wine-glass cooler had a pouring lip at each end, on which the stem of the up-ended glass rested.

In 1788, Nailsea, which is situated 10 kilometres from Bristol, began to produce cheap coloured-glass novelties that sometimes had streaks or patches of white **(17)**. Bells, walking sticks, pipes or flasks were much in demand during the 19th century, and in fact were made by the Nailsea glass-makers in their free time.

The terms 'Bristol' and 'Nailsea' glass apply to the type of product, not necessarily to the place of origin, as similar wares were made in the other English glass-making towns.

16 Opaque white glass tea caddy, last half of the 18th century. (Museum of Applied Arts and Sciences, Sydney)

15 Set of three amethyst wine bottles, early 19th century. (The Grafton Galleries, Sydney)

17 Nailsea flask in the shape of bellows, showing the characteristic white swirls. Length 31 cm. (Museum of Applied Arts and Sciences, Sydney)

Newcastle glass

The history of Newcastle glass began in 1615 when James I prohibited the use of timber to fire glass furnaces, because it was needed for shipbuilding. The glass-makers had to find coal to fire their furnaces and of the various English deposits, that around Newcastle was most suitable. Two groups of glass-makers developed the industry in Newcastle: the Huguenots and the Italians. By 1725 there were twenty-two Huguenot and ten Italian glass-houses around the city. The major Italian contribution was made between about 1730 and 1785, when the Newcastle light *baluster* drinking glass was developed. Lightweight glass was characteristic of the period after 1745, because in that year a tax on glass-making materials was imposed by weight.

Decanters

Late in the 16th century, *stoneware* decanters were imported from the Rhineland. These vessels allowed wine to be decanted from the cask for service at the table. By 1650 Lambeth delftware decanters were more popular. These were often dated and marked with the name of the wine *(168)*. Dark green bulbous glass bottles were also in use from the middle of the 17th century. The earlier clear-glass decanters made before about 1750 had loose-fitting non-ground stoppers. Very few decanters remain from the period before about 1750.

Clear-glass decanters, with ground stoppers, were first produced in 1750–1760. These were mallet- or club-shaped *(18)* and had a simple but appealing form. During this period, many 'label' decanters *(19, 20)* were made, which were engraved or enamelled with the name of the contents. The most important English glass-enamellers were William Beilby and his sister Mary, who worked in Newcastle between about 1762 and 1774.

18

19

21

18 *Newcastle mallet-shaped decanter, bearing the arms of Newcastle-upon-Tyne in full colour enamel with supporting scroll. Decorated by William Beilby,*

signed and dated 1762. (Victoria and Albert Museum, London)

19 *Newcastle mallet-shaped label decanter, enamelled in white by Beilby, c. 1762-1774. This style had*

a spire or disc stopper. Height 23 cm. (Geoffrey Wills, Cornwall)

20 *Blue mallet-shaped label decanter, gilt decorated, c. 1760-1780. (Sothebys, London)*

In 1760–1770 *faceted* decanters were popular. These tall decanters were heavily cut and had a faceted pinnacle stopper. Simple mallet-shaped decanters with plain disc stoppers *(21, 22)* were in demand during the period 1760–1780. Broader-based and slightly shorter decanters were made at the end of the century (1790 to about 1810), and many were produced in Ireland. These often had two to four rings to the neck, mushroom stoppers and fluted cutting (both narrow and thumb flutes) *(23)*. During the Regency period, more heavily cut decanters *(24)* were popular and in some the neck was extensively cut, including step-cut *(25)*, to form a type of grip that replaced the ring grip.

Between 1825 and 1840 heavy bulbous or straight-sided decanters were used *(24)*. These had broad-cut flutes and angular mushroom-shaped stoppers. Around 1835 taller decanters with spire or pinnacle stoppers *(24 right)* were produced which were used for wine, not for spirits. This was the first major

25 Step-cut decanter, c. 1825. This is extensively cut, with a heavier stopper than those made earlier in the 19th century. (Geoffrey Wills, Cornwall)

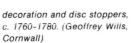

21 Mallet-shaped decanter with a disc stopper, c. 1760–1780. (Geoffrey Wills, Cornwall)

22 Pair of Bristol green mallet-shaped decanters with gilt decoration and disc stoppers, c. 1760–1780. (Geoffrey Wills, Cornwall)

23 Triple-ring decanter with mushroom stopper, c. 1800. This shape of decanter became popular c. 1780. The fine fluted cutting to the bottom of the side was in demand from around 1800. (Arthur Dibley, Sydney)

distinction in style between wine and spirit decanters. In the last half of the 19th century spirit decanters were square *(26 middle left)*, and had large round-cut stoppers. Wine decanters were made with a long neck and a bulbous body, which was sometimes engraved with motifs such as the fern leaf *(26 left)*. Towards the end of the 19th century wine decanters were lightly engraved with such classical motifs as the Greek key-pattern. Some wine decanters were made as part of a set: decanter plus glasses.

The geometric cuts of the early 19th century regained popularity from about 1885. Tall, metal-mounted claret jugs *(28)* were first produced in the 1830s and were much in demand from about 1870. Cased square decanters for travelling were produced from the mid-18th century.

Tantalus-stands were a feature of the 19th century. The decanters were visible, but sometimes locked in a case *(29)*. The name is derived from the myth: Tantalus was condemned to stand up to his neck in water without being allowed to drink. The tantalus-stand prevented light-fingered servants taking a drink, yet allowed the decanters to be admired. Prior to about 1845, plated stands were made of *Sheffield plate*. In the late 19th century, the stands were usually made of oak or electroplate, and contained square spirit decanters.

24 Left to right: Triple-ring decanter, c. 1815. This is more heavily cut than that of the previous illustration. The centre decanter, c. 1830-1840, has broader cut facets and a heavier stopper. The tall wine decanter, c. 1840, has a pinnacle stopper. (The Grafton Galleries, Sydney)

26 Left to right: Wine decanter with fern-leaf cut decoration, c. 1870. Square-cut spirit decanter, c. 1880. Tall wine decanter with curved lip, showing Art Nouveau characteristics, c. 1900. Square-shaped decanter with Art Deco characteristics, c. 1930. (The Grafton Galleries, Sydney)

27 Ruby-flashed Bohemian decanter, c. 1840. (Geoffrey Wills, Cornwall)

28 Claret jug with silver mounts, c. 1853, made by J. and H. Cresswick, London. (Geoff K. Gray Pty Ltd, Sydney)

29 Tantalus-stand of three pinnacle-stopper wine decanters, c. 1840. (Geoffrey Wills, Cornwall)

Drinking glasses

Funnel bowl

Bucket bowl

Trumpet bowl

Round funnel bowl

Bell bowl

Cup bowl

Ogee bowl

Folded foot

Double ogee bowl

Most 18th-century wine glasses had a foot of greater diameter than the bowl. The base was usually conical, rising to meet the stem. Prior to 1745, a *folded foot* was often used to protect the edge of the foot from chipping. A tax on glass-making materials was imposed by weight in 1745, so that the folded foot then became rare.

Until the middle of the 19th century, a mark was often present on the base, where the glass-maker's iron *pontil* rod (for holding the glass piece during manufacture) was snapped off. However, from about 1770 the pontil mark was often ground away or hidden with cut decoration on good-quality pieces. After 1800 a *gadget* was sometimes used instead of a pontil rod. The gadget (from which originated the modern use of the word) had a circular spring loaded clip to hold the glass during manufacture and did not mark the base.

The glass was a greyish colour and contained specks of lead resembling grains of sand. There were striations or faint ring marks around the bowl, and also a vertical mark about 1 centimetre long, extending from the edge, where it was held with a *spring tool* when soft. The bowl edge had a slight irregularity where the shears closed to make their last cut.

Wine glasses are either made in three units—bowl, stem and foot—that are then joined together, or they may be made in two units. The stem is drawn from the bowl and a separate component, the foot, attached—these are known as drawn-stem or two-piece glasses.

When dating a wine glass, consider its three components: foot, stem and bowl. By looking carefully at an 18th-century wine glass, the features described for the foot and bowl can be observed. The stem showed changes in fashion throughout the period 1685–1800 and allows wine glasses to be subdivided into five chronological groups.

1685–1735—balusters, including Silesian-moulded stems (*30*). Silesian stems are mainly from 1715–1745 and rarely to 1765.

1730–1740—plain stems or drawn stems (*31, 32*). These continued throughout the 18th century.

1740–1755—air twists (*33*).

1755–1780—opaque or enamel twists (*34, 35*).

1770–1800—faceted or cut stems (*36*).

For nearly a century after 1760 'rummers' were popular in England. Their shape originated in Roman times, and the name was derived from the

30

30 *Left: English Silesian-stem wine glass with folded foot, c. 1715. Right: Baluster-stem wine glass, c. 1695. (Sothebys, London)*

31 *Plain-stem wine glass, c. 1730. Note the greyish colour and wide raised foot. (The Grafton Galleries, Sydney)*

32 *Green drawn-stem wine glass, last half of the 18th century, probably Bristol. Stourbridge was an important source of coloured glass in the 19th century. (The Grafton Galleries, Sydney)*

33 *Funnel-bowl glass with air-twist double knop stem, c. 1740–1755. (The Grafton Galleries, Sydney)*

31

32

33

34

34 *Selection of 18th-century wine glasses. Left to right: Funnel bowl, opaque-twist 16 cm: Bucket-bowl, opaque twist, 14 cm. Double ogee bowl, close air spiral stem, 18 cm. Short funnel, baluster stem, 14.5 cm. Trumpet bowl, light baluster stem, 18 cm. (King and Chasemore, England)*

German *Roemer*. They were often used for drinking hot toddy. 'Toddy' was defined by the *Sporting Magazine* of 1780 as 'hot grog with the addition of sugar'; the grog was rum, given a spicy tang by the addition of lemon juice and grated nutmeg. Toddy was a word brought back from India where the toddy palm yielded a juice that was fermented. *Grog* was originally naval slang for alcohol, after an 18th-century Admiral, Vernon, who wore a grogram coat and was known as 'Old Grog'. *Punch* came from the Hindustani word *panch* meaning five, for the five ingredients were spirit, citrus juice, spice, sugar and fire. Because toddy is stronger than punch, toddy ladles are always smaller than punch ladles.

36 Group of facet-stem wine
glasses with engraved
bowls, last half of the 18th
century. (Sothebys, London)

35 Bucket-bowl opaque-
twist goblet, with enamel
decoration by the Beilby
family, c. 1765. (Sothebys,
London)

Usually the rummer bowl was ovoid, but sometimes was bucket-shaped.
The stem was always short and usually *knopped*. The foot was usually round,
although from about 1800 it was sometimes square. The rummer bowls were
often wheel-engraved with initials, *armorials,* sporting events (such as
cockfighting, racing and coursing), pictorial scenes or to commemorate royal
occasions.

Rummers were made until early Victorian days for use in public houses.
These glasses were often *mould-blown,* and of poor proportion. The metal (a
common term for the finished glass material) was of inferior quality and thick
in cross-section. Smaller sizes, drams, were used for gin and other spirits.

35

29

Lighting—candlesticks, candelabra and chandeliers

Although glass oil lamps were first made at the time of the Islamic empire, glass candlesticks did not appear until the end of the 17th century. The branched candlesticks of the 18th century were known as girandoles *(37)*, and the term *candelabra* only came into general use early in the 19th century. Most glass candlesticks were English, since the European preference was for metal.

Early candlestick stems had much in common with drinking-glass stems of that period. The earliest facet-cut candlestick *(38)* dates to 1742, and air-twist stems appeared at about the same time. At the end of the 18th century, candlesticks were hung with lustres, and during the Victorian era these developed into lustre vases *(39)*.

Most candelabra were made at the end of the 18th century, and they were probably not in use at all prior to the middle of the century. Glass candelabra were very popular during the Regency period and although they were used throughout the 19th century *(40)*, their popularity declined after 1820. Candelabra were far more efficient than chandeliers. Two candles at table level produced the same amount of light as ten candles hung from a high ceiling.

Chandeliers hung with faceted drops of rock crystal were first made in the 17th century. From Venice came chandeliers built up from glass flowers, because Venetian glass was far more suitable for modelled than cut decoration. English chandeliers first became popular in the early 18th century. Despite the descriptions in the brochures of some stately homes, it is now considered unlikely that any chandeliers were produced at Waterford. After 1840, chandeliers were made as copies of earlier styles.

In the 1860s kerosene came into use. This was light, so the fuel reservoir could be placed below the wick, and the kerosene moved up by capillary action to the flame at the top of the wick *(41)*. In all earlier oil lamps (using animal or vegetable oil) the fuel was either above the wick or a mechanical means was used to force fuel to the level of the flame.

Glass shades by Gallé, Daum and Tiffany are now popular collectors' items, but these date from the days of electricity. Gas was commonly used by 1850 *(42)* and electricity by 1890.

Tiffany sent two glass hanging lights to the Chicago Fair of 1893, and by 1900 his lampshades were being exhibited at international exhibitions in Europe. His lead lights were much more expensive than his blown shades and bronze shades, which sold from US$20. When it is realised that the average

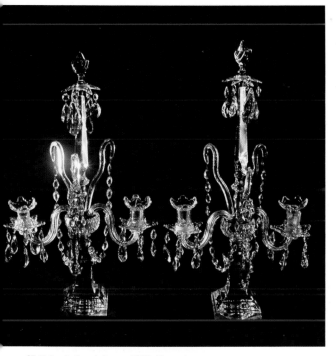

37 Pair of girandoles, c. 1775. They show the Adam influence in the top urn-shaped ornaments, and the graceful curved lines of the arms and festoons of drops. (The Grafton Galleries, Sydney)

38 Pair of Regency facet-cut candlesticks hung with icicle drops, c. 1820. (The Grafton Galleries, Sydney)

39 Pair of Victorian ruby-flashed lustre vases, c. 1870. Their design was based on that of a candlestick hung with lustres. (The Grafton Galleries, Sydney)

40 Pair of mid-19th-century candelabra, fitted with storm shades. (The Grafton Galleries, Sydney)

44 Austrian bronze and iridescent glass table lamp, c. 1900. The glass shade is attributed to Lötz. (Sothebys, London)

41 Kerosene table lamp, c. 1880. (Mrs H. McNaught, Sydney)

42 Art Nouveau wall gas-light, c. 1900. (The Grafton Galleries, Sydney)

43 Tiffany studio bronze and stained-glass Wisteria lamp, early 20th century. (Christies, London)

wage in America in 1906 was 18 cents an hour, the impracticability of some of Tiffany's production costs can be appreciated. The Wisteria lamp *(43)* was retailed at US$400 early this century. (It was sold by Christies, London, in November 1976 for approximately A$24 000.)

Early this century Tiffany had over five hundred designs for shades and another five hundred designs for lamp bases. Most, but not all, of his shades have soldered on to the shade the bronze label 'Tiffany Studios, New York'.

The French glass-makers of this time made large quantities of lamps, most of which were signed. They were also made by Lötz, of Austria, who did not always sign his product *(44)*.

Variations of this mark are included on page 51. The presence of a signature on glass adds considerably to the value. Examples of Art Deco lamps are shown as illustrations 52 and 69.

Flashed, cased and cameo glass

At the close of the Napoleonic Wars Bohemia was striving to regain her glass markets that had been closed for twenty years. The glittering Empire style was replaced by that of *Biedermeier* (1815–1850)—restrained romanticism and comfort without extravagance.

It was the close of the great Anglo-Irish period of cut, heavy lead crystal. Bohemia did not attempt to compete with this, but captured world markets with new ideas and techniques, which brought colour and technical efficiency to satisfy the newly emerging upper-middle-class taste. Two important colour developments were yellow by 1820 and sealing-wax red by 1840. Very little entirely uncoloured glass was made in Bohemia by 1820.

FLASHED GLASS *(27)* was produced by applying a thin surface layer, usually of coloured glass, to a glass vessel. A variety of contrasting patterns was created by wheel-engraving the surface to expose the glass below. Typical themes were mountain scenery, stag hunts, ruined buildings and other romantic scenes. The best examples of flashed glass were made between 1830 and 1850 *(9)*.

CASED GLASS was made of two or more layers of thick glass of contrasting colours. The layers were built up from the inside and each layer was very much thicker than in the case of flashed glass. (See Glossary for further detail of manufacture.) The outer layer was facet-cut on the wheel to form *intaglio* patterns where the bottom layer was exposed in contrast to the surface colour, which was frequently white *(45)*. The term 'overlay' is sometimes used to describe 'cased' and 'flashed' glass.

Bohemian glass-manufacturers had an efficient marketing system so their glass was widely distributed throughout Europe, and large amounts were sold in America. From 1840 other countries, particularly England, began to make glass '*a l'imitation de la Bohème*'. Some Bohemian artisans were employed in English factories, and the Richardson firm in Stroud was exhibiting glass of the Bohemian style by 1845. By the time of the London Great Exhibition of 1851, the Bohemian fashion was widespread, and continued until about 1870.

CAMEO GLASS Casing reached its highest point with cameo glass. The outer layer was thick so that it could be ground away and chiselled to show the design in relief, like a cameo. Scenes, flowers and portraits were favourite subjects. In 1876 John Northwood (1836–1902) spent several years producing a copy of the *Portland Vase* in cameo glass. George Woodall (1850–1925) followed his style. The firm best known for fine cameo glass was Thomas Webb *(46)*. In the 18th

27

Ruby-flashed Bohemian decanter, c. 1840.
(Geoffrey Wills, Cornwall)

45

45 White cased glass, c. 1840. The intaglio design is cut through the coloured cased glass, disclosing the colourless glass beneath. The amber perfume bottle, c. 1840, is an example of Bohemian cut flashed glass. (The Grafton Galleries, Sydney)

46 Thomas Webb cameo vase, 'Before the Race', by George Woodall. The circular design with one horse following the other creates a sense of movement around the saddling paddock. Height 30.5 cm. (Christies, London)

47

century the Chinese produced cameo glass known as Pekin glass *(47)*. After 1900, cheaper methods led to a decline in the quality of cameo glass.

47 Chinese example of cameo or Pekin glass, with cameo designs on the interior and exterior. Pekin glass was often used for snuff bottles. Diameter 28 cm. (The Grafton Galleries, Sydney)

Paperweights

The classic period for fine glass paperweights was the middle of the 19th century. In 1845–1855 the three most important factories were French: Baccarat, Saint-Louis (in the Vosges mountains towards the Alps) and Clichy (near Paris). Some of the paperweights from these factories bore marks and dates partly hidden in the decoration. Some Baccarat pieces were marked with a 'B' and dated 1846 to 1849. Saint-Louis pieces were sometimes marked 'S.L.' and were occasionally dated 1845, 1847, 1848 and 1849. Clichy pieces sometimes bore the letter 'C' and more rarely 'Clichy' in full. A fluorescence test with ultraviolet light usually produces a deep-blue fluorescence with Baccarat, pink

48 Chequer paperweight, with mixed millefiori canes and filigree lace. (The Grafton Galleries, Sydney)

with Saint-Louis and green with Clichy.

Venice and Bohemia began to produce paperweights in the 1840s. England began in 1848, and two leading factories were Whitefriars in London and Bacchus in Birmingham. Paperweights were produced in America during the periods 1851–1880 and 1900–1914. After the early 1845–1855 period, paperweights were again produced in France between 1878 and 1914. More recently, paperweights regained popularity in the 1950s. Paul Ysart is a famous contemporary maker in Perth, Scotland. He sometimes marks his weights 'PY'. Mid-19th-century paperweights, with their more subtle colours, had a more variable coloured glass and more detailed designs than those produced in the 1950s. Other Perth makers used 'P' marks from the 1950s.

Paperweights were produced by covering coloured glass patterns with a clear-glass magnifying dome. A common pattern was *millefiori*, meaning 'a thousand flowers'. This was made by placing a molten coloured-glass rod into a mould. When the glass had cooled, it was covered by glass of another colour and inserted into a different mould. This process was continued so as to form designs of different shapes and colours radiating from the centre of the core of the glass rod. While still hot, this rod or cane was pulled out to a length of several metres, so reducing the diameter to less than pencil thinness. When cool, the cane was cut into hundreds of slices, each having a cross-section of the same pattern. Small motifs were usually made in a larger size and stretched to final miniature size.

Filigree or lacy canes were made in the same manner, but only opaque-white and colourless glass was used and the cane was twisted whilst molten to give a ribbon effect. Filigree sections were cut into larger ribands than the *millefiori* slices.

Designs such as butterflies, flowers and snakes were made by melting coloured glass with a blowtorch, tooling to desired shapes and encasing in the clear-glass dome.

Some paperweights were made by using other materials besides glass. In the *sulphides* a ceramic medallion was encased in glass. This technique originated in France in the 18th century, but most existing examples are paperweights from the last half of the 19th century. Green glass 'dumps', doorstops or paperweights were made at Stourbridge during the paperweight era of the mid-19th century, and were decorated with patterns of interior glass bubbles.

49 *Left to right: Dated sealed bottle with a shouldered cylindrical body and high kick in base; the seal has the mark 'T.M. 1751'. Dated sealed bottle with a squat body, very high* *kick in base and a short neck that is flanged at the rim, height 19.5 cm; the circular seal bears the mark 'E. Taylor Welland 1737'. Armorial and dated bottle with a ringed rim and wide* *kick in base; the circular seal bears the arms of Chadwick and the date 1785. Height 24.5 cm. (Phillips Son & Neale, London)*

Bottles

Shaft and globe, c. 1650-1690

Bottles have always been a major product of glass-houses. A list of English glass-houses of 1696 showed that thirty-seven of the eighty-eight factories were engaged exclusively in the production of bottles.

Wine-bottles were most in demand after the mid-17th century, but were produced in small quantities before that time. Five distinct shapes were made during the first period of bottle making, 1650–1775.

1650–1690—shaft and globe, having a large neck and smallish round body.

1690–1715—onion, having a shorter neck and relatively larger body.

1715–1750—slope and shoulder, which produced a greater capacity in relation to the amount of glass used.

1750–1775—early slope shoulder, cylinder.

1775 onward—later cylinder, almost as we know it today.

The type of stopper used has affected the function and shape of bottles. During the 17th century the main function of bottles was to take the wine from the cask to the table. These bottle-decanters were only lightly stoppered. During the 17th century, cork was imported from Spain and was used to make stoppers. Bottles were stored flat to keep the cork moist and thus the bottle was airtight. The storage of many bottles, each horizontal, in bins meant that a cylindrical bottle shape was required.

Seals, initials and dates were marked on bottles from the middle of the 17th century, and identified the owner of the bottle. A blob of molten glass was placed on the side of the bottle, and the owner's mark was impressed into this by using a brass seal.

Although moulded bottles had been known since pre-Christian times and some were produced during the 18th century, free-blown bottles were generally made until the moulding processes of the 1840s.

Soda water was bottled as early as 1777 and egg-shaped bottles were soon in use. These had a pointed base, so were placed on their side, to keep the cork moist and tight fitting, to prevent escape of gas. Codd's marble-glass stopper (which did not need to be kept moist) was introduced in 1873, so torpedo-shaped bottles that stood upright were used. Inside-screw stoppers, often in porcelain, originated from about the same date. The 'lightning stopper', which worked on a wire-clip principle, was in use from about 1880 to 1920. In 1892 the modern metal Crown seal was developed, and replaced the marble-glass stopper. This seal did not become generally used in Australia until about 1907.

Relief-moulded lettering came into general use from about 1860, when more efficient metal moulds facilitated this advertising and ownership mark. The pontil mark on bottles was no longer in general use after about 1840, the exact year depending on the locality of manufacture.

Most early Australian bitters bottles were square and of American origin. Bitters was mainly a German, Dutch and American drink, rather than English. The drink and the first bottles were introduced from America during the gold rush of the mid-19th century. There were over two hundred Australian breweries at the close of the 19th century, and some of their bottles bore the marks of mining towns such as Bendigo, Kalgoorlie and Broken Hill.

Onion, c. 1690-1715

Slope and shoulder, c. 1715-1750

Cylinder (early form), c. 1750-1775

Cylinder (later form), from c. 1775

Soda bottle c. 1780

Lightning stopper c. 1880

Moulded and pressed glass

Glass moulding was used even before Roman times. Moulding was eclipsed by the invention of blowing about the time of Christ, and only regained popularity with the requirements for mass production in the 19th century.

Early 18th-century English Silesian wine glasses had moulded stems. These varied from four to eight sides and were mainly produced *c.* 1715–45. Salt-cellar and comport bases were often moulded from about 1785. Generally moulded glass became more common in Europe from about 1800. *Press-moulding* was first patented in America in 1825 by the Pittsburgh Glass Manufacturing Company, and developed by the Sandwich Glass Company, which opened in that year and closed in 1888.

Hollow ware made of pressed glass had a smooth inner surface that did not follow the curves and indentations of the outer surface, unlike glass blown into moulds.

Large quantities of white glass were press-moulded around 1870–1900, to form such items as hens on nests, covered dishes, classical figures and bowls.

50

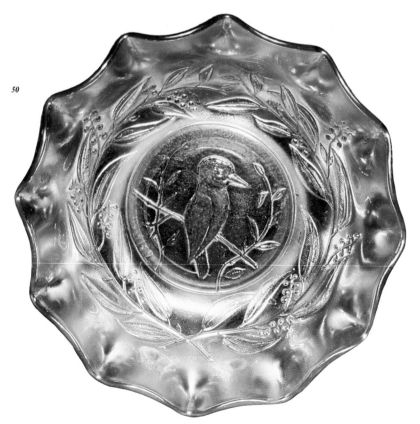

50 Carnival-glass bowl, showing a moulded kookaburra in the centre and the typical iridescent colour of carnival glass. *(Museum of Applied Arts and Sciences, Sydney)*

Between 1895 and 1920, pressed *carnival glass* or taffeta glass items *(50)* were made for sale at fairs and carnivals. The glass was a purplish or orange iridescent colour, although other colours were made.

Slag glass

The development of slag glass was part of the trend towards mass production at the end of the 19th century. Slag glass was sometimes called *agate* or *marbled glass*, because of its unique mottled appearance. The colour was usually mauve, blue, purple or white, and basket-weave was a favourite means of decoration *(51)*.

The name 'slag glass' was derived from the method of manufacture: slag from steel works was added to the molten glass, which was then press-moulded. Because of this dependence upon a local steel works, most English examples were made in the north-east, and Gateshead was the centre of the industry. The main period of production was between 1860 and 1890, and many pieces bore the diamond registration mark that signified the year in which a particular pattern was patented (see p. 249). The Tyneside glass-houses of J. G. Sowerby used a peacock's head in profile as a trade mark, and George Davidson used a lion's head also in profile.

51 Group of slag glass pieces, showing the characteristic marbled effect on the mauve and blue vases and the basket-weave design on the white plate. (Mount Victoria Antiques, Mount Victoria, N.S.W.)

51

Pâte de Verre

Pâte de verre is an interesting glass technique that was known to the ancient Egyptians. It was developed at the end of the 19th century and became fashionable during the Art Deco period of the 1920s. Moulded decoration was applied to a glass background *(52)*. Glass crystals in powdered form were packed into a mould and then fused at a high temperature. There was considerable waste due to cracking or air bubbles spoiling the finished product. For this reason, most *pâte de verre* pieces were small.

Pâte de verre had an opaque quality and a slightly rough matt surface. Its greatest feature was its colour, which was given by the addition of metallic oxides to the glass crystals before packing into the mould.

52

52 Pâte de verre lamp signed Gabriel Argy-Rousseau. (Copeland & de Soos, Sydney).

53 Collection of ruby glass, c. 1900. (The Grafton Galleries, Sydney)

54 Pair of ruby Mary Gregory vases, decorated in white enamel, late 19th century (Vandé Antiques, Sydney)

Art glass, 1870–1900

The term 'art glass' refers to decorative late 19th-century glass made for ornamental rather than utilitarian purposes. The development of such glass was a result of two factors: first, the late Victorians had a love of highly ornate and colourful decoration; second, there had been great developments in the colouring and shaping of mass-produced glass.

Art glass was an international style, with centres in England, America and central Europe. Today one frequently hears some art glass referred to as Venetian; this is usually incorrect—Venice sent no glass to the London Exhibition of 1851 and played little part in the history of art glass. This fallacy possibly arose from the fact that art glass relied for its decorative appeal on shape and colour, not cutting. These characteristics resemble those of early Venetian glass.

The most popular coloured glass of this period was *ruby glass,* or *cranberry glass* as it is called in America *(53)*. Large quantities of ruby-glass articles were made by various countries between the end of the 19th century and World War I. Less frequently, items of this type were made in other colours such as green, amber, blue or mauve.

MARY GREGORY was a generic term for free-blown coloured glass that was decorated in white enamel between 1860 and 1914 *(54, 55)*. The glass was named after Mary Gregory who used white enamel decoration on glass made for the American Sandwich Glass Company. Most of her pieces were made between 1866 and 1888. A popular picture was of a boy and girl chasing butterflies.

53

54

Hahn was the originator of this style; he was a Bohemian from the town of Jabonlec. In the late 19th century large quantities of German glass were exported to America. Perhaps because the name suited the subject better, Mary Gregory became 'immortal' and Hahn glass was forgotten. Mary Gregory glass was made in most glass-making countries until about 1914. More

56

56 Left to right: Spatter-glass vase, c. 1880. Opaline-glass candlestick with blue-glass snake grip, typical of Stourbridge c. 1870. Spangle-glass vase, c. 1880. Pair of milk-glass vases, with classical enamel head and Greek key-pattern motifs, c. 1880. (Ramornie Antiques, Sydney)

recent reproductions have a brighter coloured glass and sometimes a thicker white enamel.

MOSER ENAMELLED GLASS The Austrian Kolo Moser was an important glass designer and enamel decorator of the early 20th century. His first pieces were made just before the turn of the century, but most of his important work was done in 1900–1910. His factory in Austria is still operating. Moser executed fine gilt and coloured enamel designs, often incorporating moulded acorns in high relief (*55*). He often signed his work 'Moser', but some amethyst colour was marked 'Alexandrite Moser'—this is not to be confused with Webb *Alexandrite*, which was made in shaded three-colour designs. Enamelling was most popular in the period 1895–1914.

SPATTER AND SPANGLED GLASS (*56*) Spangled glass was decorated with flakes of

mica that had been coated with gold, silver or copper. The flakes were applied to an opaque-white or coloured glass and then 'locked in' with a layer of clear or tinted glass. Spangled glass was patented in 1886. Spatter glass was made by the addition of small pieces of different coloured glass. Like spangled glass, it was usually opaque, and the small pieces of coloured glass were covered by a clear surface layer.

MILK AND OPALINE GLASS *(56)* White glass was popular at the end of the 19th century. It was similar in colour to the ivory-coloured porcelain made by the Worcester factories and others in about 1870. White glass had been made in England and Germany (*Milchglas*) from the last half of the 18th century, but the first *opaline glass* was made in about 1815 in the Empire style. The word 'opaline' was coined by the Baccarat factory in 1823.

Milchglas had a watery appearance, and it was not until the French had succeeded in perfecting the metal of their lead glass that good-quality opaline glass could be made. Although translucent, opaline glass had a sparkle and depth of colour that *Milchglas* lacked. Opaline was also produced in blue, green and, more rarely, in other pale colours. Apart from the Empire period, the best opaline glass was made in 1840–1870. Large quantities of white or milk glass were made until 1914, but quality deteriorated with mass-production techniques.

55 Left: Blue Mary Gregory casket, decorated with children playing shuttlecock. c. 1900 (Peter Tanaka, Sydney) Right: Ruby vase decorated in enamel, attributed to Moser, c. 1900. (Ramornie Antiques, Sydney)

Smooth matt-surface glass, 1880–1914

SATIN GLASS (*57, 58 left*) During the period 1880–1914, some glass was treated with acid to obtain a smooth matt surface. One such product was called satin glass by the manufacturers in the 1880s. A variety of this, called 'mother-of-pearl', was perfected in about 1885 by Joseph Webb, an Englishman employed by the American Phoenix Glass Company. Air bubbles, manipulated into a diamond pattern, were 'locked' between two layers of glass. These bubbles could be seen through the outer casing and gave a quilted effect. Another type of satin glass, 'rainbow mother-of-pearl', was very similar in its quilted effect but had a characteristic series of rainbow colours.

Silver-plate mounts were popular, particularly with American manufacturers. Enamel or gilt surface decoration was sometimes added. The blue sugar basin (*57*) is typical of such glass, and was made in about 1885–1895. Satin glass was made until about 1914. The small jug second from the right in the same illustration is made from vaseline glass. This later 19th-century glass contained uranium and had a shiny greasy appearance like vaseline. Its glossy finish contrasted with the acid-treated matt surface of satin glass.

AMBERINA was the first shaded glass to achieve success, and was shaded from amber to red. It was patented in 1883 by an English immigrant glass-maker, who worked for the American New England Glass Company. The red shades were produced by reheating (a process called striking). Amberina was copied by the Mount Washington Glass Company, which was regarded as the focal point of American art glass. The lawsuit filed against the Mount Washington Glass Company resulted in the copy being called 'rose amberina'. However, this type of glass is known generically today as amberina.

BURMESE GLASS The shaded bi-partite technique was soon developed to give Burmese glass, shaded from lemon-yellow to salmon-pink at the top. This single-layered free-blown glass was completely yellow when removed from the fire. By striking the top half, a pink colour was obtained. Burmese glass was patented in 1885 by the American Mount Washington Glass Company, and a licence was granted in the following year to Thomas Webb in England. Webb marked his product 'Thos. Webb & Sons, Queen's Burmeseware', since Queen Victoria showed interest in his techniques (*58 right*) Production both in America and England ceased by about 1900, so articles of Burmese glass are now rare. The glass usually had a smooth matt acid-treated finish, although America produced some pieces with a glossy surface.

58 *Right: Fine example of Burmese glass, marked 'Thos. Webb & Sons, Queen's Burmeseware, Patented Rd 67648', c. 1887. (The Grafton Galleries, Sydney) Left: Satin-glass vase of a pattern style known as Federzeichnung. (Ramornie Antiques, Sydney)*

57 *Group of satin-glass pieces, and a vaseline-glass jug. The yellow domed item second from the left is a night-light shade. Note the mother-of-pearl, with its bubble decoration in a typical diamond shape. (Ramornie Antiques, Sydney)*

PEACHBLOW GLASS The name was derived from the Chinese porcelain colouring known as 'peachbloom', because peachblow glass was shaded delicately from cream to pink or sometimes violet-red. This bi-partite colour was developed after 1886, when a famous Chinese porcelain peachbloom vase from the Morgan Collection in America was sold for US$18000. Peachblow glass usually had an acid-treated matt finish, but was occasionally made with a natural finish. Peachblow glass was made for a short period only and is rare.

Art Nouveau, 1890–1910

The 19th century had produced little original design: previous styles were revived and repeated. The mass production of the new machine age made artists search for something both fresh and hand-made. The new fashion appeared almost simultaneously throughout western Europe and a little later in America. The success of Japanese art at the London and Paris Exhibitions of that time acted as a catalyst to this movement. Fine and applied arts merged; artists became craftsmen and craftsmen artists.

As a result of Admiral Perry's visit to Japan, America and Japan signed a commercial treaty in 1854. This ended a long period of isolation for Japan. With Europe eager for new ideas, Japanese art was immediately popular. The clever use of asymmetry by the Japanese was a strong influence on the asymmetrical rococo principles of Art Nouveau.

The easily identifiable characteristics of Art Nouveau are flowing lines that bend and turn back on themselves: curls of smoke, feminine curves, long hair and long dresses, twining plant forms, flowers and buds, and pastel colours (59, 60). William Morris and Arthur Liberty had a great influence on the new art form. The ideas of Morris influenced the *Arts and Crafts Movement* against the machine, so taking the first step towards Art Nouveau. Arthur Liberty worked for a London firm that bought the complete Japanese display at the London Exhibition of 1862, and about ten years later he began the famous Regent Street firm of Liberty and patronised the Art Nouveau style. Liberty visited Japan in 1888–1889.

Three collectors of Oriental art were influential at the time: Whistler, who collected blue and white porcelain in the 1880s; Siegfried Bing, who opened his Paris art shop (called Maison de l'Art Nouveau) in 1896; and Louis Tiffany, who was an American glass-maker of the late 19th and early 20th centuries.

The height of the Art Nouveau period was 1900. It would be convenient but inaccurate to believe Art Nouveau was killed by World War I: a decline in its popularity began in about 1910. Art Nouveau found its opposition in mass production, the very factor that had prompted its development. The factories climbed aboard the bandwagon of the popular movement and mass produced items in the new style. This repetition and lack of quality brought about the fall of Art Nouveau.

60 Art Nouveau vase, c. 1900, showing the characteristic soft pastel colours of the period. Such items are more readily available to collectors than the signed Art Nouveau glass, which has always been rare and valuable. (The Grafton Galleries, Sydney)

59 Bronze mermaid resting on top of a rising and curling crystal wave. The languid sensual curves of the mermaid, the long hair, restful body and semi-parallel lines of the limbs are all characteristics of the Art Nouveau style. (Mr A. D. Clifford, Sydney)

59

61

62

Tiffany and Lötz

Louis Comfort Tiffany (1848–1933) was an American glass designer, most
famous for his iridescent or lustred free-blown glass. The Tiffany trade name
(registered in 1894) for this shimmering glass was 'Favrile' *(61)*. The name
implied hand-made and individual, and was taken from an old English word
'fabrile', which meant 'belonging to a craftsman'. Favrile glass was first
exhibited in 1893.

Tiffany expressed the ductility of the material in the style of his finished
product whilst most factories producing moulded glass only capitalised on this
as a time-saving manufacturing technique. Tiffany's work is distinguished by
spiral twisted lines and veins that ran freely with a certain capriciousness, but
were dominated by a guiding principle. He never merely painted the surface of
his glass but skilfully controlled the vagaries of the melting pot, so achieving a
controlled freedom of colour and design which was part of the glass itself. The
time taken to produce some of his creations was prohibitive from a commercial
point of view.

The delicate form of the peacock's feather and tail, and the iridescent
bluish-green of the neck feathers, were Art Nouveau motifs frequently
employed by Tiffany. The iridescent surface was partially inspired by the aged

surface of excavated Roman glass; some glass buried in damp soil can attain this iridescence within a few years.

Tiffany was the son of a successful New York jeweller. An artistic young man, Tiffany exhibited paintings at the Paris Exhibition of 1878. His interest soon turned to glass design and he opened his New York firm in 1879. His product typified the spirit of Art Nouveau, which was at its peak in 1900 when Tiffany employed over a hundred glass-makers. Pieces bearing the Tiffany name alone rather than the studio name are usually more valuable. The gold comport design was popular for twenty years from about 1895. In the illustration *(61)* the Tiffany vase is probably four times as valuable as the gold-lustre comport.

The Art Nouveau style was no longer popular by the time of World War I, but the factory refused to acknowledge its demise and continued the old styles without success into the 1920s. Tiffany relinquished control of the factory in 1919 and withdrew his financial support and the use of his name in 1928. The firm continued under the name of Nash (see p. 60) until its final collapse in 1931.

The Austrian firm of Lötz also made iridescent glass *(62)*, and was exporting it to America by 1879. Iridescent Austrian glass was exhibited at the Vienna International Exhibition of 1873 by the firm of Lobmeyr which produced iridescent glass from 1863. It was copied by the Englishman Thomas Webb of Stourbridge, who was granted a patent in 1877, from whom Tiffany obtained information to further his development of iridescent glass. Tiffany's patent was issued in 1881, but Lötz did not take out a patent until 1889, ten years after Austrian glass was first exported to America.

Only the Lötz glass intended for export was signed, so the absence of a mark was not necessarily an indication of poor quality. The marks used were 'Loetz Austria'; arrows within a circle; 'Lötz Kostermuhl'; and 'Lötz'.

Lötz died in 1848 and the firm was then controlled by his widow—so the name 'Lötz Witwe'. The firm won prizes at International Exhibitions at Brussels in 1888 and Paris in 1889. At the Paris Exhibition of 1900, the Grand Prix was shared by Gallé, Tiffany, Daum and Lötz.

Lötz made the best-known Austrian iridescent glass, but other Austrian glass-houses (Bakalowits, Adolf Zasche and Joseph Palme Konig) produced a similar product around 1900.

Gallé, Daum Brothers and Legras

EMILE GALLE (1846–1904) was a French glass-maker who had a great influence on the Art Nouveau style. He took over the management of his father's faience and glass factory in 1874 and exhibited at the Paris Exhibition of 1878. By the end of the 19th century, glass typified the characteristics of Art Nouveau more than any other art form except painting.

Glass was Emile's first love, but he also designed furniture and made *faience*. Gallé was also an accomplished horticulturist, whose theme 'nature in glass' became the expression of the Ecole de Nancy that he established in 1901. Imagination was one of Gallé's greater characteristics and by 1900 he was one of the most respected decorative artists in France. He also loved literature and sometimes based his designs on a line of verse, engraving that line on the finished article. These engraved pieces were known as *verrerie parlante* (meaning 'speaking glass ware').

By 1900 the Gallé factory at Nancy employed 300 workmen; only Tiffany of New York reached the same degree of quality in mass-produced art glass. By the end of the 19th century, all Gallé was signed 'Gallé'. Because of the volume involved, much of this was not personally made by Gallé, but rather under his supervision. Initially, the glass was relatively clear and decorated with enamel, but later Gallé regarded glass as a gemstone material which he coloured and carved as if it were hardstone.

Gallé introduced his cameo glass in 1889 *(64)*. It is for this that he is most widely remembered. The glass was built up with layers of colour and then cut to leave the design in relief in one or more colours against a contrasting background *(63 centre)*. There were various methods of achieving this result and often several were used in combination to produce a single item. The cheapest method was *acid-etching,* which ate away the background to a relatively shallow depth, resulting in a frosted surface .

In about 1895–1904 Gallé produced mould-blown vases. These were made by blowing molten glass into moulds that had a design in high relief. During this period, in 1897, Gallé began to use his *marqueterie de verre* technique. Pieces of coloured glass were pressed into the body of a vase whilst it was hot and soft from the furnace. A complex design required several reheatings, so there was an increased risk of breakage. The technique was modified in the later 1890s: the glass pieces were not pressed into the body of the vase but left in relief on the surface. This later method was used until 1904.

64

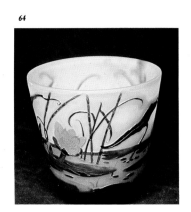

64 Gallé Cameo Bowl decorated with waterlilies and other plant forms. Signed Gallé in script and marked with a star. Post 1904, but early 20th Century (The Grafton Galleries, Sydney)

63

It was common practice to sign glass in the late 1890s; Gallé signed his pieces in fine cameo script. A date signified that a piece had been made for an exhibition of that date.

Gallé died in 1904, and his factory closed in 1931. Gallé's signature was continued ater his death, but a star was added to the mark of items produced 1904–1914. Less interesting acid etched glass was produced in the 1920s.

THE DAUM BROTHERS, Auguste (1853–1909) and Antonin (1864–1930), followed the style of Gallé. They worked in their father's glass-house before beginning on their own in 1891. Enamelled forest scenes *(63 left and right)* were typical Daum decoration at that time, and cameo glass and *pâte de verre* were also produced. During the *Art Deco* period the Daum brothers made vases deeply etched with geometric designs. The factory is still in operation today following the fashions of the time. All Daum glass bears the engraved Daum signature.

AUGUST J. F. LEGRAS, who established a factory just outside Paris, was another worker producing similar models. These were mainly cameo glass, embellished with enamel decoration. Most of Legras' work is from 1900, and in about 1907 he produced the first Coty perfume bottles that were designed by Lalique. After World War I this factory merged with the Pantin glass-house and used the marks 'Pantin' and 'De Vez'.

63 Left to right: Vase marked 'Daum, Nancy'; this tall-necked vase (called a berluze) was a form created by Daum in about 1900. Gallé bowl with deeply cut cameo decoration to exterior and interior, c. 1900. (The Grafton Galleries, Sydney) Daum Nancy vase showing typical 'rain through trees' decoration, c. 1905. (Museum of Applied Arts and Sciences, Sydney)

65

Lalique, Sabino and Etling

65 *Pair of Lalique moulded-glass quail. (The Grafton Galleries, Sydney)*

RENE LALIQUE (1860–1945) developed cast and moulded monotone glass *(65)*. Beginning in the Art Nouveau period that was always his main love, he took his style on into the Art Deco period. His early plant forms were the languid Art Nouveau iris and water lily; in the 1920s these were replaced by formalised Art Deco sunflowers, dahlias and roses. Whilst others made multi-coloured articles, those made by Lalique were monotones, mainly smoky greys and blues, but also green, brown, red, turquoise and black.

Lalique was trained as a jeweller and in the 1890s had won international fame, but he was more interested in design than in precious materials. From about 1900 his interest focussed on glass, when he had a small glass-house with four workers. He designed perfume bottles for Coty and several other perfume producers. Initially, in 1907, Lalique only designed the bottles and they were then made by Legras. However, from 1910 he was producing them in his own factory, where they have been made to the present day. His catalogue of 1932 lists about a hundred different designs for perfume bottles.

Shortly after World War I Lalique built a much bigger factory, and produced on a large commercial scale—in fact the bulk of his production occurred after World War I. He carried original *studio art* into mass production, using modern techniques to mass produce goods at reasonably low prices. This

66 Lalique moulded figure, model 833 'Suzanne au Bain', 1930. (The Grafton Galleries)

66

was the philosophy of the Art Deco age—the opposite of that of the studio artists with whom he began his training at the end of the 19th century. (The studio artists were artist-craftsmen—the wares were made and decorated by the designer.) Lalique's designs were original and his supervision of workmanship was first class, yet his production was immense. Up to 2000 items of one design were made, and when the French ship *Normandie* was launched in 1932, its main dining room (about 100 metres long, with a 9-metre-high ceiling) was panelled with Lalique glass and lit with Lalique chandeliers.

Lalique glass contained a high proportion of lead oxide, so was heavy and had a soft reflective sheen, which was finished with a smooth satin surface. Although between 1500 and 2000 models of some of his designs were made, others were 'one only' models made by the *lost-wax* casting process. These unique articles were mainly produced between 1902 and 1913.

Lalique's work was marked 'R. Lalique' until his death in 1945, when the 'R' was omitted. Today the mark is 'Lalique France'.

SABINO Another maker of glass in the moulded Lalique style was the artist Maurius Ernest Sabino, who produced under the name Sabino during the 1920s and 1930s. He established a glass-house in Paris, producing a range similar to that of Lalique: smoky, monotone colours and opaque glass. These were marked 'Sabino Paris'.

MADAME ETLING was a Paris retailer and patron of Art Deco in the late 1920s and 1930s. She later produced glass in the Lalique style, particularly ships, nudes and perfume bottles.

Art Deco, 1920–1940

The Scottish architect Charles Rennie Mackintosh rediscovered the decorative function of the straight line in 1900, and so began the trend towards geometric design in architecture and furniture. The Austrian Kolo Moser was the first to use the angular line in his glass designs during the early years of the 20th century. Only after World War I did this new style of glass-making become more popular, and the high point was the Paris International Exhibition of Modern Decorative and Industrial Arts in 1925. However, the term 'Art Deco' for the geometric designs of this period was not used until 1966. In that year an exhibition was held in Paris: called 'Les Années '25' it was based on the twenties

68

68 Art Deco vase of the 1920s. The black and orange colour combination was very fashionable throughout the Art Deco period. (The Grafton Galleries, Sydney)

and the famous 1925 Paris Exhibition.

During the 1930s the style was angular and often showed Aztec or Egyptian designs inspired by the relics of these civilisations which were being excavated at that time *(67)*. During the 1920s the shapes were more rounded *(68)*. The iris and the orchid of *Art Nouveau* were replaced by the stylised dahlia and rose. The small exclusive salon had promoted Art Nouveau, but Art Deco

was promoted by the large retail store—much of the new style, particularly in metal, was art for the masses *(69 left)*.

At the Paris Exhibition in 1925 the house was seen as a machine in which to live: concrete, steel and glass were dominant features, the interior walls were stark white and the furniture was sparse, and the pastel walls and Edwardian clutter had been swept away.

Lalique glass was very popular during the Art Deco period. Also the painter Maurice Marinot had considerable influence on glass making. He developed layered glass with bubbles and streams of colour trapped within it,

69

and also a method of eating away glass with successive prolonged acid baths.

Maurice Marinot (1882–1960) changed his vocation from painting to glass making in 1911. He was an outstanding studio glass-maker; designing, making, decorating and signing all his pieces. He first made bowls, bottles and flasks in coloured glass. From 1923 he produced massive abstract items with engraved and acid-etched patterns. These pieces often had many bubbles and streaks of interior different-colour glass embedded in the glass. He had an international reputation from 1925 until his retirement in 1937, and so influenced other glass-makers of his time. In a quarter of a century he produced only about 2500 models, some of which took a year to complete.

Marinot trained Henri Navarre and André Thuret, who later followed his style. The Daum brothers produced simplified versions of the Marinot style. *Le verre français* was part of the output of Charles Schneider's glass-house, Cristallerie Schneider, which was founded in 1908. Schneider (1881–1962) studied under Gallé and Daum. He also made pieces in the Marinot style, and some *pâte de verre*. Schneider's factory is important because it operated from just before the Art Deco period up to the present day. It produced good-quality examples of the various styles and techniques of this time. Schneider's most common mark was 'Le Verre Français' or the company name 'Schneider'. Only one of his artisans signed his work (Charder), and his style was cased glass in the bright Art Deco colours *(69 middle left, and right)*, which are usually acid-cut. The *pâte de verre* technique produced brilliant designs. Leaders in this field were Gabriel Argy-Rousseau, Francois Emile Decorchemont and Almeric Walter.

Some Important Glass Dates

2000 BC	Glass beads produced
1500 BC	Core glass bottles made
1st century BC	Glass first blown
8th and 9th centuries	Islamic glass engraved and cut
13th and 14th centuries	Islamic glass enamelled
10th century	Venetian glass begins
13th century	Venetian glass making well established
1575	Verzelini granted sole right to make Venetian-style glass in England
1676	Ravenscroft produces lead glass
1709	Glass cutting begins in England
1740	Rococo period: engraved glass at peak of popularity
1745	English glass taxed by weight
1762	Beilby enamelled glass
1780	Ireland granted free trade and glass making flourishes
1787	Glass tax increased in England
1815	Bohemian cut coloured glass develops
1825	Irish glass first taxed
1825	Pressed glass begins
1845	Glass excise Act repealed
1845–1855	Classic French paperweight period
1870–1900	Art glass
1890–1910	Art Nouveau
1920–1940	Art Deco

Some other glass-makers of the late 19th and the 20th centuries

ARGY-ROUSSEAU, GABRIEL (1885–) is a French glass-maker who produced a type of *pâte de verre* called *pâte de cristal*. This was transparent and resonant, and was generally used for vases and lamp bases decorated with relief flowers. Much of his work dates from the 1920s. His work is signed 'G. Argy-Rousseau'.

CARDER, FREDERICK (1863–1963) was an established glass designer and technician who moved to America from Stourbridge in 1903 to help found the Steuben Glass Works. This leading ornamental glass factory was sold in 1918 to Corning Glass. Carder was made art director of this company, and retired in 1933. Many factory-made pieces bear his signature, 'F. Carder'. He followed the changing fashions during his long working life, but his figures made by the lost wax process were outstanding.

DECORCHEMONT, FRANÇOIS EMILE (1880–1971) was a painter and potter who began his own glass factory in 1902. His early work included statuettes and small bowls in *pâte de verre* with decorated enamel. From 1912 he developed the use of *pâte de cristal*. He continued production until after World War II, when he turned to making opaque and marbled glass, and stained glass windows.

LOCKE, JOSEPH (1846–1936) was an engraver and enameller who studied the techniques of *cameo glass* in 1876, producing a glass copy of the Portland Vase. He went to America in 1882, and became a leader in the design of *art glass, amberina* and *peachblow glass*. His pieces are signed 'Locke' or 'Locke Art'.

MULLER FRERES established a glass-house in 1910 near Luneville in France. They specialised in cameo and moulded coloured glass.

NASH, ARTHUR J. (1849–1934) was an English glass-maker and technician who left Stourbridge to join the Tiffany glass-house in 1895. His technical skill was responsible for much of Tiffany's success.

NASH, A. DOUGLAS (died 1940) was the son of Arthur Nash and also worked for Tiffany. In 1928 he, together with his father and others, took over the Tiffany glass-house, but failed in 1931 during the Depression. He used the marks 'Corona', 'Adora' and 'Nash'. After the failure of Tiffany's, he worked successfully with other glass firms.

NORTHWOOD, JOHN (1836–1902) was an English glass-maker who specialised in cameo glass. In the 1870s and 1880s he made a series of famous cameo vases, some of which took nine years to complete. His work was continued by his son John (1870–1960), and the Woodall Brothers.

ROUSSEAU, FRANCOIS EUGENE (1827–1891) was an artist and glass-maker from Clichy who was instrumental in the 19th-century revival of *pâte de verre*. His working life was short, only 18 years. He retired in 1885 and handed over to his student, E. Leville, who continued until about 1900, when the factory was bought by Harand & Guignard.

STUART, FREDERICK (1817–1900) set up a company in Stourbridge in 1881; this company, Stuart & Sons Ltd, is still in operation under the control of his descendants, and has a name for good quality clear-glass functional ware.

WALTER, ALMERIC V. (1859–1942) was a French glass-maker who specialised in *pâte de verre*. He worked for Daum Frères in 1908–1914, and began his own studio after World War I. His pieces include sculptured figures of lizards, frogs, crabs and fish sitting on the edge of dishes. He also made bowls of coloured abstract patterns.

WEBB, THOMAS, & CO. were leading glass-makers who established a factory at Stourbridge in the 1830s and are still operating there today as Webb, Corbett Ltd. In 1886 Thomas Webb & Sons acquired a licence to make *Burmese glass*, but the firm was best known for its late 19th-century cameo glass. In the 1860s they produced Alexandrite, peachblow glass, iridescent glass, *satin glass* and other types of art glass.

WOODALL, GEORGE (1850–1925) and **THOMAS** (1849–1926) were both apprenticed to John Northwood until 1874, then worked with Thomas Webb & Sons. They are best known for their cameo glass.

YSART, PAUL (1904–) is a descendant of a Spanish glass-making family who moved from St Louis, France, to Scotland in 1915. He is famous for his paperweights, some of which are marked 'P.Y.'

Silver

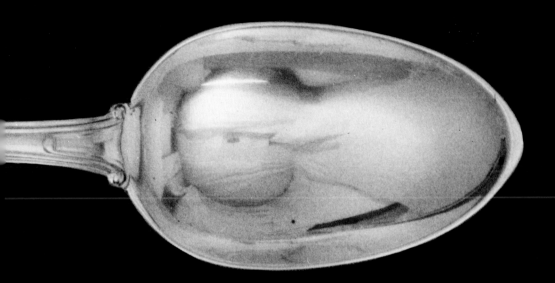

The Guift of Richard Sterne Esq.
to y̆ Honorable East-India Comp.ᵃ

70

Types of silver—hallmarks and quality

There are three categories of silver:

STERLING SILVER is 92.5 per cent silver, with 7.5 per cent of other metal (mostly copper) added to give a sufficient degree of hardness.

SHEFFIELD PLATE is formed by the heating and rolling of sterling silver onto a base, usually of copper. This silver-coated sheet is then used to make the finished product. Sheffield plate was made mainly during the period 1740–1860.

ELECTROPLATE is silver plate made by electrolysis. This process was patented about 1840 and is still used today. A metal article, already shaped, is coated with a skin of pure silver by an electrolytic process. Electroplate has a whiter, harder appearance than sterling silver or Sheffield plate. This is due to the difference in colour between plated 100 per cent silver and sterling silver with its 7.5 per cent content of other metal. Also electroplate is harder and colder to the touch than sterling silver, because it has a different rate of conducting heat from the skin.

HALLMARKS British sterling silver was always hallmarked with a series of punches applied by an assay office in a centre such as London, Sheffield or Birmingham. The sign for English silver was usually a 'lion passant' (see p. 234). This system was so well devised that from 1478 there was never any doubt as to the exact year of manufacture of British silver.

Most British silver was assayed in London, Sheffield and Birmingham. However, there were eight other *assay** offices that also marked pieces to the year of manufacture—York, Dublin, Edinburgh, Exeter, Newcastle, Glasgow, Norwich and Chester. A few pieces were made, marked but not dated, in the provinces, such as in Aberdeen and Cork. These rare provincial marks ceased in England early in the 18th century, in Scotland around 1860, and in Ireland around 1825.

The use of the hallmarking system is explained on p. 234. One important word of warning to newcomers to this system is: always go from the general to the particular—that is, date the article to within thirty years or so, which can be done from the style and from the number of punch marks, before you look at the letter that indicates the exact year of manufacture. Illegible hallmarks considerably reduce the value of an article.

London has the reputation for making consistently sound silver, but Irish silver is known for its weight and quality and may thus fetch a higher price, as can some of the rare provincial pieces. Some Sheffield and Birmingham silver was produced using large-scale methods so can fetch lower prices.

70 *Vigorous 'crossed plumes' on one of the earliest coffee pots, c. 1681, bearing the arms of Sterne. This coffee pot was presented by Mr Richard Sterne to the Honourable East India Company. Height 24.8 cm. (Victoria and Albert Museum, London)*

**Italics indicate glossary entry.*

More pertinent considerations are *line, quality, condition, age* and *weight.*

CONDITION The condition of a silver article affects its value. Unlike furniture, restoration is not as readily acceptable and significantly decreases the value of a silver item.

MAKER A silver article from the workshop of one of about twenty famous silversmiths has a higher value than a similar piece from a relatively unknown workshop. However, there were hundreds of silversmiths—so apart from the masters, there is no 'quality ladder' amongst the remainder.

Armorial engraving

72 Baroque scrolls on a set of three Queen Anne silver gilt casters by David Willaume, c. 1707. The caster covers are pierced with figures of manikins holding pipes, and other figures standing on columns. Height 22.2 cm, weight 963 g. (Christies, London)

Most silver pieces made prior to about 1830 had engraved armorials. Unfortunately, over the years, ignorance of their importance often led to their removal—*patina*, surface and history have been destroyed, and the value of the article reduced by as much as 20 per cent.

Most important collections, even Royal ones, contain silver bearing the armorials of others; the change of ownership of silver is not the prerogative of

72

modern times. The 'arms' can be identified by reference to heraldic books. The shape and decorative surround, known as the *cartouche* or *mantling*, changes according to the style of the period. By understanding this change of style, it is usually possible to identify an original armorial and distinguish it from a later replacement. Irish armorials usually have a round or oval shield set near the bottom of the mantling; English mottoes are below the crest; Scottish mottoes above.

The earliest type of armorial was vigorous 'crossed plumes', shown on the Sterne coffee pot *(70)*. This armorial was fashionable in about 1650–1685. Later armorials, in 1675–1700, were more elaborate feathery scrolls.

A system of hatching, or different types of shading, to represent different

73 Rococo armorial on an early George II oblong salver, by Edward Cornock, c. 1728; it has moulded borders and wavy corners upon four scroll feet, and the centre is crested within foliate mantling, 40 x 27 cm, 1115 g. Early 17th-century provincial bleeding bowl, with a single pierced flat handle, by Pentecost Symonds (of Plymouth), Exeter, c. 1719. Weight 100 g. Pair of George I cast candlesticks, with hexagonal domed bases and baluster columns, by David Green, c. 1719. Height 18.5 cm, weight 500 g. (Phillips Son & Neale, London)

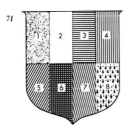

71

71 A system of hatching or shading to represent different colours on armorials engraved on silver.

74

74 *Narrow spade-shaped divided shield with 'impaled' arms, on a George III oval salver, by T. Hannam and J. Crouch, c. 1789. The salver has a thread border, and the centre is engraved with a coat of arms in a bright-cut surround; it stands on four feet. Length 49.5 cm. (Christies, London)*

76

76 *Bold, less simple Regency style arms on a William IV oval tray, by Henry Hyde, c. 1834. The tray has an unusual cast border of fourteen floral bouquets on a stylised fishscale background, and an outer border of rolled scrolls. The two handles are also elaborately decorated with leafy scrolls and bouquets, and the base bears an engraved coat of arms. Length 34 cm, weight 5670 g. (Phillips Son & Neale, London)*

colours was used on some English silver from the late 17th century (*72*): gold (*or*) is represented by dots; silver (*argent*) or white by a blank; blue (*azure*) horizontal lines; red (*gules*) vertical lines; purple (*purpre*) diagonal lines from top right (*sinister*); black (*sable*) crossed lines; green (*vert*) diagonal lines from top left (*dexter*); ermine or fur by tufts with three dots.

Symmetrical *baroque* scrolls, shells and hatching (like those on the Queen Anne silver-gilt casters, *72*) were typical of the period 1705–1740. In the period 1730–1770, *rococo* styles were in vogue.

If an imaginary line is drawn down the centre of the armorials on the

75

75 George II beer jug of the pre-rococo period, c. 1730, but bearing a later armorial of about 1800. Note the angular top corners on the shield, and the absence of cartouche. The value of this article is lessened because the armorial is not contemporary with the jug. (Christies, London)

77 Salver of neo-classical revival period, c. 1874. It has cast borders with swags and paterae, typical of the neo-classical style. The pierced gallery background has a bead border and is engraved with swags and scrolling foliage. Armorials on silver had lost their significance by about 1830. A crest in lieu of a full armorial is incorrect on a salver. Diameter 30.5 cm, weight 3685 g. (Phillips Son & Neale, London)

77

George II round *salver (79)* the oblong tray *(73)* the asymmetry of the rococo style may be appreciated.

By 1770, *neo-classical* armorials had become popular—and from about 1785 until the early 19th century, these had bright-cut engraving with broad faceted cuts that were flat rather than vertical so as to reflect light. Between about 1790 and 1800, the armorial shields were narrow and spade-shaped, and cartouches were seldom used, as seen on the George III oval salver *(74)*. Around 1800 the shields were square rather than spade-shaped, and angular top corners were used, as seen on the beer jug *(75)*. Bold, more extravagant Shield outlines,

78

78 Good-quality early
George III circular salver, by
Ebenezer Coker, c. 1762.
The shaped gadrooned
border has a rim of 'cushion'
motifs. The centre is
engraved with a rococo
cartouche enclosing
armorials in pretence. The
salver stands on four cast,
fluted claw feet. Diameter
45 cm. (Phillips Son &
Neale, London)

without cartouche (as seen in the William IV oval tray, **76**) were introduced early in the 19th century and were at their peak of demand by 1815.

A crest was a small motif above a coat of arms, such as the bird on the George II beer jug **(75)**. Crests were shared by numerous families who were not necessarily related. On large items the full armorial was generally used **(77)**, but on small items and dinner plates or candlesticks the crest alone was used, so only the motto (if present) distinguished between the various families.

The coat of arms was always in a shield. When the shield was divided vertically, the arms on the left were those of the husband and on the right those

of the wife, as shown on the George III oval salver (74). The arms were then referred to as 'impaled'. In the next generation the arms were divided into four, or 'quartered', and the shield at top left gave the family name (as seen on the same George II beer jug, 75). If a man had no sons, when his eldest daughter married her arms were placed in a smaller shield placed over the arms of her husband, as shown on the George III round salver (78). This tradition was referred to as 'in pretence'. In the next generation, the arms of the mother were no longer used. The term *accolé* was used when the shields were placed side by side, as in the George II hexagonal salver (79).

79 Rococo cartouche, containing accolé shields, on one of a pair of George II hexagonal salvers, by George Wickes, c. 1745. The salver has a shell and gadrooned border. Weight 2281 g. (Christies, London)

80

Waiters, salvers and trays

*80 Set of four George I
tazzas, by David Tanqueroy,
London, c. 1718-1720. Total
weight 1794 g. (Geoff K.
Gray Pty Ltd, Sydney)*

A waiter is a small salver of less than 20 cm diameter. Waiters and salvers
always have feet but not handles. Trays are larger items that developed from
about 1785; they always have handles but may or may not have feet. From the
last half of the 17th century until the early 18th century, the small salver known
as a tazza *(80)* was popular. It stood on a cylindrical centre column.

In the early 18th century, square salvers were made. Between about 1730
and 1740 the shape was round, and 'Chippendale' or 'Bath' borders were often
used. After about 1740 some elaborate borders were cast, but between about
1760 and 1775 *gadrooned* borders, first used in the late 17th century, returned to
popularity. By around 1775 *bead borders* were in demand, but in the late 1780s
they lost favour to *thread borders*. From about 1805 gadrooned borders were back
in fashion.

All salvers and waiters should have armorials, and most pre-1730 pieces

81

were otherwise undecorated. However, in the periods 1730–1775 and 1815–1850 *engraving* and *flat chasing* were generally used.

It is important to understand the difference in style between 18th-and 19th-century chasing, because some plain 18th-century items were spoilt by later 19th-century chasing. In the mid-18th century the style of chasing was light and open and the borders were rococo. Engraving was used together with flat chasing on a few items of this period. In the *bright-cut* period of 1785–1815, bright cut engraved decoration was popular, and after 1815 normal engraved decoration was still in demand. The style of the *classical-revival* period *c.* 1865–1914 is seen in the Victorian salver (77). Later Victorian chasing was denser than that of the earlier periods, and engraved 'C' scrolls and criss-cross *diaper* motifs were used, as shown in the Victorian salver with the cast *pierced* border (81). Later decoration reduces the value of earlier items.

81 Victorian salver, with cast pierced border. Cast borders were also used in the 18th century. Note the typical dense chasing on the matt background. (Phillips Son & Neale, London)

Some leading English silversmiths

The leading early English silversmiths had an influence on the development of silver ware over the years. These artisans (a brief portrait of some of them follows) were later replaced by the industrialists and retailers.

PAUL DE LAMERIE (1688–1751) His Huguenot parents came as refugees to England when he was a baby. Lamerie was apprenticed to Pierre Platel, and in 1716 he was appointed as Royal Goldsmith. Initially he worked in two styles: the plain Queen Anne style and the rococo style (of *gadrooning* and *cut-card* decoration). Until at least 1732 he worked in the higher *Britannia standard* of silver, which had been voluntary since 1720. From about 1730 he worked mainly in the rococo style and was the leading English rococo silversmith. He had three different marks: 'L.A.' in 1712–1732, 'PL' in 1732–1739, and 'P.L.' in script after 1739.

THOMAS HEMING (worked *c.* 1745–1773) His mark 'T.H.' was first registered at the Goldsmith's Hall, London, in 1745. On the accession of George III in 1760, he was appointed as Royal Goldsmith. Thomas Heming retired in 1773 although his mark was sometimes used until 1782. His son George then became Royal Goldsmith.

In 1775 George Heming and William Chawner were given a commission by Catherine the Great of Russia to make a double dinner service—this task required four hundred English artisans for its completion.

MATTHEW BOULTON (1728–1809) took over his father's metal button-and-buckle factory in Birmingham in 1750, and sold his wares in Italy and Holland. He began to make *Sheffield plate* in 1762, and by the end of the century his Soho factory, near Birmingham, was the largest producer of plated wares in England. By 1765 he was producing sterling silver and was involved with the opening of *assay* offices at Sheffield and Birmingham in 1773.

The *classical style* of Adam (see p. 212) was emerging when Boulton began making Sheffield plate and silver, so his wares were always in this style.

THE BATEMAN FAMILY (1709–1839) Hester Bateman (1709–1794), the widow of a gold-chain maker, first registered her mark (a script 'H.B.') in 1761. In 1790 she retired and her sons Peter and Jonathan registered their mark. However, Jonathan died the following year, and his widow, Anne, registered her mark together with that of Peter. In 1800, Anne's son William joined the partnership and their mark was 'P.B., A.B., W.B.'. Anne retired in 1805 and Peter in 1815, leaving William to continue alone until 1839.

(The Bateman women were only two of over 150 women who registered their marks and practised as effective silversmiths. Amongst them were Louisa Courtauld, Eliza Godfrey and Rebecca Emes. Some women completed the seven-year apprenticeship; others inherited the right of registration and managed their late husbands' businesses by employing other silversmiths in them.)

PAUL STORR (1771–1844) is sometimes called 'the last of the silversmiths'. At his retirement in 1839, the time of the individual silversmith had passed—the artisans had been replaced by the industrialists. He was apprenticed to the Scandinavian Andrew Fogelberg (mark 'A.F.') in 1785, and registered his first mark 'P.S.' in 1793. He made presentation trophies in the *Regency style*, working on his own and in partnership with businessmen rather than with silversmiths. Between 1807 and 1819 he worked with the Royal Goldsmiths. Between 1822 and 1839, Paul Storr was in partnership with John Mortimer.

ROBERT GARRARD (1793–1881) In 1802 at the age of nine, Robert Garrard became head of a well-established family firm, which was to endure until 1952. The firm produced silver and also sold the products of other silversmiths. The ledgers in the period 1766–1775 show that the firm bought spoons from William and Thomas Chawner; salt cellars from David and Robert Hennell; and candlesticks and *waiters* from Ebenezer Coker.

Garrard's firm succeeded Rundle and Bridge as Royal Goldsmiths in 1830 and Crown Jewellers in 1843.

Much Garrard ware was functional, but the firm did make elaborate table ornaments, typical of the mid-Victorian period. Presentation racing and sailing trophies, including the America Cup, were items on which its fame was founded. Garrard's chief designer from 1833 to 1860 was not a silversmith but a sculptor, Edmund Cotteril.

Two good books on English and London silversmiths, respectively, are Sir James Jackson's and Arthur Grimwade's, (see bibliography).

86 Typical rococo coffee pot, by David Smith and Robert Sharp, London, c. 1765. Height 27 cm. (Victoria and Albert Museum, London)

86

Coffee pots

Coffee-drinking probably began in Abyssinia during the 15th century, but this habit was only introduced to England in the Commonwealth period of 1649–1660. One of the first silver coffee pots was made in 1681 *(70)*. Until about 1715–1730, most Queen Anne coffee pots had a handle at right angles to the spout. Chocolate pots *(82)* were made in the same style as coffee pots, but had a covered hole at the top, through which a swizzle-stick could be inserted for stirring the chocolate. Although chocolate was introduced from the West Indies in the last half of the 17th century, most chocolate pots were made in the early 18th century.

    Octagonal hollow ware *(83)* was fashionable in about 1715–1730. Until about 1725, pot-lids were very highly domed, and until about 1730 the spouts were usually cast and faceted, often ending in a 'duck's head' *(83)*. Straight-sided cylindrical coffee pots *(84)* then became popular in the 1730s until shortly before 1740, when the first 'tucked-under' coffee pots *(85)* were made. This marked the beginning of the rococo coffee pot *(86)*—the *baluster* was replacing the flat-sided shape, and spouts were curly and capped with leaves.

    In the 1750s, 'Turkey' coffee pots *(87)* were first made. A pouring lip (containing a strainer) at the top of the pot replaced the spout that took coffee from the bottom of the pot. The name 'Turkey' was due to this shape resembling that of coffee pots in the Middle East, where coffee grounds settled to the bottom of the pot, and thick, sweet coffee could be poured from the lip.

82

82 Queen Anne chocolate pot, with inside circular mounting for chocolate whisk, by William Fawdery, 1707. It has a tucked-under base on a skirted cast foot, a curved spout with hinged cap, a hinged dome cover and cast scroll thumbpiece, and a looped wooden handle. Height 26.5 cm, weight 822 g. (Phillips Son & Neale, London)

83 Octagonal coffee pot, by Richard Bayled, London, c. 1716. (Victoria and Albert Museum, London)

84 Straight-sided coffee pot, c. 1730. (James R. Lawson, Sydney)

85 George II 'tucked-under' coffee pot, John Swift, London, 1750. (Geoff K. Gray Pty Ltd, Sydney)

83

85

87

Surface decoration was changing: before about 1780 coffee pots were not decoratively engraved except for armorials. Between about 1730 and 1740 they were sometimes flat-chased, but not *embossed*. The period when many, but not all, were embossed, was 1740–1765. Some plain silver ware made in previous years was embossed during the 19th century. These later-decorated and severely devalued pieces can be distinguished with an understanding of rococo fashions and by the hallmark date: for example, rococo embossing would not be expected on a piece made *c.* 1790, but would be expected on a piece made *c.* 1750. Compare the Turkey coffee pot of 1767 (*87*) with that made in 1789 (*88*).

In the mid-18th century, any floral decoration was of an open design and only covered about two-thirds of the surface area, as expected for rococo embossing (like that on the Turkey coffee pot of 1767, *87*). Some 18th century embossing of definite themes, such as a *Chinoiserie* scene, covered a greater area.

In the Adam period (*c.* 1765–1780), embossing was only of classical motifs such as *swags*—cast beaded borders (*89*) were a feature of the 1770s and 1780s.

87 Turkey coffee pot, c. 1767. The rococo embossing shows a minimum of surface decoration and a plain background. (Victoria and Albert Museum, London)

88 Turkey coffee pot, by John Schofield, London, c. 1789. The embossing is typical of 19th-century embossing, showing a matt background. The bead border of the base and lid was contemporary with a 1780s pot, and indicates that no original embossed floral decoration would be expected on this piece. (Geoff K. Gray Pty Ltd, Sydney)

89 George III coffee pot, by Daniel Smith and Robert Sharp, London, c. 1775. Adam embossing is typical of the period 1765-1780. Note the typical beaded bands. Weight 709 g. (The Grafton Galleries, Sydney)

90 Coffee pot, by Hester Bateman, London, c. 1773. This plain classical pot has gadrooned borders and urn finial. (Victoria and Albert Museum, London)

92 Victorian coffee pot, by Edward Barnard, London, c. 1854. Height 29 cm. (The Grafton Galleries, Sydney)

88

89

Restrained thread borders (97) were a feature of the 1790s. Gadrooned borders (90) finally went out of fashion between 1775 and 1800, but then came back into vogue after 1800.

Bright-cut engraving was much used between 1785 and 1815. The cuts were bevelled to reflect light (as on the George III teapot, 95). After about 1760, half-fluting on the lower sections of hollow ware was used (98), but this was much more common after about 1800. Ball feet (91) were features of the early 19th century. During the early Victorian era, 1830–1865, rococo styles were used for coffee pots (92). Provincial and Irish styles were usually a few years behind London styles.

From the early 19th century, coffee pots were part of tea and coffee services, and 19th century coffee pot styles are discussed in that section. Except for coffee pots made between c.1740–1755 and marked on the body, all coffee pots must also have some hallmarks on the cover. However, apart from those marked at Exeter no coffee pot is fully marked on the cover.

91 George III coffee pot, by Emes and Barnard, London, c. 1813. Note the typical Regency ball feet. (Geoff K. Gray Pty Ltd, Sydney)

90

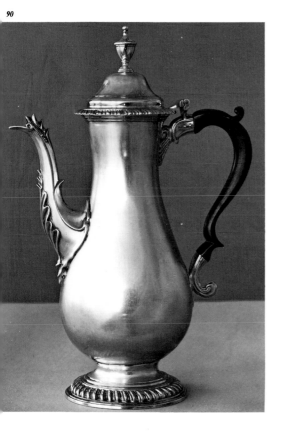

92

93

Teapots

The first teapots were made during the last half of the 17th century (*93*).
Because of the high cost of tea, these pots were very small—and very few were
made until about 1780.

Pear-shaped and octagonal teapots were made in 1715–1725. The term
'octagonal' denotes teapots not only with eight sides, but also those with seven
or twelve.

The conventional round-bullet teapots were made between 1720 and 1750
(*94*). In the middle of the century there was a change to the inverted pear-shaped
pot. Sometimes these were embossed with floral and leaf decoration. The neo-
classical style began with the drum-shaped pots, sometimes embossed or
engraved with swags. These pots enjoyed brief popularity between 1765 and
1780, but were soon replaced by oval pots (such as the teapot with stand, made
by Hennell in 1795, *95*). These oval pots remained popular until the end of the
century, in the period when bright-cut engraving was also popular. Shortly before
and after 1800, a more rectangular variation with fluted or rounded corners was
made. Stands went out of fashion early in the 19th century. Round teapots
returned to fashion in about 1815 (*96*).

Until the 19th century, hallmarks on teapots were always on the bottom
rather than the side. Teapot stands add considerably to the value of a teapot.
Covers are marked as for coffee pots; again, too many marks are as suspect as too
few. The cover should however have some marks.

94 Queen Anne round-bullet teapot, by James Smith, London, c. 1719. (Victoria and Albert Museum, London)

94

95 Teapot and stand, showing the bright-cut engraving of the late 18th century, by D. Hennell, London, c. 1795. (Victoria and Albert Museum, London)

95

96 William IV teapot, c. 1830, showing a typical solid example of the period. (Victoria and Albert Museum, London)

96

Tea services

Almost no matching tea or coffee services were made before about 1780, and only a few were made before about 1800 (such as the late 18th-century tea and coffee service, *97*). Early in the 19th century the pieces were often half-fluted and some had flat bases (like those of the George III coffee pot) *(98 left)*. In about 1805–1815, the Regency oblong shape was in vogue, and each piece often had ball feet (as in the Regency service, *98, 99*). After about 1815, round shapes were in fashion again (like the four-piece Storr tea set, *100*). From about 1820, heavy-chased and embossed decoration was used (similar to that of the four-piece George III tea set, *101*). Between 1830 and 1850, an unembossed rococo melon-shaped style was in vogue—and in the later years of this period and until about 1860, some elaborate embossing was also used (as shown on the Hennel Victorian tea and coffee service, *102*). After about 1865, the classical-revival style began, with flat-chased or engraved decoration (like that on the engraved tea and coffee service, *103*).

99 *Regency tea service, London, c. 1812. Note the oblong shape and ball feet, characteristic of the Regency style, and the gadrooned border, which had come back into vogue. (Victoria and Albert Museum, London)*

97 *Late 18th-century tea and coffee service, c. 1798, showing the thread border and bright-cut engraving of the last decades of the 18th century. Total weight 1729 g. (Christies, London)*

99

97

100

100 *Four-piece tea service by Paul Storr, c. 1816. Note the elaborately decorated pieces, partly fluted with gadrooned and shell borders. Weight 2438 g. (Phillips Son & Neale, London)*

101

101 *Four-piece George III tea and coffee service, by Joseph Wilson, 1818-1819. The bellied sides are slightly waisted, and the pieces are heavily chased with flowers and scrolls. Weight 2679 g. (Phillips Son & Neale, London)*

102

102 *Embossed Victorian tea and coffee service, by Robert Hennell, London, c. 1868. (Victoria and Albert Museum, London)*

A four-piece service with a coffee pot is much more valuable than a three-piece tea service, and hot-water pots add further to the value of a service.

Styles in the early 20th century were repetitions of former styles. Some silver tea services were made between about 1890 and 1910 with the typical flowing lines of *Art Nouveau* (*104*).

Between about 1920 and 1940 a small amount of silver was made with the sharp angular lines of *Art Deco*.

103 Engraved tea and coffee service, London, c. 1872. (Victoria and Albert Museum, London)

104 Tea service in the Art Nouveau style, Birmingham, c. 1904. (Victoria and Albert Museum, London)

106 George III tea or coffee urn, by George Smith and Thomas Hayter, c. 1794. The plain circular tapering body has a canted threaded rim and floral bright-cut engraved decoration. The square base has four ball feet. Height 49 cm, weight 3246 g. (Phillips Son & Neale, London)

106

Kettles and urns

Tea kettles were first made at the beginning of the 18th century, and were plain, sometimes octagonal, following the silver styles of this period. In the rococo period of about 1740–1770, kettles became more common (of the style of the William Grundy tea kettle and stand, *105*). Tea urns were made after about 1765, and by the last quarter of the 18th century had largely replaced tea kettles. (The George III tea or coffee urn, *106*, shows the style of that period.) From the Victorian period, kettles were again popular and generally followed the styles of Victorian tea services *(107)*. Embossing was used until about 1860, when engraving and plain lines were used and the fashion for tea urns returned.

105 Tea kettle and stand by William Grundy, London, c. 1753. Note the sparse embossing and rococo armorial. (Victoria and Albert Museum, London)

105

107 Kettle stand and spirit-burner of silver-plated copper, showing Art Nouveau characteristics. Designed by Arthur Dixon for the Birmingham Guild of Handcraft, c. 1905-1910. (Victoria and Albert Museum, London)

107

109 Silver-gilt ewer made by
Paul de Lamerie, London,
c. 1736. This illustrates the
heavy quality associated
with the Huguenot
silversmiths. (Victoria and
Albert Museum, London)

108 Silver jug, by Simon
Pantin, London, c. 1721.
Height 18 cm. (Victoria and
Albert Museum, London)

109

Cream jugs and sugar containers

The early cream jugs were in the plain rounded style of about 1715–1745 *(108)*.
These heavy jugs stood on a flat round base. Three-legged jugs were first made
in about 1730, and were also heavy *(109)*. Between about 1745 and 1765, jugs
were embossed *(110)*. Farmyard scenes were popular decoration. The jugs were
hallmarked on the base, and only a few were plain. The only 18th-century
embossed jugs after about 1770 carried classical Adam (see p. 212) motifs *(111)*.
In 1730–1770, jugs were made in the plain Irish style, so were bigger and
heavier. These Irish-style jugs often had a rib around the centre and always had
a foot under the spout, whereas English-style jugs had a foot under the handle.

Classical helmet-shaped jugs were made in about 1775–1805. Some of

108

111

112

113

114

110

111 *Left: George III pitcher-shaped cream jug, by Robert Hennel I, c. 1777. The sides are embossed with medallions and swags, and the waisted neck is decorated with flutes on a matt background. Height 14 cm, weight 141 g. Right: George III cream jug, by Francis Butty and Nicholas Dumee, c. 1772. This is almost identical to but larger than the one on the left. Height 16 cm, weight 198 g. (Phillips Son & Neale, London)*

110 *Rococo jug, by Jacob Marsh, London, c. 1761. (Victoria and Albert Museum, London)*

112 *Classical helmet-shaped jug, London, c. 1790. It is decorated with bright-cut engraving and has a thread border typical of the period.*

(Victoria and Albert Museum, London)

113 *Bright-cut cream jug, London, c. 1790. (The*

Grafton Galleries, Sydney)

114 *Helmet-shaped cream jug, London, c. 1786. It is decorated with bright-cut*

engraving and has a thread border. (The Grafton Galleries, Sydney)

115 Left: Regency jug, c. 1810. Note the gadrooned border and the oblong Regency style. Right: Heavier Dublin style jug, c. 1821. (The Grafton Galleries, Sydney)

116 Victorian rococo milk jug, by Benjamin Smith the Younger, London, c. 1840. (Victoria and Albert Museum, London)

117 Wine ewer, by Thomas Bradbury & Sons, Sheffield, c. 1858. This has Roman classical-style engraving. (Victoria and Albert Museum, London)

these jugs had punched edges, but the better-quality products had thread-mounted or bead edges *(112)*. These jugs were usually marked under the lip or on the side of the base. Between 1785 and 1810, plain helmet-shaped jugs with a flat bottom were made *(114)*. These jugs were often part of tea services, which had just come into vogue. In about 1805, oblong Regency-style jugs were made, often with ball feet *(115 left)*. A few years later these Regency jugs were fluted on the bottom half of the body. Heavy embossing was used after 1815 *(115 right)*.

During the remainder of the 19th century, jugs followed the styles of tea sets. The Victorian milk jug *(116)* shows the rococo style of 1840. The wine jug *(117)* hallmarked *c.* 1858, is a very early example of the classical-revival style that is usually considered to have emerged with the Paris Exhibition of 1867.

117

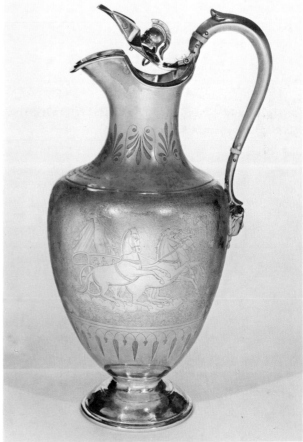

116

The late Victorian jug *(118)* shows the Japanese influence felt in Europe from the 1860s.

Before about 1760, sugar containers were simple bowls, usually with separate covers (like the George II sugar bowl, *119*). Later, the bowls had swing handles and were known as sugar baskets. Up to the late 1780s, these sugar baskets were pierced and had blue glass liners (as shown in the sugar basket, *c.* 1773, *120 left*). Later, unpierced boat-shaped sugar baskets with bright-cut decoration were more popular *(120 right)*. By about 1800, sugar basins without handles were fashionable, and these were part of matching tea services. The basins had two handles and were larger than those made today because unrefined sugar was used.

118 Late 19th-century jug, c. 1881. It has engraved Japanese motifs and a simulated bamboo handle. (Victoria and Albert Museum, London)

119 George II oval sugar box and cover, by Ayme Videau, c. 1744. It has shaped oval feet, and the bombé body and domed cover are chased with fluting, flowers and scrolls. Length 12.1 cm, weight 482 g. (Christies, London)

120 Left: Pierced sugar basket with blue liner, c. 1773. Right: Boat-shaped sugar basket, c. 1787. (The Grafton Galleries, Sydney)

118

120

119

Sauce boats

121 Sauce boat with collet foot, c. 1735. (The Grafton Galleries, Sydney)

Sauce boats were first made during the reign of George I. These early boats had a pouring lip at each end and had a scroll handle at the centre. After about 1730, sauce boats were made with only one pouring lip, and the handle was at the opposite end to this lip. The boats stood on a collet foot *(121)*. After about 1740, sauce boats were made with three feet *(122, 123, 124)*. The collet foot regained some popularity in about 1775–1800. After about 1780, sauce tureens were more popular than sauce boats.

Pap boats were small sauce boats, made between about 1710 and 1830, that were used for feeding infants or invalids. They had no feet or handles.

122 George II sauce boat, by William Grundy, London, c. 1758. Weight 563 g. (Geoff K. Gray Pty Ltd, Sydney)

122

123

123 Pair of early George III sauce boats, by John Parker and Edward Wakelin, 1765. Note the swan-neck handles and gadrooned border. Weight 82 g. (Phillips Son & Neale, London)

124 Pair of George III sauce boats, by John Schofield, London, c. 1789. Weight 782 g. (Geoff K. Gray Pty Ltd, Sydney)

124

125

126

Tankards and mugs

The difference between a mug *(125)* and the tankard *(126)* is that the tankard has a lid. Tankards were first made in the 16th century, but became more popular after the Restoration. Before about 1700, the lids of tankards were flat, then between about 1710 and 1790 the style changed to favour domed lids. Some early tankards have lids that are either new or removed from other tankards. An original lid will have a hallmark that matches that of the tankard itself. Large mugs of tankard shape are often tankards with missing lids.

Many of the tankards made in earlier periods were later heavily embossed during the Victorian period, as seen on the George III tankard of 1775 *(127)* that, like some other early tankards, was also converted to a jug by the addition of a pouring spout. Most post-Restoration tankards were not embossed, so those decorated in Victorian years can be easily detected.

The line drawings show chasing, cut-card decoration and Regency

127

Tankard, c. 1633, showing flat lid

Tankard, c. 1727, showing domed lid

Tankard, c. 1663, showing relatively plain embossing

Tankard, c. 1672, showing cut-card decoration

Tankard, c. 1827, showing extravagant Regency embossing

127 George III tankard, by Walter Tweedie, London, c. 1775. This has been embossed and converted to a jug during the 19th century. Note the heavy embossing and matt background. (Geoff K. Gray Pty Ltd, Sydney)

embossing that are exceptions to the plain late 17th-century style. Also, spiral fluting was used in the early 18th century, and flat-chased Chinoiserie decoration was used from about 1680 until the 18th century. Concentric reeded mugs *(125)* were made about 1780–1820.

Mugs were first made in the Commonwealth period, and by the end of the 17th century were cylindrical in shape. A tuck-in foot was first used in about 1715, and after about 1720 this was quite common. Mugs were small—only of quarter-litre capacity—before about 1700.

Sometimes the maker's mark was the only mark on the tankard handle, and some early tankards had unmarked handles. Body and cover must be fully and identically marked. Tankards made before about 1730 were usually marked on the body near the handle, but a few were marked underneath. After this time, most tankards were marked underneath.

Porringers, cups, bleeding bowls, quaiches and wine tasters

PORRINGERS or feeding bowls were of cylindrical shape, slightly tapered and turned in at the base *(128)*. They had two handles, and usually, but not always, a cover. Very few porringers today still have their covers. A matching cover can add 100 per cent to the value. Porringers were most popular between about 1655 and 1720. They were marked on the side or underneath, and the covers were also marked.

Quaich or cup, c. 1698

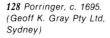

Wine taster, c. 1689. Note the raised bottom.

Porringers declined in popularity in about 1715, when cups were becoming more common. These early cups were fairly short and had a foot. Later cups were taller, like the George II two-handled cup illustrated *(129)*. **BLEEDING BOWLS** *(73)* were rather like shallow one-handled porringers. They were plain, and decorated only by the piercing of the handle. The handle was marked underneath with the 'lion passant' or 'lion's head erased' (see p. 234). Most bleeding bowls were made in about 1670–1725.

QUAICHES were two-handled low bowls, originally of Scottish origin. The word 'quaich' was probably derived from the Gaelic 'cuach', meaning cup. These bowls were made in the late 17th century.

WINE TASTERS were small bowls with a raised centre, against which the colour of the wine could be viewed. Most tasters were made in the period between the Restoration and the end of the 18th century.

128 Porringer, c. 1695. (Geoff K. Gray Pty Ltd, Sydney)

128

129 George II two-handled cup, by Fuller White, London, c. 1759. Weight 780 g. (Geoff K. Gray Pty Ltd, Sydney)

129

Wine funnels, wine labels and decanter stands

WINE FUNNELS were first made in the Restoration period, but became far more popular from around 1770. The tip of the stem was usually turned to one side to prevent the aeration of the wine whilst it was being decanted.

WINE LABELS OR BOTTLE TICKETS did not become common until about 1760. Most pieces, because they were small items, were not fully hallmarked before about 1784. Labels shaped like a vine-leaf, usually pierced with the name, were first made in about 1830.

DECANTER STANDS OR COASTERS were rare until about 1760. They were used under decanters so that wine could be moved easily along the table after the servants had been dismissed. Most stands were pierced until 1800, but then piercing was no longer fashionable. The plain style remained in vogue until early in the 19th century. Higher gadrooned edges were then in demand, and from about 1815 bacchanalian scenes and grape motifs were used. Coasters were seldom used after about 1835 until the end of the century. Pairs or sets of four coasters are very much more valuable than single items.

Pierced wine coaster, c. 1774

Wine coaster, c. 1810.

Wine coaster, c. 1815

130

*130 Pair of William III cast table
candlesticks, by John Laughton,
1701. These stand on octagonal
bases with gadrooned borders and*
*sunk circular centres, and have
baluster stems with gadroons.
Height 16.8 cm, weight 765 g.
(Christies, London)*

Candlesticks

Candlesticks are either cast or loaded (that is, made from sheet-silver and filled
with resin or other material to add weight). The first candlesticks were made
during the late 17th century, and hand-hammered sheet-silver was used. Cast
candlesticks *(73, 130)* were introduced by the Huguenot silversmiths a little
before 1700. In about 1760, *die-stamped* loaded candlesticks *(131)* were made,
mainly in Sheffield and Birmingham *(132, 133)*—and these were still being
produced early this century from old dies. However, cast candlesticks were still
mainly made in London beyond the end of the 19th century. Cast candlesticks
can be more than double the price of die-stamped loaded candlesticks of the
same period.

At the beginning of the 18th century, candlesticks were about 15

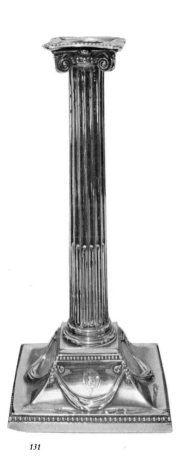

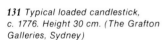
131

132

131 Typical loaded candlestick,
c. 1776. Height 30 cm. (The Grafton
Galleries, Sydney)

132 Pair of Sheffield loaded
candlesticks, by John Green & Co.,
c. 1795. Height 30 cm. (Victoria and
Albert Museum, London)

centimetres tall, but by the end of the century they were usually almost double
this size.

Nozzles or grease catchers were not introduced until about 1735–1745.
Candlestick nozzles of the mid-18th century may or may not be marked, and
then only with the 'lion passant' and maker's mark. There is little difference to
value when marks are present. However, nozzles should be marked from c. 1780
with lion passant, maker's mark and duty mark if applicable. Sunk bases (130)
were in fashion until about 1755–1765. Raised centres were then used (134).
Because of the smaller surface of candlesticks, crests rather than full armorials
were used but do not add much to their value.

Very few candelabra were made until the last quarter of the 18th century.

134

133

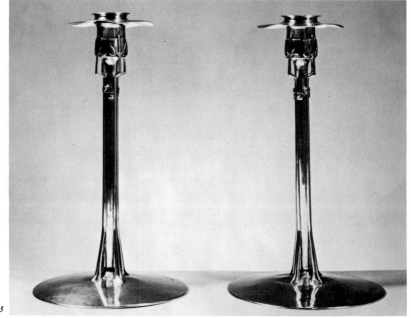

133 Classical Sheffield loaded candlestick, c. 1778. Note the bead border typical of this period. Height 17.5 cm. (Victoria and Albert Museum, London)

134 George III candlestick, London, 1770. Note the raised centre to the base. Height 16.8 cm, weight 514 g. (Geoff K. Gray Pty Ltd, Sydney)

135 Pair of candlesticks in the Art Nouveau style, bearing Birmingham marks of c. 1906 and maker's mark of Liberty & Co. (Victoria and Albert Museum, London)

135

Candelabra are rare and so more valuable than candlesticks. All detachable parts must be hallmarked, although not fully marked. Sets of two or four candlesticks or candelabra are much more valuable per unit than individual pieces.

Also, very few *tapersticks* were made because they were replaced in about 1775 by coiled wax tapers. Because of their rarity, their value is roughly equivalent to larger candlesticks of the same date.

Salt cellars, mustard pots, casters and peppers

SALT CELLARS There were four main 18th-century styles for salt cellars:

1. In about 1700–1740, trencher-type cellars were popular. These had a skirt that reached to the table, and were mostly made from sheet-silver and only occasionally were cast *(136a)*.

2. In about 1735–1785, the round style *(136b)* was common. The cellar was supported by three feet and blue liners were only used in the 19th century in such round salt cellars.

3. In about 1760–1785, the cellars were usually pierced and contained blue glass *(137a)*.

4. In about 1785–1800, boat-shaped unpierced cellars were fashionable *(137a)*.

Blue liners were only used in the 18th century with the pierced style. The liners were of glass and usually had a star cut in the base. The presence of original liners has little effect on value.

136a Trencher salt cellar, London 1721/22, with later 19th Century chasing. (James R. Lawson Pty. Ltd., Sydney)

136b Round-style salt cellar c. 1776. (The Grafton Galleries, Sydney)

137a Left pierced salt cellar with blue liner c. 1772. Right unpierced boat-shaped style c. 1795. (The Grafton Galleries, Sydney)

137b Sheffield plate salt cellar c. 1805. Oblong shape, ball feet and gadrooned edge are typical of this period. (The Grafton Galleries)

136a

136b

137a

137b

138 Typical heavy Huguenot
caster, by Paul de Lamerie,
c. 1734. (Victoria and Albert
Museum, London)

138

After about 1740, some cellars were made with a gilt lining to avoid corrosion by the salt. In the early 19th century, the oblong cellar was popular (*137b*). This often had a gadrooned border, ball feet and a gilded interior. Later in the 19th century, 18th-century styles were repeated, and pierced cellars were again popular. Matching sets of salt cellar, mustard pot and pepper pot were first used in about 1860—the salt cellars in these sets were smaller. Spice sets, excluding salt, were in use from the 17th century. Liners were sometimes used with various styles of 19th-century salt cellars.

MUSTARD POTS Before about 1760, mustard was usually placed in a 'blind' or unpierced caster. The first mustard pots were round or drum-shaped. Pierced decoration then became fashionable and glass liners were first used. From the 1770s, oval mustard pots were popular, and by the 1780s far fewer items were pierced. The bead borders characteristic of the 1870s were also used for mustard pots, until fine thread borders became the fashion in the 1790s. Mustard pots with matching salt cellars were in vogue by about 1785. During the Regency period, both the heavier round-shaped mustard pots and the typical Regency oblong shape were made. The Victorians copied previous styles, making typical early-Victorian rococo mustard pots (1845–1865).

Mustard pots are hallmarked on the body or underneath, and must also have the 'lion passant', and preferably also the maker's mark, on the cover.

CASTERS AND PEPPERS In the late 17th century, casters (*138*) were used for sugar. These were cylindrical with straight sides and accordingly were known as 'lighthouse' casters. During the same period, peppers were made for holding spices. Casters were taller (about 15 centimetres high) than peppers (about 8 centimetres high). In about 1705–1715, these vessels were rounded-pear shape (*139*). Octagonal shapes became popular in about 1715–1730. In 1715–1770, a rounded and flatter 'bun' shape was also used. In about 1705–1730, kitchen casters that had a loop handle were made.

Casters made in about 1730–1750 had a concave upper half (*140*), whereas those made in the last half of the 18th century had a double curve or baluster to the lower half of the body (*141*).

Victorian styles copied earlier Georgian ones, and Victorian rococo casters and peppers were produced (1845–1865).

Casters must always be fully marked on the lower half, and the covers should be marked with the 'lion passant' or 'lion's head erased'.

Plain drum c. 1760

Pierced drum c. 1770

Pierced oval, thread border c. 1785

Plain oval, thread border, domed lid c. 1800

Oblong, Gadrooned border, these often had ball feet. c. 1805

141

140 *George II caster, by Samuel Wood, London, 1747. Note the concave upper half, characteristic of about 1730-1750. Height 16.5 cm. (The Grafton Galleries, Sydney)*

141 *Late 18th-century caster, London, 1797. Note the double curve or baluster of the lower half pf the body, characteristic of the last half of the 18th century. (Victoria and Albert Museum, London)*

139 *Set of three rounded pear-shape casters, c. 1709. (Victoria and Albert Museum, London)*

139

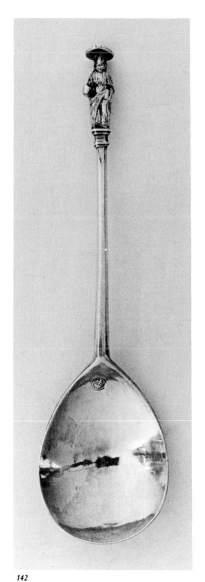

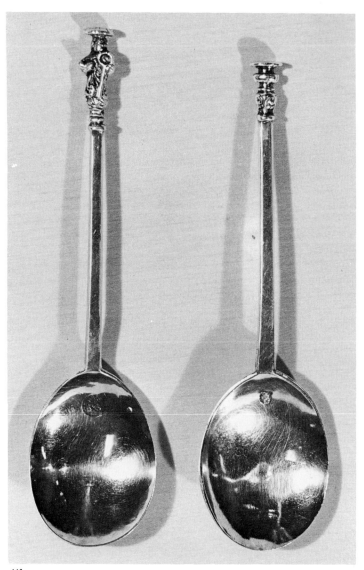

142

143

Spoons

Spoons are the most commonly found items of pre-*Restoration* silver. The coronation spoon dates from the 12th century.

APOSTLE SPOONS (*142, 143 left*) were made in sets of thirteen—of Jesus and his twelve apostles. Each figure held a book in the left hand and a characteristic emblem in the right. The bowls of the spoons were fig-shaped. Most sets were made in the late Elizabethan, James I and Charles I periods. Early *finials* were cast and fitted to the end of the stem, with a *mortise* joint that is visible.

SEAL-TOP SPOONS (*143 right*) were first made during the reign of Henry VIII. They usually had a stubby finial with a hexagonal seal to the top. London seal-top

142 Apostle spoon, 15th century. Note the maker's mark, which is a mullet enclosing a pellet. Weight 47 g. (Geoff K. Gray Pty Ltd, Sydney)

143 Left: Commonwealth silver-gilt Apostle spoon, by Edward Anthony, Exeter, c. 1640. Right: Charles II seal-top spoon, London, 1664. It bears the maker's mark 'i.l.'. (Geoff K. Gray Pty Ltd, Sydney)

spoons are rare—they should be marked with a 'leopard's head' inside the bowl and 'bottom-marked' with three stem marks.

SLIP-TOP SPOONS had a finial that was slipped or cut off at an acute angle (like a plant slip or cutting). They were seldom made after the Restoration.

TREFID SPOONS were made in 1660–1695. They had a flattened finial into which two notches were cut to form three peaks (hence the name). The stem was wide, and bore clear bold marks. This developed into a 'Dognose' 1700–1710.

HANOVERIAN-PATTERN SPOONS were made in 1710–1760. The earlier ones usually had a rat-tail strengthening motif where the stem joined the bowl, but the rat-tail was rarely used by about 1730. Until about 1760, the top of the stem was turned upwards.

OLD ENGLISH-PATTERN SPOONS were introduced in 1760. The end of the stem turned downwards (whereas the stem of forks turned upwards). This pattern was the most popular style until about 1820.

FIDDLE-PATTERN SPOONS *(144)* were fashionable from about 1805. The top of the stem resembled the shape of a fiddle or violin.

KING-PATTERN SPOONS *(144)* were made from about 1815. Scottish spoons usually

144 Some Common spoon patterns. Right to left: King; Queen; Albert; Fiddle, thread and shell; Fiddle; Old English; Old English bead. (Brufords Antiques, Perth)

144

were single struck (on the top side only). This applies also to other patterns.

SOME DATING INDICATIONS From about 1780, all *flatware* was marked at the top of the stem rather than 'bottom-marked' near the bowl. Two characteristics of the mid-18th-century spoons were the 'pictures' flat-chased at the back of some bowls, and the stretched hallmarks punched on to some stems before they were stretched and finished.

Bright-cut engraved decoration was used on flatware during the last quarter of the 18th century. The earliest, before about 1780, of this engraving was feather-edged (a narrow border of diagonal cuts) and was 'bottom-marked'. In about 1780–1805, engraving sometimes covered the whole spoon.

Scottish and Irish spoons usually had a very short pointed bowl, and sometimes a pointed stem.

146

146 *Pair of rococo sauce ladles, London, c. 1756. (The Grafton Galleries, Sydney)*

145

145 *Set of Art Deco coffee spoons, c. 1930. (The Grafton Galleries, Sydney)*

Sheffield plate

Sheffield plate was made for just over a hundred years, from the 1740s to the 1840s, when it lost popularity to the newly introduced *electroplate*, and was seldom made after the 1860s.

This was the only system of plating by which the silver-coated sheet was produced first, then the article made from this sheet. For electroplate, the article was shaped from a base metal first, then the silver skin applied. This important distinction helps in the identification of Sheffield plate. Evidence of this technique was seen in most hollow ware, at the seam where the sheet is joined. Breathe on the seam to see it better. The wine coaster *(147)* shows clearly the joining of the sheet. However, some hollow ware is formed by *raising*.

The silver-coated sheet was made by wiring a thick sheet of silver to the top of a small copper brick. The silver and copper were fused by heating, and then rolled into a thin sheet of copper coated with silver.

The silver used for Sheffield plate is of sterling standard and is not pure silver. For electroplate pure silver is used, which has a colder, brighter appearance.

The socket handles, finials, feet and other fixtures of hollow ware were die-stamped in two or more sections. The seams are visible on Sheffield plate so are helpful in identification.

Decorative mounts applied to Sheffield plate are either of silver or of lead, covered with silver. On electroplate, however, the mounts are part of the original shape of the article. When the base metal of an electroplated piece is copper, the mounts are also in copper so that when the silver skin wears through on the high points the copper base of the mount is visible. For Sheffield plate pieces, the mounts show only silver or lead when the coating has worn off. This is a very useful guide to identification.

Pieces that have been silver-plated on to a copper base are sometimes mistakenly considered to be old Sheffield plate, particularly when they are of an old style. However, electroplated articles with copper bases are being produced today, and are often copies of an old style.

On later Sheffield plate, from about 1830, the base metal was sometimes nickel, so that worn patches did not show copper, but a silver-coloured base metal.

The inside of hollow ware and under-surfaces of waiters were tinned. Double-sided silver was first used in about 1765, but tinning continued to be an

147 Sheffield plate coaster, showing seam and rubbed-in shield. (The Grafton Galleries, Sydney)

148 Edge of Sheffield plate entrée dish, showing lapped edge. (The Grafton Galleries, Sydney)

alternative method for finishing Sheffield plate.

The changes in manufacturing techniques are a useful guide to dating Sheffield plate. There were changes in the method of lapping the silver over the edge of the article. However, Sheffield plate always has a definite edge (148), unlike electroplated articles.

Decoration on Sheffield plate was always flat-chased, not engraved, because engraving would cut through to the base metal. Armorial or crest engraving was done on shields that were then let into the desired position. After about 1789 these shields were made from thick Sheffield plate, but after about 1810 they were made from pure silver. These later shields are slightly whiter than the surrounding plate, and stand out clearly when breathed on.

Few pieces of Sheffield plate are marked. In fact marks were forbidden between 1773 and 1784 in order to avoid any confusion with silver hallmarks.

149 Sheffield plate Argyle or sauce-warmer, showing cylindrical shape, c. 1770. (Shepherds Market, Sydney)

Electroplate

The process of electroplating *(150)* was patented by Elkington of Birmingham in 1840. Within a decade it was widely used by such firms as the P & O Steamship Company, and numerous clubs and hotels. Electroplating was a cheaper manufacturing method than the Sheffield plate process, because the article was shaped in base metal first, then was silver-plated. For Sheffield plate a silver-coated sheet was produced first, then the article was made from this sheet.

The first electroplated articles made, however, were not cheap. An Elkington 1847 catalogue lists engraved electroplated tea trays at £32, and an engraved electroplated tea kettle at £17. The same kettle unengraved was £16 5s. These prices were greatly reduced in subsequent years.

Although Elkington perfected the process, experimental non-commercial items had been electroplated during the first decade of the 19th century. Elkington licensed Charles Christofle of France to use his patent in 1842. By 1850 Christofle was producing large quantities of electroplate, particularly in the Louis XV and XVI styles. The embossed decoration of these styles was much simpler to do by using the electrolytic process than the Sheffield plate process. With an eye to promoting French products, Napoleon III placed a large, plated dinner service in his palace for use on state occasions.

In the 19th century, all Christofle pieces were available in the same shape in both silver and silver plate. This was important at a time when appearances counted for so much. Guests were never able to detect the composition of their host's Christofle flatware.

The basis of electroplating lies in the fact that an electric current passing through an electrolytic solution causes silver from one terminal to be deposited on the article to be plated, which is attached to the other terminal.

Elkington made his name and fortune with a popular household line of goods that differ little from those we use today. When he died in 1865 he was employing over a thousand workmen and left an estate valued at £350 000— indicating the success of the electroplating system during its first twenty years.

Elkingtons also made electrotypes—reproductions of sculptured pieces. The model was sculptured and then electrolysis was used to deposit a fine layer of the metal—either silver, gold or copper—over the model. By this means very fine bronze sculptures could be reproduced simply. The plaque illustrated *(151)* was modelled by the French artist Leonard Monel-Ladeuil who worked for

Elkington from 1859 until his death in 1888. The plaque is from the 'Milton Shield' (now in the Victoria and Albert Museum), and won a gold medal at the Paris Exhibition of 1867.

There is no uniform system of marking for electroplate as there is on sterling silver. Pieces were marked with the name of the country of origin after

150 *Art Nouveau electroplate dressing-table tray. (The Grafton Galleries, Sydney)*

111

151 Electrotype, by Elkington, c. 1860. (The Grafton Galleries, Sydney)

1890. The letters EPNS, EPBM, EPGS indicate electroplated nickel silver, Britannia metal and German silver respectively. Some late 19th-century marks resemble silver hallmarks, but can be distinguished by the absence of a 'lion passant'.

Some Useful Silver Dates

1478	Date letters first used for English hallmarks
1697–1720	Compulsory higher Britannia silver standard
c. 1715–1730	Octagonal shapes in hollow ware
c. 1730–1755	Flat-chasing
c. 1740–1770	Rococo period
c. 1760–1775	Gadrooned borders again in vogue
1784	Monarch's head first used for hallmarks
c. 1775–1788	Beaded borders
c. 1785–1800	Thread borders
c. 1785–1815	Bright-cut engraving
c. 1780–1820	Concentric rings used on items such as mugs
c. 1800 onwards	Gadrooned borders again fashionable
c. 1815–1850	Flat-chasing again used
c. 1815	Engraved decoration
c. 1821	Leopard's head uncrowned used for hallmarks
c. 1891	Victoria's head no longer used for hallmarks

Ceramics

Introduction

Any material made of fired clay is called 'ceramic'. This word is derived from *keramos* (Greek), meaning 'a potter's earth'.

The Chinese vase in the illustration *(152)* shows the two ingredients usually, but not always, present in most ceramics: the matt *body**, also called paste, and its glassy skin, called *glaze**. The body is modelled from clay, then the liquid glaze is applied. In most of Europe and the Orient, the glaze was applied to the dried but unfired body, and the article was *fired** once. With English porcelain during the 18th century the body was usually fired before the glaze was applied and again to fix the glaze. Where a glaze was not applied to the fired body, the article is known as *biscuit*.

The two basic types of ceramics are earthenware, also called pottery, and *porcelain*, sometimes called china. Earthenware has been made for thousands of years all over the world. It began in Egypt and Mesopotamia. At first the clay was baked in the sun and later, as techniques developed, it was fired at a relatively low temperature in a kiln. It is opaque and not even a strong light can pass through it. It is porous and requires the application of a glaze to make it waterproof. The clay particles are not *vitrified* or fused.

Porcelain is translucent to varying degrees *(153)*. It is fired at a much higher temperature than earthenware, and made from materials that will vitrify so that it is not porous, even without glaze.

Porcelain is of relatively recent origin. It has been made in China at least since the 9th century AD, and in Japan from the 17th century. It was not made in Europe until the 18th century, although an *artificial* or *soft-paste porcelain* was made in very small quantities in Italy and France towards the end of the 16th and 17th centuries respectively.

The Western definition of porcelain requires thinness of body and translucency. The Chinese laid more emphasis on the capacity to emit a resonant sound when struck. The fine Tang Dynasty (618–906) *stonewares* (which can be regarded as coarse, opaque porcelain) developed into the first translucent porcelains.

152 Chinese vase, with green glaze and brown body or paste. (The Grafton Galleries, Sydney)

**Italics indicate glossary entry.*

153 Spode porcelain plate, c. 1825. The shadow of the hand illustrates the translucent nature of porcelain, which distinguishes it from earthenware. (The Grafton Galleries, Sydney)

Glaze—celadon and flambé

Three basic methods of decorating ceramic surfaces are well illustrated by certain techniques of the ceramic pioneers, the Chinese:

1. The first coloured glaze, celadon, was used in China in the 3rd century. The Chinese first used *flambé* glazes in the Sung dynasty (960-1279).

2. Overglaze colours were first used in China in the 14th century. The article was glazed and the colour, known as enamel, was applied and fired at a low temperature. A wide range of colours was available because many pigments could be found that were stable at low firing temperatures.

3. Underglaze decoration, usually blue, was also first used in China in the 14th century. Cobalt was used because it is stable at high firing temperatures, so retained its colour.

CELADON GLAZES *(154)* were first made in the 3rd century; they were most used during the Sung Dynasty (960–1279). The beauty of celadon ware lay in the green glaze, which was lustrous and smooth. This covered the hard vitrified stoneware body that had the strong classical contours typical of the Sung Dynasty. The glaze clung like velvet, becoming part of the beauty of the shape. Any decoration was carved or moulded in low relief, usually under the glaze.

154

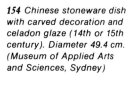

154 Chinese stoneware dish with carved decoration and celadon glaze (14th or 15th century). Diameter 49.4 cm. (Museum of Applied Arts and Sciences, Sydney)

Similar wares were made in Korea and Japan. Plates, bowls and jars are the more common items in existence today.

FLAMBE GLAZES *(155)* were introduced in the Sung dynasty (960-1279) and developed fully in the early 18th century. These glazes, like the celadons, gave intrinsic beauty to ceramic ware. The colourful glassy glaze was applied to a white or greyish-white stoneware body. There was always some *crackle* present, and the glaze had minute pores and bubbles. *Flambé* glazes had a tendency to run, sometimes forming a welt towards the bottom of the piece. In early pieces the glaze did not run under the base, but in later pieces it did run and was ground off.

A popular colour was *sang de boeuf*, or 'ox blood', which was a rich deep-red colour, sometimes splashed with blue or grey. Of the other colours used, the blues and green were more in demand. At the end of the 19th century, large quantities of *flambe*-glazed pieces were made for the European markets. This prompted some European manufacturers to produce similar pieces: Doulton made 'Chang', 'Sung- and *flambe* glazes in the early 20th century. Bernard Moore was a pioneer in this field (see p. 180).

155

155 Chinese porcelain vase with crimson flambé glaze, Ch'ien Lung period (1736-1795). Height 43 cm. (Museum of Applied Arts and Sciences, Sydney)

Overglaze enamels

Ceramics are fired at a high temperature to fix the glaze. Most substances used as pigments disintegrate at these high temperatures, so cannot be applied before the glaze is fired. The few *high-temperature* or *grand feu colours* are cobalt-blue, manganese-mauve, iron-brown, reds, greens and copper-red. Antimony produces a yellow suitable for high-temperature *faience*, but not for underglaze porcelain. There is a greater choice of low-temperature or *petit feu* colours, because these are applied over the glaze and fired at a low temperature—and many pigments are stable at these low temperatures. These overglaze or *petit feu* colours are known as enamels. Each colour is applied and fired separately.

Polychrome overglaze enamels were used on porcelain during the Ming period (1368–1644), and popular colours were red, green, turquoise-blue and yellow *(156 left)*. During the reign of K'ang Hsi (1662–1722) and Yung Cheng (1723–1735), a fine style of overglaze enamelling was perfected. Later, these pieces became known according to their enamel as *famille noire* (black), *famille verte* (green), *famille jaune* (yellow) and *famille rose* (pink) *(156 centre)*.

In the early 18th century the Chinese made armorial porcelain *(157)* using overglazing enamelling for export to European families: a copy of the family arms was sent to China, where a large dinner service was made with an *armorial* on each piece. These armorial services were in great demand until large-scale production of porcelain began in Europe.

The size and type of armorial is a guide to dating this ware. The earliest pieces, made in about 1725, had large armorials with elaborate mantling or scroll work surrounding the armorial. In about 1750 the coat of arms was

156 *Left to right: Chinese porcelain globular jar painted in four overglaze enamel colours, 16th century. Height 20.5 cm. (Museum of Applied Arts and Sciences, Sydney) Famille rose Chinese plate, c. 1730. (The Grafton Galleries, Sydney) Chinese Mandarin overglaze enamel mug, late 18th century. (The Grafton Galleries, Sydney)*

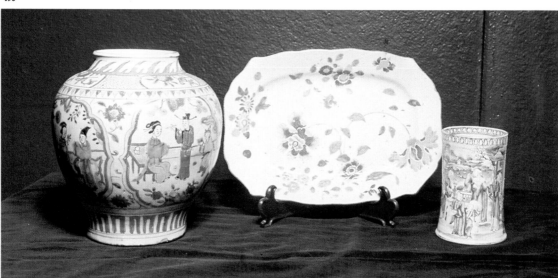

158

158 Group of so called Cantonese enamel pieces, c. 1830. Cantonese ware was produced in large quantities for export and is still being produced today. After 1890, most but not all pieces were marked 'Made in China' on the base. (The Grafton Galleries, Sydney)

157 Chinese soup tureen made for the European market, mid-18th century. It has a large armorial. (The Grafton Galleries, Sydney)

157

smaller and the mantling simpler. In about 1770 the coat of arms was a simple shield, and by about 1790 the coat of arms was set in a small spade-like shield.

By 1770 large quantities of enamelled ware known as 'Mandarin porcelain' *(156 right)* was produced for export. This ware was decorated with many figures of Chinese mandarins or nobles, sometimes with brown surrounding panels. Bulk imports of Chinese porcelain to England were stopped in 1792. However, by 1825 the Chinese were exporting the so-called Cantonese porcelain *(158)* to many countries, particularly America. This ware was enamelled with green leaves, pink flowers, and groups of pheasants and people. Cantonese porcelain is popular and common today, mostly dating from the late 19th and 20th centuries.

Underglaze blue-and-white

159

159 Blue-and-white saucer dish, early 15th century. The freedom of the painting is a major characteristic of Ming blue-and-white ware. (Christies, London)

In the 9th century the Persians discovered that the blue pigment, cobalt oxide, withstood the high temperatures used to fire their soft earthenwares better than other pigments. By the 14th century, the Persians were exporting their 'Mohammedan blue' cobalt pigment to China. There are three important phases in Chinese underglaze-blue porcelain:

1368–1644—Ming

1662–1722—K'ang Hsi

1736–1795—Ch'ien Lung.

During the early Ming period, the refining processes used for cobalt pigment resulted in a glaze that had a dull grey colour. Ming ware often had a mixed grey (almost black) and pale blue colouring *(159)*. Sometimes the design outlines were darker than the wash shading, and the painted decoration often featured formal interpretations of natural objects.

160

160 Group of underglaze porcelain pieces, K'ang Hsi period (1662-1722). The dark blue pigment contrasts with the pure white background. The shape of the tall vase was much in demand on the European market during this period. (The Grafton Galleries, Sydney)

122

In the K'ang Hsi period the potting was finer and lighter. Cobalt refining was further developed until it was possible, particularly by adding some Persian cobalt pigment, to achieve beautiful dark purple and silvery colours (*160*). The porcelain was whiter than that of the Ming period. The painted decoration was less formal than that of Ming, with precipitous mountains, waterfalls and sensitively drawn plants showing an expression of natural beauty. A popular style of the period was the 'cracked ice' background, which was painted to give a translucent faceted effect, suggesting thawing ice cracking on the surface of a frozen stream. This theme seems to symbolise spring, and often painted

162 Nanking porcelain of the late 18th century. Note the greenish tinge in the white porcelain, in comparison with the K'ang Hsi jar. (The Grafton Galleries, Sydney)

prunus blossom was used to add to this effect *(161)*.

Prior to the 17th century, Chinese exports had been confined to the Middle East and Portugal. In 1603 the Dutch captured a Portuguese ship and took Chinese blue-and-white porcelain to the European markets. There was soon a high demand for Chinese ware in Europe. Most early Chinese blue-and-white wares exported to Europe were decorative rather than functional. However, the trade developed in the 18th century towards more functional wares that were similar to European designs.

The Ch'ien Lung period (18th century) was known for its blue-and-white dinner services. This porcelain ware was known as Nanking, named after the city through which it passed en route to Europe. However, the ever-increasing demand led to mass-production techniques, and quality and colour began to decline. Many 18th-century pieces had a greenish tinge to the white porcelain, due to the presence of iron impurities, and the surface was dimpled or pitted *(162)*. The 'rice grain' technique, still used today, was developed in the 18th century. The vessel was pierced with elliptical holes, so that on glazing these filled with translucent glaze.

161

161 K'ang Hsi (1662-1722) prunus-blossom jar. The cracked ice and blossom are symbolic of spring. (Victoria and Albert Museum, London)

Stoneware

This is an important ceramic group that lies midway between earthenware and porcelain. It is vitrified by mixing a fusible rock (*petuntse*) with the clay and firing to a much higher temperature than that applied to earthenware. Stoneware and porcelain, both of which contain petuntse, are fired at about 1300°C, whereas earthenware, which is composed of clay only, is fired at between 900° and 1040°C. Earlier earthenware was fired at even lower temperatures.

The difference between stoneware and porcelain by European definition is that porcelain is translucent whilst stoneware is not.

Because stoneware is vitrified it is not porous and does not require glaze to make it waterproof. However, much of it is glazed for decorative purposes. Most stoneware will not stand extreme changes of temperature and therefore it is not used for cooking utensils, but rather for holding liquids, etc.

Although China first made stoneware during the Chou Dynasty, 1000–300 BC, European stoneware was made much later—from the 14th century. By the

164

164 Dwight or Elers red stoneware mug, decorated with a prunus branch in imitation of the Chinese late 17th-century ware. Height 9.2 cm. (Jonathan Horne, London)

163

16th century, the Rhineland of Germany produced large quantities of stoneware. Most pieces were containers for liquids such as beer and wine. These early mugs, jugs and tankards were decorated in moulded pictorial reliefs. Inscriptions were often used, and later the decoration was usually impressed or incised. These were usually *salt-glazed*.

Rhenish stoneware *(163)* was exported to England, where some pieces gained the name 'tiger ware', because their mottled–brown glaze resembled the skin of a tiger. This 'tiger ware' was made during the 16th and 17th centuries, mostly at Cologne and Frechen. In the 19th century, stoneware with a bluish glaze was produced. This later 'Cologne ware' had serial numbers stamped into the base of each piece. The Villeroy and Boch factory (a large manufacturing concern, employing 6000 workers in 1899) marked its wares in this way.

Fine stoneware was made in England in about 1670, by John Dwight of London. Some pieces were made in Nottingham and Staffordshire, where the stoneware industry is still operating today. A fine red stoneware *(164)* was introduced to Staffordshire by the Elers brothers at the end of the 17th century. These pieces were thrown and turned on a lathe, then decorated with a dab of clay pressed onto the surface with a metal die.

163 Rhenish stoneware jugs with silver mounts, bearing English marks of the 16th century. As foreign silver imported to England was assayed in England, the silver mounts could well be German with English hallmarks. (Victoria and Albert Museum, London)

125

165

Decorating earthenware surfaces— slipware, tin glaze, Whieldon and white glaze

The clay used for the low-temperature-fired earthenware bodies often resulted in an unattractive surface. It was therefore necessary to evolve various techniques to produce a surface either attractive in itself, or suitable as a background for design. Four important types of earthenware surfaces were developed:

1.   Slipware, in which a refined clay covered the body of the rougher clay.

2.   Opaque, often white, tin-glazed wares.

3.   Coloured, Whieldon-glaze wares.

4.   White Staffordshire salt-glazed stonewares.

These were introduced in an attempt to compete with the fine white porcelains, which were at first imported from China and in the last half of the 18th century were produced in increasing quantities in Europe. However, before the end of the 18th century, the popularity of porcelain and of the *creamware* produced by Wedgwood soon gained an advantage over the surface-coated earthenware.

SLIPWARES were first made in Roman times in the Middle East and in Europe. In England, slipware developed its own characteristic style, and marked the beginning of English decorative ceramics. The earliest authenticated English piece dates to 1612. Slipware is still made by studio potters, but it was most popular during the period 1660–1760.

'Slip' is the term used for fine clay diluted to a cream-like consistency with water. The brick-coloured body, formed from inexpensive clay, was coated with a surface layer of refined slip clay. The surface was then decorated in various designs, sometimes by applying coloured slips. The simple method of feathered or combed slip is shown in the illustration of the English press-moulded earthenware dish *(165 left)* . The white slip covered the clay body, and the brown slip lines were formed by drawing a bristle or thin object across the lines to form a series of loops. This method began in the early 18th century.

A few pieces were decorated by cutting or carving through the outer surface layer of slip to expose the darker body below. This was the *sgraffito* or scratched technique.

The black Jackfield ware *(165 right)* in which a red body was covered with a glossy black slip, was made at a pottery in Jackfield, Shropshire, from about 1750 to 1775. Most pieces were black, but some were decorated with Jacobite emblems, mottoes and inscriptions in oil-gilding and unfired painting. A similar product was made in Staffordshire before 1750. Staffordshire produced most Jackfield pieces and the term is very much a generic one.

GILDED WARE In the early oil-gilding method, gold sizing was painted on the ceramic surface with a brush. Gold leaf was then applied whilst the sizing was still tacky. No firing took place and the gilt wore off with use. Lacquer-gilding was a later method, in which gold leaf was ground with lacquer and applied to the ceramic surface with a brush. However, this gilt also wore off. The best method was honey-gilding, which was used on early English porcelain. Gold leaf was ground and mixed with honey, then applied to the ceramic surface. The piece was lightly fired to give a soft, rich and durable gilt coating that was thick enough to be chased and tooled. In about 1780, mercury-gilding was introduced. An amalgam of gold and mercury was applied to the surface. The mercury evaporated when the piece was fired in a *muffle* kiln. The resultant bright, durable gold surface was not as attractive as the coating applied by honey-gilding. During the late 19th century, a liquid gold that did not require burnishing was used. This produced a thin film resembling lustre painting.

166

TIN-GLAZED WARES Earthenware surfaces were often coated with a glaze that contained opaque-white tin oxide. This provided an excellent basis for the addition of painted decoration. The technique was known to the Babylonians, was developed by the Persians in the 8th century AD, and was then spread by the Moors to Spain in the 11th century. Tin-glazing had reached Italy by the 15th century, and was most employed in the early 16th century. The technique arrived in northern Europe in the 16th century and flourished in 1650–1750.

In Italy, tin-glazed ware was known as *maiolica*, although articles were made elsewhere in this Italian style. *Maiolica* was finely potted and decorated with characteristic high-temperature colours of blue, green, yellow, orange, purple, brown and black *(166)*.

In France, Germany, Spain and Scandinavia, *faience* was made. This was similar to the delftware made in Holland *(167)* and England *(168)*. These wares were first painted with Chinese-style decorations, but later simple, more original, motifs were used. Early delftware and *faience* had an attractive characteristic derived from the method of manufacture. The lightly fired clay body was covered with a powder-like glaze that was decorated before firing. The chalk-like nature of the surface was unsuited to any but the most simple designs, applied with bold strokes. In the second quarter of the 18th century a lead overglaze was used at Bristol—it was given the Dutch name 'kwaart' having first been used in Holland. *Faience blanche* was a style in which the tin glaze was only decorated with a central coat of arms and a wreath-like design around the edge.

In the first half of the 17th century, the Dutch town of Delft assumed a leading role in Holland for the manufacture of tin-glazed wares (delftware). It became famous for imitations of Chinese porcelains that were made with tin-

167 Two 17th-century Dutch Delft tiles. Mauve, produced from manganese, was a popular high-temperature colour. Scenes of children at play and of biblical stories were in demand. The tile on the right shows a bedroom scene of Potiphar's wife and a servant, marked 'Gen. 39:12'. This passage reads, 'And she caught him by his garment saying lie with me, and he left his garment in her hand and fled and got him out.' (The Grafton Galleries, Sydney)

167

glazed enamels, and its finest period was 1640–1740. From late in the 17th century onwards, *polychrome* wares (*169 left*) were made.

In England tin-glazed earthenware was also called delft, because of the Dutch influence on the English product. The production of delft 'galley ware' began in London in the last half of the 16th century. The English ware differed from the Dutch Delft and no maker's marks were used. The English glaze was smooth and even, but the Dutch glaze had a 'porridgy' grey, pitted appearance

168

169

169 *Left: French faience earthenware tray painted in polychrome, early 18th century. Width 21.4 cm. Right: Dutch Delft earthenware wall plaque, c. 1700. Width 29.8 cm. (Museum of Applied Arts and Sciences, Sydney)*

168 *Left: English delftware wine jug marked 'Sack 1645'. Sack was an early name for sherry. (Museum of Applied Arts and Sciences, Sydney) Right: German Hanau faience wine jug or Enghalskrug, marked 1705 on the pewter lid. Hanau was one of the oldest German faience factories. Decoration of flowers, birds and dots were typical Hanau decorations in 1661-1700. (The Grafton Galleries, Sydney)*

due to its higher lead content. The Dutch blue was more opaque and the polychrome palette was stronger and more boldly used (*169 right*).

During the second quarter of the 17th century, the English began to develop a characteristic style of delftware. This was made at several factories in London (particularly at Lambeth), in Bristol from about 1680 and in Liverpool from the first quarter of the 18th century. Smaller quantities were also made at Brislington near Bristol, and at Wincanton in Somerset.

Dated and labelled wine bottles were made and dated between 1639 and 1672. Large dishes now called 'blue dash chargers' were made from the mid-17th to the mid-18th centuries. These had blue diagonal dashes around the rim, and were often decorated with paintings of monarchs from Charles I to George II. Towards the end of the 17th century, many pieces of apothecary equipment were produced in delftware. A new palette of red, green, yellow and blue was introduced in England from about 1696, but tin-glazed earthenware lost popularity by 1800, and was replaced by porcelain and Wedgwood's creamware.

WHIELDON-GLAZE WARES Thomas Whieldon, the famous 18th-century Staffordshire potter, was involved in the development of semi-translucent lead glazes. These so-called Whieldon glazes were usually applied to moulded, thinly potted earthenware bodies. The term 'Whieldon' is generic, because Whieldon did make other types of pottery, and other potters used these coloured surface effects *(170)*. As with most early pottery, very few pieces, and none of Whieldon's, were marked.

Whieldon glazes were also applied by the elder Ralph Wood (1715–1772) (see p.147) to figures and groups particularly, but not exclusively. From about 1790, translucent lead glazes were replaced by opaque enamel colours that had a tendency to flake.

English pottery at the end of the 18th century had a definite local character, because many of the leading potters were trained in the same factories, and traditional ideas were passed through several generations. Wedgwood was a partner of Whieldon from 1754 to 1759. Josiah Spode was an apprentice of Whieldon from 1749 to 1770, when he began his own factory. Aaron Wood was also an apprentice, and William Copeland a partner.

WHITE STAFFORDSHIRE SALT-GLAZED STONEWARES Thomas Whieldon and Ralph Wood were. both apprenticed to John Astbury, who developed white Staffordshire salt-glazed stonewares in about 1715. This early 18th-century white stoneware was yet another result of the attempt to compete with porcelain. A type of white slip coating was applied to the moulded stoneware body, and was sometimes decorated with painted enamel. The earliest pieces made were slip-coated with a fine Devonshire clay. Some of the salt-glazed stoneware pieces were partly mottled in a Whieldon-type glaze, and were known as Astbury-Whieldon ware *(171)*. Many of these early 18th-century white Staffordshire stoneware pieces were also painted in porcelain-type styles so as to achieve the closest possible resemblance to porcelain.

White Staffordshire salt-glazed stoneware was most popular between 1720 and 1780, then was largely replaced by creamware and porcelain.

There are two products that can be mistaken for early white

171

170 English earthenware plate with 'tortoiseshell' glaze of Whieldon type, c. 1760. Diameter 24 cm. (Museum of Applied Arts and Sciences, Sydney)

171 Astbury-Whieldon pottery group of officer, piper and drummer, c. 1745. Note the touches of Whieldon glaze. This sensitive early Staffordshire potting differs markedly from the provincial style of 19th-century Staffordshire figures. (Earle D. Vandeka Antiques, London)

Staffordshire salt-glazed stoneware. Earlier stonewares were also salt-glazed, but were usually light grey or brown. The Turner and Castleford stoneware of the end of the 18th century is also similar in appearance. At this time, porcelain and creamware were well established, and this white stoneware was developed as a durable product, not as one that was to mimic porcelain.

Pottery with coloured body rather than coloured glaze—creamware, basalt and jasper

CREAMWARE European potters had often attempted to produce white ware, but because white clays often lacked plasticity a white *slip* or tin-glazed covering was applied to a coloured body. It was not until about 1740 that a refined whitish or cream-coloured earthenware body was developed in England. This creamware *(173, back)* soon became popular throughout Europe, ousting tin-glaze earthenware, slipware and the early 18th-century white Staffordshire salt-glaze stoneware. By about 1760, creamware had become the standard English pottery, and Leeds, in Yorkshire, became one of the major manufacturing centres of this product. Most pieces were unmarked until about 1770 and have a transparent lead glaze.

Wedgwood perfected creamware and coined the name 'Queensware' in 1765, following an order for it from Queen Charlotte. In France creamware was known as *faience-fine* or *terre de pipe,* in Germany *Steirgut,* in Sweden *flintporslin* and in Italy *terraglia inglese.* In 1779 Wedgwood went on to develop pearlware, which had a whiter body emphasised by a characteristic bluish glaze. This was in full production by the early 19th century.

BLACK BASALT In about 1768, Wedgwood perfected black basalt stoneware *(172 right)* from Egyptian black, which was a popular standard unglazed stoneware made by various Staffordshire potters prior to 1760. Black basalt was a very hard material that took a polish without glaze. It could be cut and polished on a

172 Left: Wedgwood blue jasper stoneware copy of the Portland vase, c. 1850. Height 26 cm. Right: English black basalt stoneware teapot, Staffordshire, c. 1810. Height 14 cm. (Museum of Applied Arts and Sciences, Sydney)

172

lathe or lapidary wheel. From about 1800, basalt pieces were mass-produced in the Wedgwood factory from moulds, yet they still retained crisp sharp features. Basalt was also made by other factories, notably Spode, well into the 19th century.

JASPER In 1774, Wedgwood invented another hard, fine-grained stoneware, for which he is probably best remembered: blue jasper ware, with white cameo decoration *(172 left, 173 right)*. He had been experimenting with high-fired materials for some years before this, probably in an attempt to find the secret of porcelain. He claimed that this jasper ware was 'coloured through its whole substance', as indeed earlier pieces were. However, after 1780, the colour was applied as a surface wash, known as 'jasper dip'. The colour was pastel: blue was the most popular, and lilac, sage-green, yellow or black were also used. Jasper ware was imitated in Staffordshire and in Europe. Two successful British producers were Adam and Turner *(173 left)*. Jasper ware was used for reliefs, portrait medallions and cameos *(174 right)*, which were usually in white and suited the classical taste of the day.

173

173 Back: English creamware plate with blue painted Chinoiserie scene, probably Leeds, c. 1790. Diameter 24.2 cm. Left: English blue jasper stoneware scent bottle, impressed 'Turner', Staffordshire, c. 1780. Height 10 cm. Right: English blue jasper stoneware scent bottle, Wedgwood, c. 1780. Height 11.2 cm. (Museum of Applied Arts and Sciences, Sydney)

English 19th-century stoneware types

In the early 19th century, stoneware was developed further to compete with the new *bone china*, as in the last half of the 18th century creamware was developed to compete with *soft-paste porcelain*.

TURNER'S BODY In 1785–1825 a white refined semi-porcelain stoneware was produced, which became known as Turner's body *(174 left)* after the potter John Turner (1738–1787). This stoneware was typically used for relief-decorated mugs and jugs, which often had a royal-blue painted rim and sometimes had a silver mount. Such pieces were also made by others, particularly the Adam factory.

The 'Castleford' Yorkshire ware (1790–1825) and the 'Herculaneum caneware' from Liverpool (1810–1820) were similar to Turner's body. Relief-moulded jugs *(175)* and other wares were made by the Ridgway factory and others in 1835–1870.

IRONSTONE-TYPE BODIES In 1813, Charles Mason was granted a patent for his ironstone china. The name indicated both toughness and delicacy. Ironstone was a partially fused earthenware, with characteristics of both earthenware and stoneware. Mason's china was often decorated in bright oriental colours to satisfy the market demand caused by the restriction of Chinese porcelain imports to England in the last years of the 18th century. It was similar to Spode's *stone china* that had been introduced in 1805. Mason was particularly remembered for his dinner services.

174

174 *Left: Turners-body mug, showing typical relief decoration and coloured bands, early 19th century. (The Grafton Galleries, Sydney) Right: English six-sided stoneware cream jug with cameo scenes, impressed 'Turner', Staffordshire, c. 1800. Height 7 cm. (Museum of Applied Arts and Sciences, Sydney)*

175

Many English potters between 1830 and 1880 made versions of this successful ironstone china, using names such as 'stone ware', 'stone china' *(176, 177)*, 'granite china' and 'opaque china'.

Mason was declared bankrupt in 1848, but continued in a smaller way until 1853. The factory was bought by Ashworth, who continued to use the old Mason's mark and patterns for some time. In 1968 the Ashworth factory restored the original name, Mason's Ironstone China Limited.

DOULTON STONEWARE There were two Doulton factories: one in the London district of Lambeth, famous for its stoneware *(178 left)* and earthenware; the other in the Staffordshire town of Burslem, more famous for fine porcelains (made from 1884).

John Doulton's earthenware factory at Lambeth began in 1820, making ginger-beer bottles, covered pans, mugs and jugs. From 1846, his son, Henry

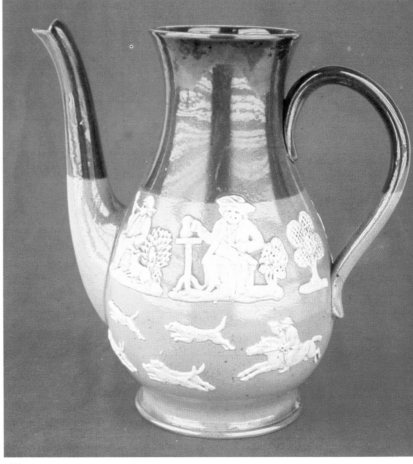

177

177 *Late 19th-century Doulton stoneware coffee pot, marked 'Doulton Lambeth, England'. (The Grafton Galleries, Sydney)*

Doulton, made enormous quantities of such utilitarian items as sanitary pipes. After the 1862 London Exhibition, the Lambeth Doulton factory produced some decorative earthenware, and exhibited some art pieces at the 1871 and 1872 London Exhibitions, which were a revival of decorative salt-glazed stoneware. Students from the Lambeth School of Art decorated the stoneware

176

176 *Left: Spode ironstone-type double-handled dish, with blue-painted mark 'Spode Stone China' and pattern number 2886, c. 1818. Right: Hicks & Meigh single-handled ironstone-type dish, bearing the printed Royal Arms mark and words 'stone china', c. 1806-1822. (The Grafton Galleries, Sydney)*

and signed their own pieces. This was the beginning of art pottery in England, which continued into the 20th century.

Late 19th-century English art pottery was a protest against mass production and repetition, but at the same time was a by-product of the machine age. The style of each piece was determined by the artists themselves, even though they were often working for a large factory. No two pieces were the same: originality could be seen in the form, glaze, incised or painted decoration.

William de Morgan (1839–1917) was also well known for his art pottery *(178 right)*. De Morgan's firm specialised in surface decoration, sometimes purchasing the undecorated blanks from other factories. Persian colours were popular and themes for decoration included birds, beasts and the sea. Many pieces were impressed with de Morgan's name or initials. The painters of each piece marked their work with painted initials. De Morgan's initials and the words Bushey Heath were also used by some of his ex-employees after his death.

178

178 Left: Doulton Lambeth salt-glazed stoneware vase, with pâte-sur-pâte decoration, by Florence Barlow, 1883. Height 37 cm. Right: English earthenware bowl painted with mythical animals and foliate designs, from the workshop of William de Morgan, c. 1900. Diameter 27 cm. (Museum of Applied Arts and Sciences, Sydney)

Transfer-printing, copperplate monochrome

Transfer-printing began in England in the middle of the 18th century, when it was first used on enamel and porcelain. The inventor is unknown, although the Liverpool printers John Sadler and Guy Green developed the technique. These independent decorators were most successful after 1756, and Wedgwood sent much of his earthenware to them for printing.

Early printing was overglaze *(181)*, often in red, purple or black; blue underglaze was first used in England in about 1760. Between 1780 and 1850, underglaze-blue was used by the many Staffordshire and Yorkshire potters to

180 Chinese late 18th-century hand-painted blue-and-white porcelain plate, of the type that inspired the willow pattern design. (The Grafton Galleries, Sydney)

181 Worcester porcelain-lidded cream jug c. 1770, decorated with overglaze printing. This technique was popular c. 1757-1774. (Alan Landis Antiques, Sydney)

180

179

181

179 English 19th-century blue-printed willow pattern earthenware plate, with the lovers fleeing across the bridge, and pagoda, fruit tree and phoenix birds. (The Grafton Galleries, Sydney)

produce thousands of patterns *(182a, b)*. Much of this blue ware was exported to America, where there was no similar industry until about 1840.

An engraved copper plate was inked with ceramic pigment, and a print (or transfer) was made on paper so the pattern could be transferred to the earthenware. These transfers were usually in two or more sections according to the shape and size of the article. Joins in the pattern are often visible on the borders of large meat plates.

At the end of the 18th century, the very fine overglaze 'bat-printing' was developed. The design was transferred on soft flexible glued sheets or 'bats', and was mainly used on porcelain. The design consisted of dots rather than lines and the process remained popular until 1820 *(183a, b)*.

The famous willow pattern *(179)*, with the two or three figures on the

182a

182a Spode Tiber pattern earthenware plate, c. 1812, showing the river Tiber with the Castle of St Angelo to the right, and Trojan's Column and St Peter's in the centre. The Spode mark is in blue. (The Grafton Galleries, Sydney)

bridge and the two doves above, is one of the most famous of blue-and-white patterns. This English design was probably inspired by one of the 18th-century Chinese export wares *(180)*. Willow pattern was thought to have been designed by Thomas Minton when he was apprenticed to the Caughley factory, but this

182b

182b Spode Indian
sporting series pattern
earthenware tureen
stand, c. 1810, showing
hunters mounted on
elephants hunting a
buffalo. The stand is
marked 'Spode' and
'Hunting a Buffalo'. (The
Grafton Galleries,
Sydney)

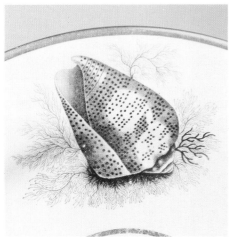

183a

183a The detail possible
with Bat printing was
particularly fine.

183b Barr Flight and Barr
porcelain plate, c.1810,
decorated with overglaze
Bat printing. This form of
printing was popular c. 1795/
c. 1820. (The Grafton
Galleries, Sydney)

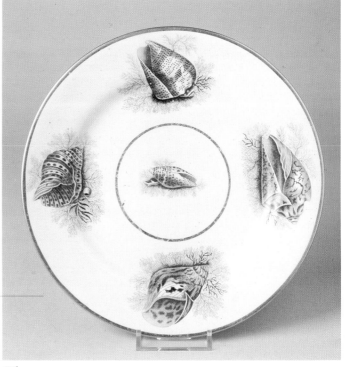

183b

is unlikely because 18th-century willow pattern plates have not been found. The willow pattern was probably designed in the early 19th century.

Blue-and-white transfer wares were in fact a creation of the engraver rather than of the potter. However, most of the engravers of the original copper plates were unknown. Only the larger potteries employed their own engravers; others bought engraved copper plates from engraving firms. There was no Copyright Act until 1841, so a pattern or a border is not always proof of the factory of origin.

184

184 John Ridgway stoneware plate, c. 1835, marked "JR, Napier Imperial Stone". This is typical of the new underglaze colours, other than blue, which were first used from c. 1825. (Museum of Applied Arts, Sydney)

During the second quarter of the 19th century, other monochrome underglazes were used, mainly black, green *(184)*, red, purple or brown, but blue remained the most popular.

In the 19th century ceramic printing increased in Europe.

Prattware, polychrome copperplate, and lithographic printing

PRATTWARE is an English term for late 18th-century and early 19th-century earthenware that was painted in high-temperature underglaze colours—typically ochre, dull green, blue and brown *(185)*. The colour was usually applied with a sponge. This technique was very popular until about 1850, particularly on export goods intended for America.

Prattware is a generic term, because many potters used these underglaze, sponged 'earth' colours. William Pratt, a master potter, died in 1799. In 1812 his two sons founded the famous Staffordshire polychrome printing firm F. & R. Pratt.

POLYCHROME UNDERGLAZE COPPERPLATE PRINTS From the middle of the 19th century it was possible to print in more than one underglaze colour. This polychrome process is associated with F. & R. Pratt, although several other firms used the same technique. At least four copper plates had to be cut for each design, one for the black outline and detail, and one for each colour separation, usually red, yellow and blue. These were placed precisely in register (positioned exactly one on top of another) with the aid of two circles marked on each side of the design on each plate. These registration marks are usually visible on the finished article.

The printed picture was transferred on paper to the article, which was then placed in a hardening kiln. The high temperature allowed the oil from the coloured inks to be burned off, and the metallic oxides to mature into the final colour. The article was then glazed.

Pot-lids were some of the first items decorated by the new process. Some twenty-four different polychrome bear lids *(186a)* were made until about 1875. These were made for pots of hair oil, which contained bear grease. There were about sixty different coloured Pegwell Bay subject lids for fish and shrimp paste, and numerous lids for meat paste. This printed earthenware was on Pratt's stand at the 1851 London Exhibition and was probably developed in the late 1840s. Contemporary events were recorded, such as in the 1851 London Exhibition series. There are at least ten different Duke of Wellington lids.

After about 1900, the lids were produced for decorative purposes only, rather than for functional use.

After the success of the pot-lids, Pratt made tea services, trinket boxes, toilet jars, bottles and jugs. Nine other firms made similar articles between the middle and end of the 19th century.

185

186b

LITHOGRAPHIC PRINTING A lithographic monochrome ceramic printing process was patented in England in 1839. The colours used were blue, pink, green, purple, grey and black. A polychrome lithographic process patented in the 1850s was not perfected until the 1870s *(186b)*. The lithographic transfer did not produce the quality of the earlier copper plate. It was usually over glaze.

185 English Prattware earthenware jug, moulded with a figure, 'Peace', and painted in underglaze colours, c. 1800. Height 23.5 cm. (Museum of Applied Arts and Sciences, Sydney)

186b A Bavarian porcelain plate c. 1900. This is typical of the later, usually overglaze, lithographic process. (The Grafton Galleries, Sydney)

186a Bear earthenware pot-lid for hair oil (which was made from bear grease), mid-19th century. (The Grafton Galleries, Sydney)

186a

Lustre and majolica

LUSTRE Copper-lustre decoration began in Spain in the 14th century. In about 1810 it was first used in England, but in a restrained form. Most English lustreware *(187)* was made from about 1830, and was often called Sunderland lustre, as much of it was made in that town. Relief-moulded jugs were popular, and some bore personal, historical or religious messages, and were splashed with pink lustre.

There are two types of English lustre: a complete cover of silver or copper *(188 left and centre)*, and silver or copper used in conjunction with other enamel colours. The overall silver lustre, emulating silver plate, was mainly made in the period 1840–1870.

MAJOLICA Despite the name, the English majolica, with its lead and later semi-translucent glaze, was mostly technically quite different from the earlier Italian tin-glazed *maiolica*. Majolica *(188 back)* was a typically Victorian earthenware introduced by Minton in 1850. Other factories soon produced similar ware. Some early Victorian majolica however did have an opaque white glaze completely covering the body as did the much earlier Italian maiolica.

Probably the most common examples of majolica today are the green-

187 Earthenware frog mug showing the Sunderland Bridge, decorated in pink lustre, c. 1840. (The Grafton Galleries, Sydney)

187

188 *Left to right: English earthenware jug with copper lustre, mid-19th century. Height 12.5 cm. English earthenware jug with silver lustre, mid-19th century. Height 14 cm. English Victorian majolica plate, c. 1870. (Museum of Applied Arts and Sciences, Sydney)*

leaf relief-moulded fruit sets of plates and *comports*. These were popular with Minton (who coined the name), Wedgwood, Davenport and others.

Staffordshire earthenware figures

The simple English country style of Staffordshire figures **(189)** contrasts with the more European origins of *stoneware, delft* and porcelain. Staffordshire earthenware figures were first made in the early 18th century, and were produced until the end of the 19th century.

THE WOOD FAMILY In 1754, the elder Ralph Wood (1715–1772) began in the Astbury-Whieldon style using coloured running glazes. He turned away from symbolic modelling towards realism, and is credited with originating the *Toby Jug*. The glazes followed the technique of each period. His son, Ralph Wood (1748–1795), continued using his father's techniques and often used the same moulds. His work is difficult to distinguish from his father's until about 1790, when he began to use overglaze enamel decoration. He is also credited with introducing the underglaze decoration known as Prattware (see p. 144). Enoch Wood (1759–1840), a cousin, founded a firm that operated until 1846. Although the quality of his products was not as good as that of the Ralph Woods' his modelling was highly regarded.

JOHN WALTON (1780–1835) began making earthenware figures in about 1810. The name 'Walton' is usually moulded on a ribbon at the back of his models, and he frequently used *bocage* **(190)**, like an espaliered fruit tree. Although

189 *Staffordshire earthenware figure 'Autumn', c. 1760. (Museum of Applied Arts and Sciences, Sydney)*

147

191

191 *Staffordshire flat-back earthenware figure of a zebra, c. 1860. (The Grafton Galleries, Sydney)*

190 Early 19th-century Walton- type earthenware figures, with bocage. (J. M. Gedye, Batlow)

bocage was seldom used for porcelain after about 1770, when earthenware figures and bases were also plain, it was used on earthenware figures in the early 19th century. This was probably an attempt to give the cheaper mass-produced earthenware figures the standing of the earlier costly porcelain ones. The colouring of the Walton school was opaque, and was often applied with a stiff brush that gave a graining effect. The Walton style was followed by many potters of the early 19th century. Today, marked reproductions are not uncommon.

RALPH SALT (1728–1846) worked from about 1812 to 1846. Some pieces were marked 'Salt' on a scroll similar to that used by Walton. He often modelled sheep, and some of his other titles are 'Gardens', 'Bird's Nest', 'Shepherdess' and 'Fire'—but other potters used similar titles. Charles Salt (1810–1864), his son, worked in a style very similar to that of his father. Some of his models were impressed 'Salt' on the back of the plinth.

JOHN AND RALPH HALL worked from about 1804 to 1849. Their best-known model was 'The Cobbler and Cobbler's Wife', which was made in more than one size.

OBADIAH SHERRATT (1775–1846) had a characteristic robust style of modelling but most of his models were large and badly modelled. His best-known theme was 'Bull-Baiting with Dogs'. (This sport was only banned in 1835.) Other Sherratt models were 'The Death of Monrow' modelled in 1830, which shows Lieutenant Monrow being carried off by a tiger, and 'Polito's Menagerie' which inspired the 'Wombell's Circus' produced by other potters in about 1850. The 'Red Barn Group' is accredited to Obadiah and his wife Martha in 1828. Two of his religious groups were 'Christ's Agony' and 'The Sacrifice of Isaac'.

VICTORIAN STAFFORDSHIRE FIGURES In 1840–1900 figures were produced in large quantities at cheap prices, for the modest homes of the period. They were completely moulded, unlike earlier pieces that had been at least partly modelled by hand. Victorian figures were larger and more rounded, the pottery was smoother, harder and whiter, and the colouring usually covered the whole surface—a bright dark blue was very popular. Underglaze colouring was used again by about 1823. The figures depicted the Empire, religion, animals, sport and the theatre—all related to the highlights of Victorian life. Very few of these figures are marked, and some were made in Scotland. Most Victorian figures have flat backs and are known as *'flat-backs'* (*191*).

Japanese porcelain

The Japanese ceramic industry was centred on the large western island of Kyushu, adjacent to the coasts of China and Korea. Although these countries had an influence on the Japanese industry in its earlier days, a local Japanese character developed later. Japan first made translucent porcelain at the beginning of the 17th century.

KAKIEMON The school of Kakiemon porcelain began with Kakiemon I (1596–1666), a potter who devoted himself to discovering the secrets of Ming overglaze red enamel. In about 1642, Kakiemon I successfully fired porcelain with the coveted red enamel decoration. By far his greatest characteristic was a fine asymmetrical balance, with a subtle use of unfilled space, as shown in the illustrated jars *(192)*. The hereditary house of Kakiemon is now in its twelfth generation, but its golden age was 1684–1704. Work from this period inspired the development of early European porcelain: Kakiemon ware was copied at Delft, Meissen, Saint-Cloud, Mennecy, Chantilly, Bow, Chelsea and Worcester. These Kakiemon-inspired patterns are often known as the 'Arita style' from the area on the island of Kyushu where the Kakiemon family worked.

NABESHIMA AND HIRADO wares were two other very fine examples of Japanese porcelain, also made in the Arita pottery district. These wares were under the patronage of the House of Matsura, and quality control was strict. Nabeshima porcelain was first made in 1722, and flourished in the early 18th century. Hirado porcelain was at its best in 1751–1843. The later 19th-century Hirado wares were mass-produced, and their quality often declined.

IMARI was another Japanese porcelain popular in Europe. It was first made in the early 17th century. It lacked the fine quality of some other Japanese porcelains, but had appealing colours that attracted the export market. The colour scheme was copied in China in the first quarter of the 18th century, and copied later by Meissen, Derby and others. Imari porcelain was underglazed with blue and overglazed with iron-red, sometimes with a touch of gold *(193)*. The iron-red was difficult to fire as an underglaze together with the blue, because it required a different firing temperature to that required for cobalt-blue. The Chinese occasionally fired iron-red and cobalt-blue together as underglaze, but the resultant colour was not very good. The Japanese Imari achieved a successful colour combination by firing the iron-red as overglaze after the blue had been fired as underglaze.

192 Pair of Kakiemon porcelain quadrangular jars and covers, decorated in red and blue overglaze enamel, from the period 1673-1687. These four visible surfaces show a subtle use of unfilled spaces, also a command of asymmetrical balance and vitality in the brushwork. These are the dominant principles of the Kakiemon style. (Christies, London)

Imari porcelain is in fact named after the port for shipping this ware to Europe. The buyers (mainly the Dutch) were not allowed to visit the pottery district itself, which was fourteen kilometres from Imari, as the Japanese wanted to prevent their porcelain techniques being discovered by competitors.

KUTANI or **KAGA WARE** of the 19th century is popular today because of its red and gold colour *(194)*. This porcelain was made in the village of Kutani, in the remote province of Kaga on the north coast of Japan. It had a strong Japanese character and showed little influence from China, mainly because of the geographic isolation of Kutani. Porcelain was first made in this area in about 1650, and was initially decorated in green and red. These first pieces were seldom marked. Later, in the 19th century, the ware exported to Europe was marked in red with the Chinese character meaning 'happiness'.

SATSUMA Perhaps the most common Japanese ceramic available to collectors is Satsuma ware *(195)* from the late 19th or early 20th centuries. This light, porous semi-porcelain earthenware had a soft crackled glaze decorated with elaborate

193 Imari porcelain, with the typical underglaze-blue and overglaze iron-red. The plate on the left has the Japanese sixteen-leaf chrysanthemum motif within the decoration, and this motif is repeated in the sixteen lobes of the plate. (The Grafton Galleries, Sydney)

195 Japanese Satsuma vase, late 19th century. (The Grafton Galleries, Sydney)

193

195

overglaze enamels. Satsuma earthenware was first made in the last decade of the 18th century in the Satsuma province, in the south-western corner of Japan. The style was brought to Japan by Korean potters in the last years of the 16th century. The plain Korean stonewares were then developed into the decorated Satsuma ware of the 19th century. The original mark, a cross within a circle, was that of the prince of Satsuma.

After 1862, international exhibitions held in London, Paris and America launched Japanese art styles onto an enthusiastic world market, and influenced the development of Art Nouveau *(196)*. However, this success led to a decline in the quality of Satsuma ware. By 1900, mass-production techniques were used and the item was often overdecorated. The local Japanese character of the Satsuma ware was lost in the attempt to produce articles to please the European market. The term 'Satsuma' became generic for buff-coloured, crackled overglaze enamelled ceramics, and most production in fact took place in Tokyo, Kyoto and other centres outside the Satsuma province.

196

194 *Japanese 19th-century Kutani porcelain. Kutani ware was first made in the Kaga province on the remote north coast of Japan. Dish and lidded bowl showing typical Kaga colouring. (The Grafton Galleries, Sydney) Square tea caddy. (Mrs Roy Hudson, Sydney)*

196 *Japanese Satsuma saki-pourer, late 19th century. This style helped to inspire the Art Nouveau movement. Note the soft curves, semi-parallel lines and pastel colours. (The Grafton Galleries, Sydney)*

197 Meissen porcelain dish, with moulded cornucopia border, c. 1735. The painting follows the Japanese Kakiemon style. Diameter 44 cm. (Museum of Applied Arts and Sciences, Sydney)

The beginning of porcelain in Europe

ITALY An artificial or soft-paste porcelain was made in Florence for perhaps as few as eight years, between about 1575 and 1583. This was the first European porcelain. The kilns were patronised by the influential Medici family and the product became known as Medici porcelain. The style was underglaze blue, and it imitated the rare Ming blue-and-white underglaze porcelain being imported in limited quantities through Venice. The paste was white clay and *frit*—this composition is hardly distinguishable from powdered glass. Specimens are extremely rare: only 59 are known to exist, and many of them are in the Victoria and Albert Museum.

GERMANY The manufacture of true or hard-paste porcelain in Europe began in Germany in the first twenty years of the 18th century. In the late 17th century, lead crystal was being made in England, and increasing quantities of oriental porcelain were being imported to Europe. In 1694, King Augustus II of Poland succeeded to the title of Elector of Saxony and almost immediately ordered his financial adviser, von Tschirnhaus, to initiate local production of the new lead glass and porcelain. This state interest established the industry in Germany, and later in other European countries.

In 1704 a young chemist, J. F. Bottger, was placed under the supervision of von Tschirnhaus and in 1708 he succeeded in producing white porcelain at Meissen. This was perfected by 1719 and was the first true porcelain to be made in Europe. Meissen is about twenty kilometres from Dresden, so this product was sometimes known as Dresden china, particularly in England.

A brilliant young painter, J. G. Horoldt, decorated Meissen porcelain in about 1720–1735. Many of his pieces were in the oriental style, particularly in the Kakiemon (*Arita*) style *(197)*, which had been the aim of King Augustus.

Soon after 1733, J. J. Kaendler began to develop the technique of modelling. He worked until 1770, but most of his models were made in about 1740, and were in the rococo style.

FRANCE Soft-paste porcelain was made in France as early as 1693 at the Saint-Cloud factory. Other soft-paste factories soon followed: Chantilly in 1725, Mennecy in 1734 and Vincennes in 1738 (it moved to Sèvres in 1756). Despite this early start, it was not until the middle of the 18th century that fine-quality porcelain was developed in France. From 1760 the French began to produce work in their own unique style *(198)*, breaking away from the influence of the Arita style of Meissen. They used rich colours, gilding, exotic birds, floral and court scenes. This was the first regal European porcelain style, and it influenced other countries at this time.

Like Meissen, Sèvres owed its existence to state aid—the factory could well have failed had it not been taken over by King Louis XV in 1759. Until 1770 the factory produced soft-paste porcelain, but from 1772 hard-paste porcelain began to be made, and from 1804 it was the only product of Sèvres.

198 Sèvres porcelain panel, showing the rich blue and gilt that replaced the Arita style in Europe after the Seven Years' War (1756-1763). This was the first truly European style to influence porcelain painting. (The Grafton Galleries, Sydney)

198

The beginning of English porcelain— glassy-paste, bone-ash, soapstone and hard-paste

The first English porcelain was made in Chelsea, London, in about 1745 *(199)*. This innovation had been completely dependent upon private enterprise, unlike the development of Meissen and Sèvres porcelain. Its design followed that of the European porcelain, but until the end of the 18th century most English products were soft-paste. Other European countries produced mostly hard-paste porcelain, like almost all oriental porcelain.

Soft-paste porcelain is fired at a much lower and more critical temperature, so more articles are wasted. Many soft-paste pieces have warps or *fire cracks*, and are sometimes discoloured by hot liquids or marked by steel knives. Soft-paste porcelain can be easily cut with a file, whereas unglazed hard-paste porcelain is much tougher and can roughen a finger nail. Unglazed soft-paste porcelain stains because it is slightly porous. Unlike hard-paste porcelain, which is usually fired once only, soft-paste porcelain is fired once for the body, then the glaze is fired at a lower temperature. Soft-paste porcelain glaze is thus thicker, blued and sometimes forms pools, whereas hard-paste

199 Examples of Chelsea porcelain in the 'red anchor' period, c. 1754. Plate marked with a red anchor, having slight imperfections in the glaze concealed by the painted decoration, three spur marks on the base and a ground foot rim. Finely modelled perfume bottle, showing a priest blessing a young woman. Height 11.5 cm. (The Grafton Galleries, Sydney)

199

porcelain glaze is glittery and thin. Overglaze enamels sink into soft-paste but not into hard-paste porcelain. This is sometimes easily detected with the finger tips. Hard-paste porcelain glaze often does not cover the *foot rim* to the same extent as that of soft-paste porcelain. Soft-paste porcelain looks granular where it is chipped, whereas hard-paste porcelain looks like glass. Soft-paste porcelain has a warmer, softer feel than hard-paste porcelain. Hard-paste porcelain is usually more thinly and finely potted, particularly in foot rims.

Before 1790 there were only twelve English porcelain factories, and these fell into four groups according to the composition of the paste. The first used a glassy *frit* paste (glassy-paste group: early Chelsea, early Derby and Longton Hall). The second used *bone-ash* paste, so produced heavy greyish bodies that were almost opaque and often showed fire-cracks (bone-ash group: Bow and Lowestoft, later Chelsea and Derby). The third made distinctly thinner and finer *soapstone* paste, and particularly fine foot rims and walls for cups and dishes (soapstone group: Lund's Bristol, Worcester, Caughley and some Liverpool). The fourth produced the first true hard-paste porcelain (hard-paste group: Plymouth, Bristol and Newhall).

Glassy-paste group

CHELSEA (1745–1769) Before the Seven Years' War (1756–1763), the Chelsea factory made some porcelain in the Arita-Meissen style. This was the 'red anchor' period of 1752–1756. The factory closed for a year in 1756 during an illness of the proprietor, Nicholas Sprimont, and when it reopened the Sèvres style was adopted. This was the 'gold anchor' period of 1756–1769. Bone-ash and gilding were used for the first time, figure bases were more rococo and elaborate, and bocage was popular.

Chelsea figures were slip-cast rather than *press-moulded*. A fluid slip was poured into plaster moulds and so gave smoother, finer detail.

Small toys and scent bottles were made in the 'red anchor' period (when they were undecorated) and in the 'gold anchor' period (when they were gilded and painted).

Chelsea plates normally had three spur marks on the base, where they stood on stilts in the *glost firing*, i.e. when glazed and refired. Blemishes on the surface were concealed with painted decoration, and excess glaze was often ground from the foot rims.

The Chelsea factory operated at a lower output from 1763 until it was sold in 1769 and taken over by Derby in the following year. This Chelsea-Derby factory produced fine porcelain, indistinguishable from Derby, up until 1784—also, some Derby products were decorated at Chelsea. This was the *neoclassical* age: pastel colours were fashionable, less bocage was used on figures, and bases became simpler and often square.

LONGTON HALL (1750–1760) This factory produced the first Staffordshire porcelain, but its life was short and its output small. The paste was similar to that used at Chelsea, but the glaze had a waxy feel. Flower painted decoration was well executed. Moulded overlapping-leaf-shape dishes were characteristic of Longton Hall, and these were often pale green and yellow, with touches of pink. A few figures and some underglaze-blue functional wares were made, but table wares cracked when subjected to very hot water. The factory closed during 1754–1756, and after reopening its output was small.

DERBY (1750–1848) The pioneer days up to 1800 were dominated by the strong personality and energy of William Duesbury. He joined the factory in about 1756 after working in London as a decorator for the products of the Chelsea, Bow and Longton Hall factories. When Longton Hall factory closed in 1760, Duesbury most likely bought its moulds. He took over the Chelsea factory in 1770. This Duesbury-Derby period was thus closely linked with the decoration and shapes of Chelsea, Bow and Longton Hall.

The early Derby paste was glassy-frit, until the secret of bone-ash paste was disclosed in 1770 when Duesbury took over the Chelsea factory. Fine quality decorative ware was the major product until 1770. By 1777 only seventy people were employed at Derby. Few items were marked until 1780.

Figures were made in relatively large quantities. These were *slip-cast (200)* and had three or four patch marks on the base *(201)*, caused by the pads of clay on which the figures stood whilst being fired. Although other factories occasionally had such marks, they are generally a useful indication of a Derby piece. Some of the early Duesbury figures had 'dry edges' (glaze-free edges) to the base of figures.

Early figures (1756–1760) were pale coloured and lacked gilding. From 1760 to 1770, higher rococo bases were popular, colours were stronger and darker, and bocage or leafy branch backgrounds were fashionable. After the classical revival of about 1770, square bases were sometimes used, pastel colours were popular, and bocage was no longer in vogue.

200 Derby porcelain figure of a boy, c. 1760. This is slip cast, with finer detail than Bow figures. Height 25.7 cm. (Museum of Applied Arts and Sciences, Sydney)

Because of Duesbury's training and interest in decoration, Derby ware was well painted. Two important landscape artists were Zachariah Boreman and 'Jockey Hill'. The famous flower painter William Billingsley was apprenticed at Derby in 1774, and had established his style within ten years.

Derby biscuit, or unglazed porcelain (202), reigned supreme in England from about 1770 until the end of the century. These unglazed figures were more costly and were well finished, for imperfections could not be hidden under paint or glaze.

202

202 Derby biscuit porcelain figure of a dog, c. 1780. (The Grafton Galleries, Sydney)

201 Pair of Derby porcelain figures of Shakespeare (base only shown) and Milton, c. 1765. The figure of Shakespeare is based on Scheemakers' statue of 1740 in Westminster Abbey. Note the typical Derby patch marks. Heights 29.2 cm. (Museum of Applied Arts and Sciences, Sydney)

Bone-ash group

BOW (1747–1776) This was the second English porcelain factory, established in east London by 1747. The Bow factory used a heavy, greyish bone-ash paste that had a wide range of critical temperatures in the kiln, so wastage was kept to a minimum. However, many pieces showed small fire cracks, which, with other pastes would have meant rejection. The low firing temperature gave a

204

203

characteristic almost opaque body.

Unlike most European dishes, those made at Bow had foot rims that were not *applied* but made, as in China, with only one angle to the rim. Transfer printing was used and functional blue-and-white wares were the main products. Overglaze polychrome enamels were used, but were only of average quality, and often followed the Arita style. By 1754, the annual turnover of the Bow factory was £18 000, and 300 potters and 90 painters worked for the factory.

Many press-moulded figures were made. These were heavier than the slip-cast Chelsea and Derby figures *(203)*, and often had a square hole at the back where an *ormolu* candle-holder could be inserted. The figures had oval faces and receding chins in the period 1750–1755, and had flat bases until 1760. After this time, the bases were higher and had rococo characteristics. Shells were a popular Bow motif, and were often incorporated in the base. The Bow factory output had decreased by 1767 and was very small by 1770.

LOWESTOFT (1757–1799) This factory, in a small fishing village on the English east coast, used a bone-ash paste that was almost indistinguishable from that of Bow. Tea wares were by far the most common product *(204)*. Until 1770 these were usually decorated in underglaze-blue, sometimes also with an attractive relief-moulded design. Some of the designs were copied from those of

160

Worcester, but the ware itself had a thicker and less finely potted shape.

Lowestoft cream jugs often had a handle that 'kicked up' after meeting the body at its bottom junction point. Cups and saucers sometimes had three small rough marks around their rims where they were rested upside down in the kiln. Only a few figures were made at Lowestoft.

In about 1770, enamel colours were popular, and often were applied in the style of late 18th-century Chinese export table wares. This led to the incorrect term 'Chinese Lowestoft' for late 18th-century Chinese export porcelain.

Soapstone group

LUND'S BRISTOL. WORCESTER The Worcester factory, which still operates today, was formed in 1751 from the Lund's Bristol soft-paste factory, which operated from 1749 to 1752. The Bristol soft-paste porcelain when unmarked is almost indistinguishable from Worcester in body and shape.

Here we consider the 'Dr Wall' or first period (1751–1776) and the 'Davis/Flight' period (1776–1793). In the 18th century, the Worcester factory produced a trim, finely potted body that was the neatest of English ware during the period. This fine potting was the main characteristic of the soapstone group (205).

Early Worcester paste usually showed a green translucency, although this was sometimes clear or yellow; it was never orange. Later in the 18th century, there was far less green coloration.

Worcester tea wares did not crack when subjected to hot water, as did some other thicker soft-paste porcelain. The glaze-free line inside the foot rim was characteristic of the 1760–1790 period, but the technique of wiping the glaze so that it did not run down the foot rim was also employed at Caughley and some Liverpool factories. The Worcester foot rim had a 'V' section. The inside flange of the teapot covers was often unglazed.

Underglaze-blue was used during the first period. Overglaze transfer designs often in black were in use by 1757. Between 1760 and 1780 the scale-blue ground was more popular (206). Panels within the scale-blue ground were decorated with exotic birds and flowers. The Sèvres influence was greatest in 1770–1787, gilt was not applied to blue and white Worcester. Painted wares had an outline crescent mark, whereas printed wares had a hatched or filled-in crescent mark. Fluted shapes were fashionable from c. 1775, and the

205

205 Thinly potted Worcester porcelain leaf dish, c. 1760. Note the raised veins that were possible with this fine soapstone paste. (The Grafton Galleries, Sydney)

finely potted bodies were well suited for this. Only a few figures were made at Worcester.

CAUGHLEY (1775–1799) The Caughley (pronounced 'car-flee') factory was near Worcester, only a few kilometres away up the river Severn. It was originally an earthenware factory, but in 1775 porcelain was introduced there by the ex-Worcester potter Thomas Turner. In that year, the Worcester engraver Robert Hancock joined the Caughley factory and greatly improved the quality of engraving on Caughley wares. The Caughley factory copied Worcester in many respects, but the potting was a little thicker. The Caughley foot rim was always rectangular and usually very deep (207). Caughley paste usually showed a straw-coloured or orange translucency; sometimes this can be a greenish colour similar to Worcester. Blue-and-white tea wares represented three-quarters of the Caughley output, and most pieces were blue printed. Gilt was applied to Caughley underglaze-blue often by outside decorators.

The factory was sold to John Rose of Coalport in 1799.

LIVERPOOL (1754–1800) There were seven factories at Liverpool, some using soapstone paste. At their best, their ware approached that of Worcester in quality. No marks were used. Functional wares were produced, with plain shapes and simple designs (often of an oriental nature). The combined output of the Liverpool factories was small, and the average length of operation of these factories was less than ten years.

Hard-paste group

The first English hard-paste or true porcelain was made by the apothecary William Cookworthy at Plymouth. In 1768 he discovered the two essential ingredients, kaolin and petuntse, in the local Cornish clay which was fired to a high temperature of 1400°C. He was granted a patent which he sold to businessman Richard Champion of Bristol in 1774. When Champion ran into financial trouble in 1778, he sold the patent to a group of Staffordshire potters who later established the Newhall factory. Thus there were indeed three English hard-paste factories, but the same patent was passed from one to another so that they did not all operate at the same time.

The patent held back the development of English porcelain for twenty years, because the use of this particular formula for Cornish clay and china stone (petuntse) was generally denied to other English factories until the patent lapsed in 1796.

PLYMOUTH (1768–1770) This factory was the first holder of the patent and because it was still in the experimental stage, manufacturing faults often occurred. The surfaces were pitted and the glaze was speckled and of uneven thickness. Plates and cups were not made, because these were difficult to fire at high temperatures. Leaf-shaped pickle trays, mugs and sauce-boats were mainly produced. A blackish-blue underglaze was used and the designs were mainly of oriental style. Only a few figures were made. Bow, Chelsea and Longton Hall ideas were copied. The polychrome enamel decoration stood out from the glaze, as characteristic of hard-paste.

Plymouth ware was very similar to that of Bristol, although it was more primitive and less developed.

BRISTOL (1770–1781) William Cookworthy established the Bristol hard-paste porcelain factory in 1770, and the wares produced were very similar to those of Plymouth. In 1774 Cookworthy sold the patent to Richard Champion. Under

206

207

207 Caughley porcelain teacup, showing the characteristic deep foot rim. (Peter Edge, Sydney)

206 Worcester porcelain dish with scale-blue background, c. 1770. Diameter 18.4 cm. (Museum of Applied Arts and Sciences, Sydney)

208

Champion, the Bristol factory developed better techniques and produced more classical ware. The firing of plates and cups was mastered, and these formed a large part of the factory's output. Vases were often hexagonal in shape, in the Arita style, because of difficulties in firing. Gilding and polychrome decoration, of flowers and birds, were popular. Underglaze-blue and transfer printing were rarely used.

NEWHALL (1781–1835) This factory had the sole legal right to manufacture hard-paste porcelain until 1796. Newhall was thus able to attempt to compete with the flood of Chinese tea wares coming into England at the beginning of this period. The factory's output was mainly comprised of tea wares, which had classical shape and oriental-style decoration (208). Other popular decorations were floral *swags*, garlands of green leaves and pink roses, and simple rural scenes. Attractive bat-printed designs were used in 1805–1815 (183). Fluted wares decorated with gilt were made in 1800–1810, and were very similar to Worcester wares. Their 'Mandarin' styles (156) were popular at about the same time.

After 1812 the Newhall factory began to make bone china, which was thinly potted and had an even glaze. When the patent lapsed in 1796, Newhall lost its advantage, and other factories became far more prominent.

208 Group of Newhall hard-paste porcelain pieces. Teapot has pattern number 195 listed as early as 1787; this silver shape was made as late as 1803. Bowl and jug have pattern number 173, found as early as 1782; this pink scale border with brown outline was popular for many years. The white basket pattern cup and saucer have pattern number 171 and are found between at least 1782 and 1814. The blue-and-white transfer-print

Bone china and early 19th-century porcelain—Worcester, Derby and Spode

Several events of the last decade of the 18th century gave an impetus to English porcelain production. Until this time English soft-paste porcelain could not compete with the Oriental and European hard-paste products.

English tariffs reduced the import of Chinese porcelain from the 1780s. The English East India Company ceased bulk imports by 1792.

Champion's patent on English hard-paste expired in 1796. Whilst a small quantity of hybrid English hard-paste had been produced from *c.* 1790, the expiration of this patent was a great asset to the industry.

The introduction of *bone china*, reputedly by Spode in the 1790s, gave English manufacturers a lead they were to maintain throughout the next century.

Bone china was a fine white body made from similar ingredients to hard-paste porcelain, plus up to 40 per cent bone ash. Bone china was fired at a critical temperature of 1260°C. It withstood very hot water and did not scratch with steel knife blades. Bone china was an immediate commercial success, although the trade name 'bone china' was not used until early in the 20th century. After about 1815, most English porcelain was bone china.

Most early 19th-century pieces were not marked, and products of different factories were very similar because the techniques of large-scale production had defeated the individuality of the previous fifty years. However, after about 1790, pattern numbers were painted onto the base of each piece, so that individuals and retailers could place orders for particular items. (See Appendix, p. 245.)

Bat-printing was popular in 1795–1820 *(183)*. Then and until about 1825, all printing, except blue, was overglaze. Hand-painted underglaze-blue was only rarely used after about 1800, when the cheaper technique of transfer-printing was introduced. Fine painting of landscapes and flowers, and the use of *Imari* colours *(209)* and gilding were features of the early 19th century.

Teapots were globular *(204)* before 1790, then oval 1790-1825 *(209)* and rounded (often with feet) after 1825 *(213)*. Few spoon trays were made after 1800. Teacups made in 1820 had twice the capacity of those made in 1800 and were similar in size to those of today. Some factories had made cups with handles since the mid-18th century, but after 1820, all teacups had handles. A fluted or spiral fluting on tea wares *(238)* was a characteristic of most factories in about 1790–1810, and suited the thinner, harder pastes of this period.

209

209 Early 19th-century oval porcelain tea service. Imari colours were particularly popular with various English factories at this time. (Mrs L. Moy, Sydney)

210 Left: Derby porcelain dish, showing Imari and gilt colours popular around 1815. Right: Rockingham porcelain plate, c. 1835, with a typical ground (background) on which painted or gilded decoration was frequently superimposed. (The Grafton Galleries, Sydney)

Among the leading factories in the early 19th century were the three Worcester factories, and the Derby and Spode factories. The Worcester factories did not switch to bone china during the first few years of the 19th century. Their early wares, at this time, were of a hard-paste type.

Worcester (1751–present day)

FLIGHT & BARR WORCESTER The original Worcester factory was managed by Flight and Barr until 1807, then continued by various members of the Flight and Barr families until 1840, when amalgamated with Chamberlain Worcester.

CHAMBERLAIN WORCESTER Robert Chamberlain left the original Worcester

210

factory in 1788, and decorated and sold Caughley porcelain in his own decorating establishment until the early 1790s. During the 1790s Chamberlain began to manufacture his own porcelain, which showed fine painting, sometimes of delicate shells and feathers. Some teapots and sugar bowls were marked 'Chamberlain Worcester' inside the lids. Finely painted and *encrusted* Chamberlain Worcester ware was made in the 1830s. In 1840, the Chamberlain factory and the Flight, Barr & Barr factory amalgamated.

GRAINGER WORCESTER Thomas Grainger, an employee of the Chamberlain factory, branched out on his own in 1801. At first he bought white porcelain from other factories and then decorated it. From 1805, he produced his own porcelain. Like the Chamberlain wares, Grainger pieces were sometimes marked inside the lids. During the 19th century, the Grainger factory produced shapes and designs according to the fashions of each period, so the wares were very similar to those of other factories and were in fact rarely marked. In 1889, the Grainger factory was taken over by the Worcester Royal Porcelain Company, but continued to use the Grainger mark until 1902.

Derby (1750–1848)

William Duesbury, the owner of the Derby factory, died in 1786. The firm was then operated by his son, also William, until he died ten years later. The Derby factory then passed to Michael Kean, who followed the Duesbury styles until the management of Bloor and the 'Bloor Derby' period of 1812–1848, when the quality of Derby ware declined. Fine landscape painting, *Imari* colours and gilding were features of this factory (*210 left*), and after 1782 table wares were mainly produced.

SPODE (1797–1833) When his father died in 1797, Josiah Spode took over the well-established Spode earthenware factory. At about this time, the Spode factory introduced bone porcelain and in the early 19th century was well ahead of the other porcelain factories in this regard.

The Spode output was very steady—by dividing the pattern number by 150, the approximate 19th-century year of manufacture can be obtained. For example, pattern number 300 divided by 150 gives 2, thus indicating the year 1802; pattern number 3000 indicates 1820.

Bat-printing was used on Spode porcelain and, after 1810, most pieces were marked 'Spode'.

In 1833 the firm was taken over by Copeland & Garrett (see p. 171).

211

211 Spode porcelain vase, c. 1820, typical of the Regency period. (D. J. Clifford, Sydney)

Other early 19th-century porcelain factories

There were numerous other factories operating at the time of Worcester, Derby and Spode, and the most important were Swansea, Nantgarw, Mason, Wedgwood, Minton, Coalport, Ridgway, Rockingham, Davenport, and Copeland & Garrett.

SWANSEA (1814–1820) and NANTGARW (1813, 1817–1820) These two short-lived Welsh factories were unique because they continued to make soft-paste porcelain in the face of competition from bone china. The Nantgarw factory was moved to Swansea in 1814, but Billingsley re-opened Nantgarw in 1817. Both factories produced an extremely translucent paste, and functional ware was the most common product. Particularly fine flower decoration was carried out by Billingsley, and some was also done by London decorators.

MASON (1800–1813) and WEDGWOOD (1812–1822) These two major earthenware factories both made porcelain for a short time in the early 19th century, and the Wedgwood factory again produced porcelain from 1878.

In 1813, the Mason factory discontinued porcelain production in favour of Mason's famous ironstone. Mason porcelain was similar to that of other factories, and had a *craze*-free glaze. The main product was tea ware, and the handles of teacups had a characteristic thumb-rest spur.

Mason offered to sell porcelain to Wedgwood's London showroom in 1810, and so may have prompted Wedgwood to begin porcelain production in 1812. The Wedgwood factory made mainly tea ware. The glaze was particularly white, shapes were classical, and the decoration was often a finely painted landscape.

MINTON (1793–present day) Minton porcelain was first made in about 1797, and followed the styles of the period although porcelain production ceased between 1817 and 1823. Fine painting was characteristic of the Minton ware made in the 1830s. From 1824, the bone-china body was whiter than that of earlier wares, and floral encrusted decoration (212) was popular after 1824—although most factories made encrusted porcelain in the period 1820–1840. The encrusted porcelains of the 1820–1840 period have become known generically as Coalbrookdale as they were so much made by the Coalport factory, which was near the place called Coalbrookdale.

212 Minton documented encrusted rococo porcelain vase, c. 1835-1845. (The Grafton Galleries, Sydney)

COALPORT (often called Coalbrookdale, 1796–present day) In the early 19th century there were two Coalport porcelain factories—the best known was that of John Rose, which was opened in about 1796. Rose took over and also

213

213 Rococo porcelain tea service, typical of about 1840. Such items are often wrongly attributed to Rockingham. (The Grafton Galleries, Sydney)

produced at the Caughley factory between 1799 and 1814. The Coalport product was at first a heavy hybrid hard-paste porcelain. The rival Coalport factory (Reynolds, Horton & Thomas Rose) produced similar wares in 1800–1814. John Rose bought this rival factory in 1814 and moved his Caughley production to that site—and in about 1820, Billingsley-type roses featured in decorated Coalport wares. At this time, the Coalport factories began to use a lead-free *feldspar* glaze, which produced a very white product.

RIDGWAY (1808–1855) By 1850, this firm probably made more tea and dessert services than any other factory at the time. Ridgway pattern numbers were distinctive (see p. 246). The factory began to produce porcelain in 1808, and large quantities were made by 1830.

ROCKINGHAM (1826–1842) Prior to the mid-19th century, porcelain was made in the rococo style, and the products of the Rockingham factory in Yorkshire were typical of this period—in fact, much English porcelain of the mid-19th century has been wrongly attributed to Rockingham (*213*). The Rockingham paste was softer than that produced by the Minton, Ridgway and Spode factories, and the glaze was often finely crazed. Gilt decoration and coloured grounds *(210 right)*, especially green, were characteristic of Rockingham ware. On tea wares, only the saucers were marked—but pattern numbers were used.

DAVENPORT (1793–1887) This factory was started in 1793 by the Davenport family, at Burslem in Staffordshire. The Davenport factory produced fine earthenware, and began to make porcelain in 1800. From 1830 Davenport wares followed the Coalport style, often with painted landscape decoration. Fine multicolour printed earthenware was also made in the mid-19th century.

COPELAND & GARRETT (1833–1970) This firm began by taking over the old Spode factory in 1833, and the Spode product was continued until Parian porcelain (see below) was introduced in the 1840s. After 1847, the firm continued as Copeland. The quality of the Copeland & Garrett porcelain was always good, and the painted decoration, particularly landscapes, was outstanding.

White wares of the last half of the 19th century

PARIAN WARE *(214 left)* became popular in the middle of the 19th century. It was originally created to imitate the fashionable and costly marble quarried on the Greek Island of Paros. Statuary Parian was a highly vitrified *biscuit* porcelain, which was silky, lustrous and suitable for delicate detail.

The making of Parian figures required great skill. The figures were cast in moulds from a *slip* that had a creamy consistency. The casts were then assembled and joined with slip, then refired in a low-temperature biscuit oven. The figures were then refired at high temperatures. The resultant fired figure was only three-quarters of the size of the original cast.

Parian figures were very popular in Victorian homes, as they were as effective but cheaper than the soft-paste biscuit figures of Sèvres, Berlin, Vienna and Derby that had been so much in demand during the last half of the 18th century.

The Minton and the Copeland & Garrett factories were both experimenters with the production of Parian figures during the 1830s, with only partial success on the part of Minton. In 1842 Copeland & Garrett released the first piece of what was to become known as 'Parian statuary'—the 'Apollo as the Shepherd Boy of Admetus', from the original marble by R. J. Wyatt,

215

215 Goss porcelain vase, early 20th-century. The words 'Votes for Women' are painted at the top of the smiling woman's face. This was made at the peak of enthusiasm for the Women's Suffrage movement. (Miss Joyce Bowden, Sydney)

R. A. Minton finally achieved success at about the same time, and launched the celebrated Minton statuary. By the 1850s, most English porcelain factories were producing Parian figures—and these remained popular until the end of the century.

BELLEEK (1863–present day) This Irish factory was founded in about 1863 by a London architect, Robert Armstrong, whose interest in ceramics had arisen whilst he was designing factory additions for the Kerr & Co. Royal Porcelain Works at Worcester. In company with Kerr, Armstrong visited the Castle Caldwell Estate in County Fermanagh in Ireland, from where the owner, John Caldwell Bloomfield, had sent feldspar and china clay to Kerr's factory in the 1850s. The Irish clay proved superior to English clay, particularly for the manufacture of Parian. Bloomfield also supplied Irish feldspar, via the Mersey and the canal system, to various Staffordshire potteries.

Armstrong decided to produce porcelain in Ireland, so as to undercut the Staffordshire factories and capture the American market. He obtained the financial support from a wealthy Irish storekeeper, David M'Berney. By 1863, M'Berney and Armstrong had established their factory at Belleek on a small island in the River Erne. The river was navigable to small coastal craft, which facilitated transport to America.

English designers and artisans were employed. The cost of finely made, luxury goods was subsidised by profits from more functional ware such as dinner services. The fine lightweight Belleek porcelain *(214 right)* had an iridescent glaze that was suggestive of mother-of-pearl. Shells and flowers were popular motifs for fine, plastic decoration, and openwork baskets were produced. The *lustre* glaze was invented in France at about the same time as the Belleek factory was established, and the Belleek factory acquired manufacturing rights, protected by patent, for this glaze.

When partners Armstrong and M'Berney died in 1884, the firm was acquired by a group of more profit-minded local businessmen. Luxury goods were discontinued and many of the finer artists were dismissed. Armstrong's two sons, and some of the better artists, emigrated to America, where they successfully duplicated Belleek at the Trenton pottery.

Belleek porcelain was marked, usually with an Irish harp, wolfhound and castle, and the words 'Belleek Fermanagh'. After 1891, the mark 'Ireland' was added.

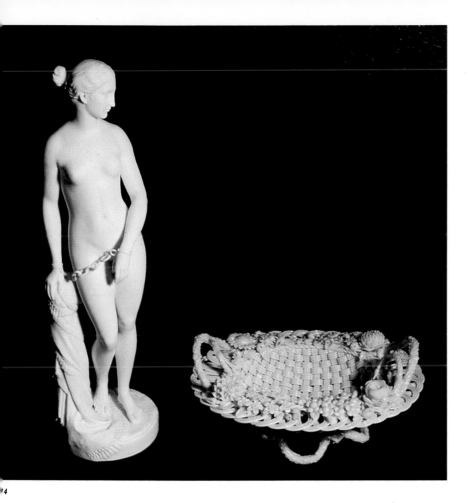

*4

GOSS (1862–1940) William Goss left the Copeland factory and had established his own Staffordshire factory by 1862. Fine Parian-type busts were made, and the porcelain resembled that of the Belleek factory. Between 1885 and 1920, glazed porcelain ornaments (usually small jars), bearing coats of arms of towns and cities, were produced in large quantities. Production continued until 1940, but in 1929 the Goss Company was taken over by Cauldon Potteries Ltd.

PÂTE SUR PÂTE This was produced from 1870 until 1939. *Pâte sur pâte*, meaning 'body on body', had the effect of a ceramic cameo *(216)*. White layers of semi-translucent Parian china were built up layer by layer over a coloured Parian background. After tooling, an attractive cameo effect was obtained. The technique was developed at the Sèvres factory and an employee, Marc Louis Solon, brought it to the Minton factory in 1870. Solon made individual pieces, and signed his work. He trained other Minton craftsmen, who marked their work with initials. *Pâte sur pâte* was also made by most of the leading English porcelain-makers between 1875 and 1890. Much of this was signed by the respective artists.

214 Left to right: Minton Parian porcelain figure of a Greek slave, after an original by the American sculptor Hiram Powers, 1848. Height 36.5 cm. Right: Belleek porcelain basket, c. 1885. Length 22.6 cm. (Museum of Applied Arts and Sciences, Sydney)

216

216 Pâte-Sur-Pâte porcelain plate modelled by F. Schenk, late 19th Century. Impressed monogram GJ and crescent mark of George Jones Factory. (Mr. D.J. Clifford, Sydney)

217 Late 19th-century Minton porcelain vase, showing the Japanese influence that developed from London and Paris exhibitions of the 1860s. (Private collection)

217

Late 19th-century and Art Nouveau porcelain

Some of the finest porcelain was made during the late 19th century, and today often has greater value than rarer items made a hundred years earlier. The styles in some respects were a revival of those of the late 18th century: pastel colours, classical lines, and the French Louis XVI revival style. Oriental influences were again seen, but from Japan rather than China *(217)*. In 1853, after two centuries of isolation, Japan had opened its doors to Europe. At the international exhibitions in London and Paris in the 1860s, the Japanese exhibits, showed their influence on European art.

By the late 19th century most ceramics were marked, and such words as 'Limited', 'Royal', and 'England' were specific from a certain period. (See Appendix, p. 244.) Among the most successful factories of this period were Royal Worcester, Minton, Doulton, Derby, and Moore Bros.

ROYAL WORCESTER (1862–present day) This factory was a leader of the period, sharing first prize with the Minton factory at the Vienna Exhibition of 1873. Some of the best painters of the day were employed, and they followed Japanese and French styles. The working lives of some of these painters are:

Reginald and Walter Austin (1910–1930)—birds, fruit and flowers, including Australian wildflowers, after the Australian artist Ellis Rowan.

Harry Davis (1898–1969)—landscapes, sheep and fish.

Ernest Phillips (1890–1929)—flowers.

William Powel (1900–1950)—English birds.

Frank Roberts (1880–1915)—fruit.

Richard Sebright (1891–1947)—fruit.

Walter Sedgley (1899–1929)—flowers, birds.

Harry Stinton (1896–1963)—cattle.

James Stinton (1885–1951)—game birds.

John Stinton (1889–1938)—cattle.

Edward Townsend (1918–1971)—fruit, sheep.

George Owen was an outstanding Worcester craftsman, famous for reticulating, or piercing, porcelain vases *(219)*. Some items took months to create—each small piece was cut out with an oiled knife while the clay was wet. He worked during the 1880s until the early 1900s and usually signed his work with an incised 'G. Owen'.

Royal Worcester ware was marked to the year of manufacture by a series

218 *Worcester porcelain vase painted by Harry Stinton, c. 1911. Height 22 cm. (Russell Brooks, Sydney)*

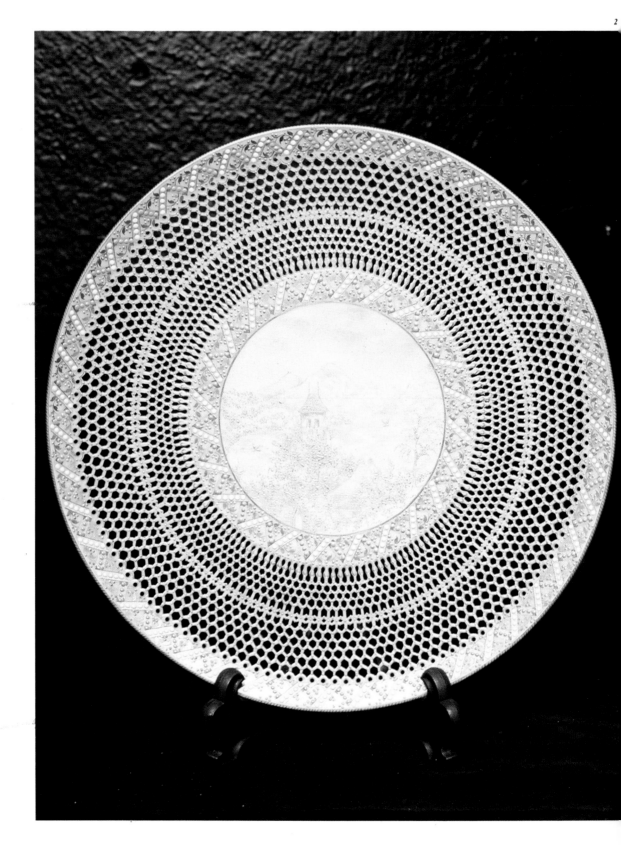

of dots and other marks. (See Appendix, p. 251.)

There were several factories in Worcester during the late 19th century. The original and Chamberlain factories had amalgamated in 1840, to be known as Chamberlain & Co. In 1852 this factory was taken over by Kerr & Binns and was known by that name until 1862, when the name Worcester Royal Porcelain Co. Ltd was first used. The Grainger Worcester factory operated under that

220

219 Worcester porcelain plate, with pierced decoration by George Owen, c. 1882. Diameter 19.7 cm. (Museum of Applied Arts and Sciences, Sydney)

220 Late 19th-century Royal Worcester porcelain cup and saucer, showing the influence of the Art Nouveau style. (The Grafton Galleries, Sydney)

name until taken over by the Royal Worcester factory in 1889. The modeller James Hadley established his own Hadley's Worcester factory in 1875, but this was taken over in 1905 by Royal Worcester. Another small, less important factory, Locke & Co., operated in Worcester between 1895 and 1902.

THE MINTON FACTORY added 's' to the name 'Minton' from 1873. The globe mark was used in 1863–1872, and late in this period the globe was crowned. For a hundred years after 1842, small cyphers were impressed into the body—these were in a series of three and represented the month letter, potter's mark and year cypher.

THE DOULTON FACTORY began the production of porcelain, in addition to the

221

221 Moore Brothers porcelain vase, decorated with black-and-gilt Greek key pattern motifs, c. 1880. (The Grafton Galleries, Sydney)

earlier earthenware, in 1884. Burslem in Staffordshire was the site of the porcelain factory, while the Lambeth factory in London produced stoneware.

The ceramic ware made by Royal Doulton in the Art Deco period was marked 'Royal' and 'England' after 1902, but 'Made in England' was not used until 1930. The Doulton lion stood on a duke's coronet until 1922, when this

224

coronet pedestal was removed.

THE DERBY FIRM closed in 1848, but some of the employees carried on the Derby tradition in a new factory at Derby. The Derby Crown Porcelain Co. Ltd was established in 1876 and used a crown mark in 1878–1890. The word 'England' was added to the factory mark from 1890. The words 'Made in England' were not used by this factory until about 1921. Year cyphers were used from 1882 onwards.

THE MOORE BROTHERS FACTORY *(221)* operated at Longton in Staffordshire between 1872 and 1905. The mark 'Moore Bros' was used during this period. The globe mark was used from about 1880; the word 'England' added from *c.* 1891. Bernard Moore took over the factory in 1905.

223

22

222 Late 19th-century porcelain tea service, showing typical pastel colours, Japanese bamboo motifs and swags of the classical revival period. (The Grafton Galleries, Sydney)

223 Art Nouveau Austrian vase, showing pastel colours, matt surface and languid long-haired maidens, c. 1890-1910. Note the semi-parallel lines of limbs, hair and plant branches. (Private collection)

224 Typical Art Nouveau porcelain vase, c. 1895, marked 'Amphora, Austria'. (Private collection)

The Art Nouveau style was at its peak around 1900. It began in about 1890 and finished in about 1910. The Austro-Hungarian empire was strong during this period, and Austria exported large quantities of decorative articles *(223, 224)*. Pastel colours, matt surfaces and linear geometric lines were typical of this Austrian secession movement.

225

226

Early 20th-century and Art Deco ceramics

225 Doulton porcelain flambé vase, early 20th century. (D. J. Clifford, Sydney)

226 Royal Doulton vase marked Chang with incised initials of Harry Nixon and marked Noke, impressed date for 1927. Height 17 cm. (The Grafton Galleries, Sydney)

Art Deco ceramic decoration had its beginnings in the waning years of Art Nouveau prior to World War I. There were two main trends in ceramic decoration: one style used simplified shapes and glazes so as to produce a version of Chinese, Korean and Japanese stoneware *(225, 226)*, and the other used figurative or abstract designs to decorate lamp bases, bowls and plates *(227, 228, 229 centre and right)*.

Some of the leading ceramic artists of this period were:

BERNARD MOORE (worked in these glazes *c.* 1905–1916) was one of the first European potters to master the early Chinese *flambé* glazes *(229 left)*, and was famous for his glaze effects, often red with black silhouettes of landscapes. His work was usually marked 'BM' or 'Bernard Moore'. He had a skilled team of

228 Art Deco porcelain
plate, marked 'Cauldron
Tango Pattern'. Geometric
patterns and bright colours
such as orange were
fashionable. (Colin Lennox,
Sydney)

227 Art Deco earthenware
tea service, c. 1930. This
illustrates the rounded
shape of the 1920s, and the
angular painted decoration
of the 1930s. (Copeland &
de Soos, Sydney)

artists who usually signed their work with monograms of their initials.

WILLIAM MOORCROFT (worked *c.* 1898–1945) from the peak of Art Nouveau until the end of the Art Deco period. He was designer for James Macintyre & Co., Burslem, and was in charge of their art pottery department from 1898. His early work was decorated with plant forms. After the closure of Macintyre's art pottery department in 1913 he established his own factory. Bright monochrome lustre glazes were produced until the 1920s. *Flambé* glazes began in 1919, and were fully developed by the late 1920s *(230)*. He used the mark 'Moorcroft' and impressed signature 'W. Moorcroft'. His son Walter took over in 1945.

NOKE, CHARLES JOHN (worked *c.* 1889–1936) was art director at Doulton from 1914 to 1936. He supervised the production of *flambé*, Sung and Chang glazes *(226)*. Also, important figures were made during his directorship. He was succeeded as art director by his son Cecil Jack in 1936. Both signed their work Noke, but the father had two dots below his signature.

231 Wedgwood porcelain
'Fairyland' lustre bowl. (Miss
Nora Firth, Sydney)

229 Three vases of the Art
Deco period. Note the bright
colours and geometric patterns
on the examples in the centre
and on the right.
*Left to right: Red-lidded
earthenware vase, c. 1916,
by Bernard Moore, bearing his
mark on the base as well as
an impressed mark 'Snow',
which indicated a particular
type of crystalline glaze.
Earthenware vase, c. 1925,
marked 'Meramis made in
Belgium D1337' and with a tin
glaze design that was built up
by hand in layers. Lidded
porcelain vase, c. 1925,
marked 'Rosenthal, Selb,
Bavaria Kad Wemdner'.
(Copeland & de Soos, Sydney)*

230 Moorcroft vase, c. 1930
(Serendipity Antiques,
Dubbo)

MAKEIG JONES (worked *c.* 1915–1931) designed and painted bone china with lustre decoration at the Wedgwood factory. Some decoration was derived from Chinese and Japanese styles. A style decorated with birds, butterflies and dragons, was known as 'Dragon Lustre'. Another style with fairy subjects was known as 'Fairyland Lustre' *(231)*.

CLIFF, CLARICE (worked *c.* 1913–1963) was a designer and painter famous for brightly coloured medium-priced tea services and vases. An outstanding style called 'Bizarre' *(232)* was very popular between 1929 and 1939. She was art director at Wilkinson's Royal Staffordshire pottery and its subsidiary, the Newport factory, in 1930–1939. A team of painters would sometimes work on a production line hand-painting quantities of Miss Cliff's designs. In 1932 a 21-piece tea service cost A\$3.50, which was about the week's wages of a painter. Some pieces until 1963 have her name, but the magic died with the bright colours of the Art Deco period. Marks are variations of 'Hand Painted Bizarre

Clarice Cliff, Newport Pottery, England' and 'Wilkinson Ltd, England'.

COOPER, SUSIE (worked *c.* 1922–1930s) specialised in stoneware bowls, jugs and vases with incised designs, depicting a strong *celadon* and Art Nouveau influence. She established her own company in 1932; it had a deer as a factory mark. In the 1930s similar designs were made in bone china.

THE DOUGHTY SISTERS—Dorothy (worked *c.* 1933–1945) and Freda (worked *c.* 1931–1970) both worked as modellers for the Royal Worcester Company. At an exhibition in 1931 Freda produced models of children *(233)* that sold well despite the economic depression, and these have continued to be popular to the present day. One famous series was based on the old rhyme 'Monday's child is fair of face, Tuesday's child is full of grace . . .'.

Dorothy produced very accurate bird models in limited editions. In 1935 a pair of birds cost A$200. A recent auction price of a pair in America was approximately A$32 000.

232 Clarice Cliff earthenware 'Bizarre' vase, c. 1930. 'Bizarre' was a style and a trade name not a pattern name. (Copeland & de Soos, Sydney)

233 Royal Worcester porcelain group of children, 'Babes in the Wood', an example of Royal Worcester children's groups popular from the early 1930s. (The Grafton Galleries, Sydney)

Typical shapes and decoration, 1745–1940

This section illustrates some styles of various periods between 1745 and 1940. The duration of styles varied according to public demand, and often different factories copied others' styles. However, the illustrations in this section consolidate the fashion trends outlined in the ceramic chapter.

235 Changing shapes of porcelain vases between about 1820 and 1930. Left to right: Regency spill vase typical of the Bourne factory, c. 1807-1830. (Newman's Antiques, Sydney) Minton encrusted vase, c. 1835, bearing pattern number 1505. Royal Worcester pastel-coloured vase, c. 1885. Art Deco Royal Doulton vase, c. 1930. (The Grafton Galleries, Sydney)

Often made in creamware, c. 1770   Typical of Davenport, c. 1815- 1825   Newhall bone china, c. 1814-1831   Hard-paste Newhall china, c. 1782-1787   Hound handle typical of America, c. 1852-1867

Newhall jug, c. 1800

Soapstone Caughley chocolate cup, c. 1790-1795

Earthenware teacup, c. 1825

Spiral fluting typical of Worcester and other fine potting factories, c. 1783-1793

Newhall with handle typical of Staffordshire, c. 1820

Early English globular teapot, soft-paste Bow, c. 1753

Liverpool teapot of globular shape, typical of 1775

Oval Worcester teapot of the Flight, Barr & Barr period, c. 1807

Worcester of the Davis/Flight period, c. 1780

Oval Mason, early 19th century

Oval silver Newhall, late 18th century

Rococo revival, early Victorian Coalport

Style of Chaffers, Liverpool, c. 1760-1765

Newhall bone china, c. 1814-1820

Typical early soft-paste sauce boat, Bow, c. 1752

Sugar basin, typical of Chamberlain Worcester, c. 1800

234 Left to right: Blue-and-white sparrow-beak jug, typical of Nanking export porcelain of the late 18th century. Blue-and-white porcelain jug, typical of c. 1800. Earthenware jug, c. 1780. Porcelain jug, early 19th-century. (The Grafton Galleries, Sydney)

236

236 Changing styles in Porcelain plates between about 1755 and 1885. Left to right: Chelsea 'red anchor', c. 1755. 'Derby' type made by various factories, c. 1820. Plate typical of c. 1840, bearing pattern number 5263, probably Copeland. Wedgwood porcelain plate with pink hibiscus flowers, showing Art Nouveau influence of the end of the 19th century. (The Grafton Galleries, Sydney)

238

237

238 Group of porcelain cups and saucers showing changing styles. Left to right: Chinese 18th-century blanc-de-chine that influenced Bow and Chelsea. Late 18th-century Chinese export ware. Fluted, thinly potted spiral-fluted late 18th-century ware, possibly Worcester. Larger, heavier English cup with rose decoration, c. 1825. (The Grafton Galleries, Sydney)

237 Left to right: Late 18th-century jug, Chinese export porcelain. Late 19th-century porcelain jug, with smudged blue typical of the period. Blue-and-white transfer-printed earthenware jug, c. 1800–1830. (The Grafton Galleries, Sydney)

Some Useful Ceramic Dates

6000 BC	Earthenware Middle East
4500 BC	Glazing Middle East
3500 BC	Potters Wheel Middle East
Chou Dynasty (1122–256 BC)	Chinese stoneware
3rd century AD	Chinese celadon glazes
9th century	Persians use cobalt-blue pigment on earthenware and produce tin-glazed enamels
Tang Dynasty (618–907)	Chinese porcelain
Sung Dynasty (960–1279)	Porcelain and celadon glazes perfected
Ming Dynasty (1368–1644)	Overglaze enamels and blue-and-white underglaze decoration
14th century	German stoneware first made; Persian cobalt-blue pigment imported by the Chinese
15th century	*Maiolica* produced in Italy
16th century	Stoneware perfected in Germany; tin-glazed enamels produced in northern Europe
1575–1583	Small quantity of artificial, Medici porcelain produced in Italy
Early 17th century	Porcelain manufacture begins in Japan
Late 17th century	Soft-paste porcelain introduced in France, although not significant until mid-18th century; *flambé* glazes develop in China; stoneware produced in England; Chinese porcelain imported in relatively large quantities into Europe
Early 18th century	Hard-paste porcelain at Meissen; Chinese armorial porcelain as Famille rose group of overglaze enamelling was fully developed
c. 1740–1780	Whieldon influences English earthenware
c. 1740–1800	Creamware significant; tin-glaze enamels wane
c. 1745	English soft-paste porcelain begins at Chelsea
c. 1748	Excavation at Pompeii and Herculaneum begins
c. 1755	Honey-gilding
c. 1756	Transfer-printing at Worcester

c. 1760	French styles supplant Meissen influence after Prussians capture Dresden in 1756; black basalt ceramic
c. 1770	Hard-paste porcelain in France
c. 1774	Blue jasperware
c. 1775–1800	Neo-classical styles
c. 1785	Mercury-gilding
c. 1770–1800	Biscuit made at Derby
c. 1785–1825	Turner's body
c. 1780–1840	Blue-and-white transfer decoration widely used
c. 1780–1835	Prattware
c. 1790	Opaque glazes replace translucent glazes on English earthenware figures
c. 1796	Champion's hard-paste patent expires; bone china introduced
1789	French Revolution
c. 1800	English pattern numbers become more generally used
c. 1805	Spode stone China
c. 1813	Mason's ironstone
c. 1815	Feldspar china introduced by Spode
c. 1820–1840	Encrusted decoration revival
c. 1847–1900	Pot-lids and polychrome printing
c. 1830	English lustre
c. 1840–1900	Flat-back Staffordshire figures
c. 1840	Samson figures in France; Parian ware
c. 1863	Belleek
c. 1870	Doulton 'art pottery'
c. 1885	Goss
c. 1890–1910	Art Nouveau
c. 1920–1940	Art Deco

Furniture

241 Oak chair, second ha
of the 16th century, with
linen-fold decoration. Th
chair shows panelled and
pegged construction.
(Victoria and Albert
Museum, London)

241

The age of oak—before 1660

Cromwellian oak joint stool

Elizabethan oak cupboard with cup-and-cover supports below middle shelf

Mid-17th century oak dropside gateleg table

Cromwellian oak refectory table

Prior to the Restoration in 1660, most northern European furniture was made of oak, and was heavier in both construction and appearance than that made in later years. Screws were not used and glue only occasionally. Before 1650 *mortise and tenon**joints, secured by wooden pins, were in general use.

TECHNIQUES *Turning* in England was first carried out in the middle of the 16th century. The early styles were plain, but during the Elizabethan period turning was bulbous and accentuated. Plainer styles then returned, particularly during the austere Commonwealth period in the mid-17th century. *Split balusters* were used as decoration, and were pinned or glued to flat surfaces.

During the Elizabethan period, inlay was used as a form of decoration, often for the fronts of cupboards. This technique had been introduced from Italy, through Germany and Flanders. Small pieces of different coloured woods, such as ebony, box or fruitwood, were inlaid into the oak.

CHESTS The early oak chests were simple lidded wooden boxes made of planks, and were held together with iron nails or wooden pins *(239)*. The wooden planks often split, as they expanded and contracted with changes between damp and dry, and hot and cold weather. During the 16th century, oak panels were fitted into frames that allowed the wood to expand and contract without splitting. These panels can be seen in the 16th-century chest and on the back of the 16th-century chair illustrated *(240, 241)*. From the end of the 16th century some chests, later known as mule chests, had drawers fitted in the bottom so that small items could be moved without disturbing the main contents. Chests of drawers were not made until about 1650.

TABLES Before about 1660, tables were made from long planks of oak or elm. These tables were usually narrow and the diners sat only on one side and at the

Italics indicate glossary entry.

239 Late 15th-century iron-bound chest, made from planks nailed together. The wood often split as it expanded and contracted. (Victoria and Albert Museum, London)

240 English 16th-century chest. The wooden panels are carved with linen-fold decoration. (Victoria and Albert Museum, London)

239

240

242

242 Elizabethan oak court cupboard, with gadrooned frieze on gadrooned and fluted baluster support. Width 116.25 cm. (Christies, London)

ends. The *gateleg table* was made in the beginning of the 17th century.

CASE FURNITURE Court cupboards *(242)* were in general use by about 1570. These derived their name from the French *court*, meaning short. Court cupboards had no doors; only open shelves for cups or plates, and sometimes a drawer. There were usually three shelves, the bottom one just above the floor, and the shelves were often supported at the front corners by '*cup-and-cover*' supports. A drawer was often included in the friezes of the top and middle shelves.

The cupboard or press was closely akin to the court cupboard. It had a central door, which was often flanked by splayed sides, and also often had drawers included in the friezes.

243

244

Cupboards for food storage were sometimes called 'hutches'. These were fitted at the front with an open screen of turned balusters for ventilation.

The degree of decoration and bulbous Elizabethan *cup-and-cover* turnings are an indication of date.

CHAIRS Very few chairs were made before the beginning of the 17th century, and these were for the heads of important households—stools or benches were used by most people. In the 17th century, chairs were made with wooden seats and backs *(243)*, and some were upholstered in velvet, silk or Turkey work *(244)*. Side chairs in sets were not made until the Commonwealth period, in the middle of the 17th century.

243 Carved and joined English oak chair, typical of the early 17th century. (Victoria and Albert Museum, London)

244 English oak armchair, upholstered in Turkey work, c. 1635. (Victoria and Albert Museum, London)

The Restoration—the beginning of cabinet-making, 1660–1685

With the *Restoration* there was a leap forward in home furnishing. New ideas were introduced from Europe, particularly from the Low Countries, which had been the sanctuary of Charles II during part of his exile in the Commonwealth period. The austerity of the Commonwealth styles was rapidly replaced by the ostentation of the new royal style, although the provinces were slower to follow the new fashion.

The *baroque* style predominated during the late 17th and 18th centuries. It

245 Late 17th-century marquetry. This pine table-top has been veneered with walnut, cherry and other woods. (Victoria and Albert Museum, London)

245

196

was a move away from the classical, sometimes repetitive, style of the Renaissance. Bernini (1598–1680), who designed St Peters in Rome, can be regarded as the creator of the baroque style. Baroque was characterised by symmetry. It gave way to the asymmetrical *rococo* style in about 1730.

TECHNIQUES Two important new technological developments were made: the wood screw, and efficient glues. The screw introduced in 1675 had a filed thread, non-centred slit and very little taper. Machine-made tapered screws were not introduced until the London Great Exhibition of 1851.

More efficient glues and Dutch veneer-cutting techniques led to the development of floral *marquetry* *(245)*. Veneers were slices of figured wood used to decorate the structural timber, which was often oak or pine. These slices were sawn by hand and were usually about 1.5-3.0 millimetres thick. New woods such as ebony and amboyna were imported from the East and the West Indies. Walnut had been used only to a minor extent in Elizabethan times, but now replaced oak as the major furniture timber and was used for solid pieces and for decorative veneers.

A simple form of marquetry involved gluing together two different-coloured slats of veneer with a thin sheet of paper between. The design was cut with a fine fretsaw and the sheets were then separated by soaking in water. The cut-out pieces from wood of one colour were used to fill the spaces in the other.

Grinling Gibbons, the Dutch carver and sculptor who settled in London by 1671, had an influence on carved motifs of fruit and flowers to decorate furniture.

Parquetry was originally a French term for a process whereby blocks of the same wood were laid on floors in such a way as to contrast the grain, and it became used for furniture veneers of the same wood, applied on the same principle of the contrasting grain forming a pattern.

Small quantities of *lacquered* furniture had been imported from the East during Elizabethan times, but during the Restoration period large quantities of such popular items as cabinets, *coromandel screens* and panels were imported. The great demand for these lacquered articles soon led to the development of European *japanning (246)*. The term 'Japanware' refers to articles lacquered with the European imitation of oriental lacquer.

CHAIRS Cane for the seats and backs of chairs was introduced to England from Holland, and was imported from the East Indies. Spiral or 'barley twist' turning

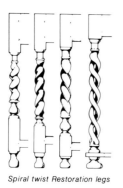

Spiral twist Restoration legs

(247) was typical of the Restoration period, and was also introduced from Holland. The English style of turning gave deeper hollows and a smaller diameter than those turned in Holland, and the Dutch items had a close, more rapid twist. Completely upholstered wing chairs were first made in the Restoration period, and some of these chairs had a back that reclined for sleeping.

CHESTS Chests of drawers were first made in the middle of the 17th century. Early drawer bottoms ran from front to back—from the mid-18th century they ran from side to side. The fronts or sides of chests were often decorated with applied moulding and panels, known as wainscot after a type of oak *(248)*. This decoration was only fashionable for a short while in London, but persisted in

246 English cabinet, c. 1670. The cabinet has been japanned in the Chinese style, and the stand is of carved and gilded wood in the European style. (Christies, London)

247 French armchair, c. 1670. English and European styles were very similar at this time. The twist-turning and cane are characteristic of the period. (Victoria and Albert Museum, London)

247

246

248

the provinces well into the 18th century. Drawer pulls were of brass and were single-drop- or fantail-shaped *(248)*.

MIRRORS The use of gilding and *gesso* became more popular during the Restoration period. The Vauxhall glassworks was established in 1663 and produced expensive mirrors from the late 17th century. However, France led the world in mirror production at this time.

CLOCKS The clock pendulum was introduced to England just prior to the Restoration. Early long-case clocks had a glass disc at the front to allow the pendulum to be seen.

248 Oak chest of drawers, c. 1660-1680, with wainscot decoration and drop handles. (Victoria and Albert Museum, London)

Cast drop handle, late 17th and early 18th centuries

250

250 French armchair, second half of the 17th century. This walnut chair is ornamented with carved flank panels, and has the vertical look of the period. (Victoria and Albert Museum, London)

William and Mary, 1688–1702

This was a period between the ostentation of the Restoration and the elegant simple styles of the early 18th century. Many craftsmen came from Holland with William and Mary, and the Revocation of the Edict of Nantes in 1685 led to many Huguenot craftsmen seeking refuge in England.

249

249 Late 17th-century Dutch chair. This walnut piece shows the style of Daniel Marot. (Victoria and Albert Museum, London)

252

252 Long-case clock, c. 1700. The trunk door has bird and floral marquetry, and the surround has scroll marquetry. The sides of the trunk have walnut panels and boxwood stringing.; (King & Chasemore, Pulborough)

Daniel Marot (1663–1752) was a French-born architect, decorator and designer who was influential in England during this period *(249)*. As a French Protestant he sought refuge in Holland in 1684, the year before the Revocation of the Edict of Nantes. Marot was employed by William of Orange and, after the Prince's accession to the English throne, worked in England between 1694 and 1696 and again in 1698. He was a pioneer, introducing design to a craft previously dominated by carpenters and joiners.

CHAIRS During the late 17th century, a vertical look developed. This vertical style was particularly apparent in the chairs of the period—seats were smaller and backs higher *(250)*. Often the top rail and the front stretcher were arched or curved. *Balusters* replaced twist turnings, and the cresting at the top of the chair back rested on top of the baluster uprights, whereas earlier that century it was tenoned in between the uprights. *Bun feet* were usually round or octagonal, and the legs of both chairs and tables were often linked by serpentine X-shaped stretchers *(251)*. Although cane was still used for chairs, upholstery was becoming more popular and the first upholstered *drop-in* seats were made. The production in England of silks, velvets and brocades for upholstery and bed hangings increased considerably, and fewer imports from France and Italy were necessary.

CASE FURNITURE China collecting was a popular pastime of the late 17th century. Large quantities of Chinese blue-and-white K'ang Hsi porcelain were imported and collections were often displayed in glass-fronted cabinets and in corner cabinets with glazed or panelled fronts. These corner cabinets were often japanned. Chests or cabinets without stands had bun or *bracket feet*. The first glass-door bookcases were made during this period, and the fall-front (sloping lid) writing bureau was in use by the end of the century. There was a trend towards taller furniture, characterised by the various types of glass-door cabinets made during the period. Some of these cabinets had mirrored doors. Other cabinets had a sloping front to the bureau, and were known as bureau bookcases. The secretaire bookcase had a drop-front (vertical front) to the writing compartment.

MIRRORS The mirrors of this period were tall, in accordance with the high ceilings of the time, and were expensive and uncommon. Toilet mirrors or stands with small drawers were in use by 1700, and usually had curved, crested tops and a drawer at the base of the stand.

251 *Late 17th-century English side table, with floral marquetry in stained horn. Note the X-shaped stretcher and drop handle typical of the period. (Victoria and Albert Museum, London)*

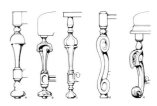

Typical legs of William and Mary period

CLOCKS Long-case clocks were often elaborately veneered (252). Other clocks, called bracket clocks, were displayed on carved and gilded brackets.

Queen Anne and early walnut, 1702–1725

This period produced the first typically English furniture. Its simplicity of line differed from late 17th-century English furniture, which had a strong European character—although some of the early 18th-century items still showed a European influence. Proportion and shape were more important than applied decoration or elaborate carving, and serpentine curves became part of the article—superseding the arches or scrolls applied to furniture in the William and Mary period. Styles remained much the same after the death of Queen Anne in 1714 until the death of George I in 1727. In the mid-1720s, mahogany was introduced and although walnut continued to be used, it was far less popular than during the first quarter of the century. *Marquetry*, japanning and gilding were used to a lesser extent than in the William and Mary period, japanning being mainly used on bureau cabinets, long-case clocks and corner cabinets.

CASE FURNITURE was made of pine and decorated with a fine walnut veneer (253). Drawers were usually of oak and were finely dovetailed. At the beginning

Queen Anne walnut dropside dining table

Early 18th century japanned hanging corner cabinet

253 Chest of drawers with beautifully matched walnut veneers and feather-banding. It has bracket feet and no cockbeading on the drawers, c. 1710-1715. (The Grafton Galleries, Sydney)

254 Bureau cabinet, with burr-walnut veneer on oak, early 18th century. The drawers are separated by a single half-round moulding, which indicates it was made c. 1710-1715. Note the bun feet and the well between the writing surface and the top drawer. Height 217.5 cm, width 100 cm, depth 55 cm. (Victoria and Albert Museum, London)

Escutcheon, first half of the 18th century

of this period, in about 1710–1715, drawers were separated by simple half-round mouldings. Later, two smaller half-round mouldings were set side by side. *Cock beading* was first used on drawers in about 1725. Feather or herringbone borders were used with the walnut veneer, but lost favour in about the 1720s when mahogany was introduced and by about 1730 were no longer used.

In the Queen Anne period, the first small kneehole desks were made. These had drawers on each side and a small cupboard at the rear of the kneehole. Fall-front bureaus of this period often had a 'well' beneath the writing surface and above the top drawer (*254*).

On chests, *drop handles* remained popular until about 1735; the more elaborate handles with matching backplates and keyhole escutcheons lost popularity slightly earlier. Bracket feet were more often used than bun feet during this period. At the end of the 17th century, chests on chests (tallboys) were made, in which the top (usually not veneered) was above eye level.

CHAIRS The best chairs were veneered, and some were decorated with marquetry inlay. The curved line dominated the design of Queen Anne chairs *(256)*. The legs were usually *cabriole,* and the feet were hoof-, club- or pad-shaped in 1700–1750, and ball-and-claw-shaped in 1710–1760. A wide vertical *splat* (often vase- or fiddle-shaped) joined the bottom rail to the curved top rail and usually followed the curve of the sitter's back. The drop-in seats were round. Stretchers lost favour in the first few years of the 18th century.

Good chairs have always been expensive because more labour is required to make a chair relative to its size than most other items of furniture. An existing inventory, made just prior to Queen Anne's accession, lists a set of eight chairs at 26s each. This is equivalent to more than A$1000 each, at today's values.

256 Carved mahogany Dutch chair, c. 1725, in the Queen Anne walnut style. (Victoria and Albert Museum, London)

255

255 Louis XIV ormolu-mounted boulle commode, c. 1700. It is inlaid with designs in brass, scarlet tortoiseshell and pewter, and contains three drawers in the bowed front. Note the French styles were usually some years ahead of those of England. Width 119 cm. (Sothebys, London)

Queen Anne oak table with pad feet

Early Georgian mahogany—Palladian, 1725–1740

English elbow chair with
vase-shaped splat c. 1730

The removal of a tax on West Indian timber resulted in mahogany becoming the major cabinet-makers' timber by about 1725. The earlier imports were very hard, dark and heavy—but later that century, the timber was lighter in weight and in colour. The early mahoganies were known as Spanish mahogany, and came from the islands of San Domingo, Cuba, Jamaica and Puerto Rico. By the end of the century most of the lighter mahogany came from Honduras, where a faster-growing and less dense timber was produced.

In the later 1730s the first book of a series on furniture design was

257

258

257 Bureau bookcase, with marquetry of tortoiseshell and engraved brass inlay, c. 1720-1730. Note the three Corinthian columns supporting the top pediment, which indicates an influence from ancient architecture. (Victoria and Albert Museum, London)

258 English settee, c. 1735. It is painted white and gold, and is based on a design by William Kent. Note the heavy swags in comparison with those of the lighter neo-classical, late 18th-century style. (Victoria and Albert Museum, London)

published, *The Gentleman's and Builder's Companion*, by William Jones. Most of the designs engraved in this book were of the classical Palladian school, based on the architectural ideas of the 16th-century Italian architect Andrea Palladio.

Columns and pediments, inspired by early Roman architecture, were a feature of this classical style *(257)*. The significant point in these designs was that they were copied from large, public—not domestic—buildings. The result was a style that was often too grand for houses, particularly for furniture.

The leading English influence in the Palladian style was William Kent (1684–1748). He was an architect, landscape gardener, interior designer and furniture designer *(258)*. Each item of furniture was usually designed for a specific position in a particular room, so often appeared to be massive and of an architectural scale when placed elsewhere. As an architect Kent saw a room as a whole, not as a series of items of furniture. During this period mahogany was available in wider boards than walnut, and was used at first as solid timber more often than as veneer.

Pedestal desks usually stood in the middle of the room. Handles were either lion masks, with brass rings through the mouth, or circular brass loops. The simple bail handle was first made in the middle of the 18th century.

Kent's side tables usually had a marble top supported by a substantial carved and gilded base *(259)*; the base was often in the form of an eagle or dolphin. Card tables had paw feet and deeply carved knees—these were also used on chair legs. At the end of the period, round tea tables were made that had a central column and three cabriole legs.

George I corner chair with club feet

Loop handle of cast and engraved brass, early 18th century

259

259 Gilt console table with marble top, designed by William Kent for Chiswick House, c. 1725. (Victoria and Albert Museum, London)

260

Mid-18th century—rococo, 1740–1765

The rococo style began in France as early as about 1700. Rococo was a lighter and more fanciful, asymmetrical style than baroque—and a contrast to the heavy *Palladian* style. The English preferred classical styles, so the Palladian movement continued to be in demand. The influence of the rococo style on English furniture did not become important until the 1740s, and continued to be resisted by those of the classical school.

Chinoiserie was both fashionable and fanciful, Chinese *card fret* decoration often being used *(260, 261)*. Gothic arches and pinnacles were far lighter than those of earlier designs. Mirror frames *(263)* and *console tables* gave scope to rococo designers. As both were supported by the wall, their design was not restricted by the need for supporting legs. This allowed the full expression of the light, airy rococo character, which was far removed from the weight-bearing columns and pediments of the Palladian style.

Not all chairs of this period had ball and claw feet; many had straight legs

62

262 Mahogany settee in the rococo style, c. 1760. (Victoria and Albert Museum, London)

260 English mahogany bureau bookcase, c. 1760. The fret decoration, keyhole escutcheons and ogee feet are characteristic of the rococo period. Case furniture does not fully interpret the period: note the mirror frame (263) and settee backs (261, 262) that follow and exploit the rococo linear style fully. (Victoria and Albert Museum, London)

261 Mahogany settee, carved in the Chinese style, c. 1748. (Victoria and Albert Museum, London)

Chippendale mahogany tea table

Side table with bail handles, c. 1760

Mid-18th century chest on chest

in keeping with Chinese and Gothic taste. China cabinets were popular items of the period. They had bars of *astragal* moulding that were lighter than the earlier glazing bars. Oriental lacquer cabinets usually had japanned stands with straight legs. In about 1765, the rococo style was losing popularity and there was a revival of the use of marquetry, particularly on *commodes*. It was lighter and covered less of the background than did the earlier Stuart marquetry. A new style of loop handle was made in which the large backplate was replaced by two smaller, circular or rococo plates. The French style of *ormolu* mounts on the corners and feet of commodes became fashionable. From the middle of the century, the baseboards of drawers ran laterally and were no longer placed from front to rear.

The best-known cabinet-maker of the period was Thomas Chippendale (1718–1779). He led a successful cabinet-making firm, which was continued by his son, also Thomas, into the 19th century. Chippendale published his book *The Gentleman and Cabinet-Maker's Director* in 1754. This was accepted both by society and the trade, and influenced design to such an extent that English mid-18th century rococo furniture was often considered to be of 'Chippendale' style. (Chippendale was a versatile man—when the rococo was replaced by the neo-classical style of Adam, he did not resist the change but adopted it, making the furniture for Adam's interiors.)

William Vile (who died in 1767) was a leading Royal Cabinet-Maker, who continued to make pieces in the classical style, even through the rococo period.

263 *Early George III
giltwood mirror in the
rococo style of Thomas
Chippendale. It has a divided
rectangular plate and the
frame, base and cresting are
carved. 116 x 80 cm.
(Christies, London)*

263

*Rococo escutcheon from
'Chippendale's Director', 3rd
edition (1762)*

Adam and neo-classicism, 1765–1800

'Neo-classic' does more than describe a late 18th-century classical style copied from Greece and Ancient Rome. The term distinguishes between the light, smaller scale style of the late 18th century and the heavier architectural style of the Palladian period of 1725–1740. The inspiration for the neo-classical lines

264 *Stripped pine break-front bookcase, Adam style, c. 1780. (King and Chasemore, Pulborough)*

264

came from recent excavation at Pompeii and Herculaneum, and the smaller scale domestic buildings brought to light, of which the Palladians had had no knowledge. The swing from rococo occurred first in France, and was then welcomed in England. In the late 18th century there was a relatively large English middle class, which provided a greater demand for smaller, functional, good-quality furniture.

Straight simple lines were typical of the new style *(264)*, and decoration was subordinate to form, with Roman motifs such as rams' heads, *paterae* and urns. Light-coloured woods such as satinwood and Honduras mahogany complemented the pastel colours used by Adam and Wedgwood. West Indian satinwood was introduced by 1760; East Indian by 1780.

CASE FURNITURE A new style of brass handle was introduced in about 1777: the backplate was octagonal in shape and was stamped from sheet-brass, with shells and similar decoration raised in relief. A lighter 'French' bracket foot was developed, which was tapered and splayed outwards at the base. By about 1790, round machine nails replaced square hand-made nails. Wide drawers now had baseboards slotted into a bracing strut across the centre.

CHAIRS A significant change in chair design in about 1770 was the straight, usually tapered but sometimes baluster-shaped leg *(265)*. These legs were often fluted and had *spade feet*. The upholstery materials used were silk *damask* and tapestry or leather for dining chairs.

266 Earliest form of sideboard, Adam period, with a pair of urn-shaped knife boxes. (Christies, London)

266

Mahogany fall-front bureau

Double-pedestal desk

265 *Louis XVI gilt chair, late 18th century. (Victoria and Albert Museum, London)*

ROBERT ADAM (1728–1792), the Scottish architect, was the leading personality in the *neo-classical* style. After several years in Italy studying classical architecture, he returned to England in 1758—and the new style was well established by 1765. During his working life of over thirty years, Adam designed many important English houses and was architect to George III for a few years. Like William Kent he designed furniture and other items for his interiors. Formal room arrangements still dictated the positioning of furniture around the walls, rather than functionally within the room. Dining tables were usually *dropsided* with folding legs, so that they could be folded and put to one side when not in use.

An important Adam innovation was the sideboard, which was a side table flanked by pedestals **(266)**. Knife boxes were widely used at this time; they were either vase-shaped **(266)** or in the form of a box with serpentine front and lift lid. *Wine coolers* were sometimes designed *en suite* with sideboards.

Adam influenced not only architects and cabinet-makers, but also potters such as Wedgwood, and silversmiths. Many large cabinet-making firms operated during the neo-classical period. George Seddon of London employed 400 craftsmen in 1786. Robert Gillow of Lancaster and London began in about 1760 and had a large export business by the early 19th century. There were hundreds of smaller firms throughout England making furniture of good quality.

Hepplewhite and Sheraton, 1780–1806

Furniture of the late 18th century was influenced by the designers George Hepplewhite (who died in 1786) and Thomas Sheraton (1751–1806). Although they were both trained as cabinet-makers, no furniture is known to have been produced by either. However, they produced design books that had an influence on public taste and on the work of cabinet-makers. Hepplewhite's *The Cabinet-Maker and Upholsterer's Guide* was published in 1788, two years after his death. Thomas Sheraton's *The Cabinet-Maker and Upholsterer's Drawing-Book* was published in four parts between 1791 and 1794. The books presented a fresh interpretation of the neo-classical style, although their ideas were not new. Both Hepplewhite and Sheraton favoured a lighter and simpler version of Adam's style, designing furniture for middle-class as well as stately

Hepplewhite side chair

Sheraton sideboard

Sheraton bow-front chest of drawers with typical French feet

Stamped backplate from a trade list, c. 1790-1810

Dining chairs,

Camel-back dining chair

Carlton house desk

Powdering or wig stand

Fluted four-poster bed

Pembroke table

Brass-bound wine cooler

Corner washstand

Corner cabinet

267 One of a pair of Hepplewhite mahogany open armchairs. Note the characteristic curves. (Christies, London)

267

'D' end dining table, late 18th century

homes. Hepplewhite favoured curves like those of the Louis XV style *(267)*, but his influence was brief and examples of his style were rare. Sheraton, however, preferred the vertical look of Louis XVI and his chair backs almost always had a straight line on top even when the overall shape of the back was oval.

The fashionable light-coloured woods of the period *(268)* were often decorated with painted garlands of flowers. Some chairs were painted all over, or japanned. The chairs usually had cane seats and squab cushions. Upholstery was mostly of woven horsehair, and *stuffed-over seats* were fastened with brass-headed nails or sometimes trimmed with braid.

The 'D-end' dining table was popular until the end of the century. A new pedestal type, which had leaves and could also be dismantled, was made. Breakfast tables had one pedestal, dining tables had two or more; both types had brass feet. These pedestal tables continued to be popular until the first quarter

of the 19th century. Card and side tables were usually semicircular and were often inlaid with satinwood. They stood on square tapered or turned legs that had a characteristic fineness *(269)*.

The *bow-front* chest of drawers was a common household item. Round brass paterae-shaped drawer knobs were in use by the end of this period. The wooden mushroom-shaped knob was frrst made at the close of the 18th century and had a more delicate shape than the later (Victorian) turned knobs—it also had a metal screw instead of the wooden screw characteristic of Victorian knobs.

The sideboard developed from a decorative table to a piece of furniture with storage space in the form of drawers and cupboards. Sideboards were usually D-shaped, and some had a serpentine front and stood on square tapered or turned legs.

268 English bureau bookcase of inlaid satinwood, c. 1790. (Victoria and Albert Museum, London)

269 Sheraton satinwood card table, on finely tapered Sheraton legs and spade feet, c. 1790. (The Grafton Galleries, Sydney)

Regency, 1800–1825

This style lasted longer than the rule of the Prince Regent (1811–1820): it began before 1800 and continued for at least the first quarter of the century. In addition to the earlier Roman influence, an Egyptian influence was evident (particularly during the first decade of the 19th century), and modified Greek

Dropside supper table

Convex mirror surmounted with eagle

Regency Davenport with slide top

Canterbury, c. 1805

Canterbury, C. 1820

Chiffonier with mirrored back and brass gallery

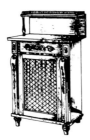

Brass inlaid chiffonier with brass grill to door

Brass inlaid sabre-leg dining chairs

Three-pillar dining table on splayed legs with brass cup castors

Four-tiered rose-wood whatnot with brass castors

Mahogany card table

Mahogany breakfast table, c. 1800

Mahogany drum top library or rent table, c. 1800

Regency rosewood centre table on platform base

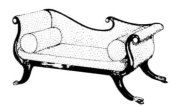

Regency mahogany framed couch with bolsters

Sea chest on bracket feet—turned screw-on feet are more usual

Hall chair with naval scene painted on back

ideas continued throughout and slightly beyond the period, in fact until about 1835. The classical scholar Thomas Hope (1768–1831), who had an enthusiasm for archaeology, published his book *Household Furniture and Interior Design* in 1807; it included furniture based on Greek, Egyptian and Roman designs. The French

Regency toilet mirror, c. 1805

270

***270** French or Italian throne chair, c. 1805, believed to be that of Napoleon I. (Victoria and Albert Museum, London)*

'Empire' style *(270)* influenced furniture design in other countries; it was inspired by Napoleon's campaigns in Egypt and Syria between 1798 and 1801 *(271, 272)*.

Oriental motifs, simulated bamboo, lacquer and japanning were still fashionable. Balls were often-used Regency motifs on mirrors, backs of chairs

272

and as feet on tea services, particularly during the first decade of the 19th century. Dark timbers with exotic grains, sometimes inlaid with brass, were Regency favourites, and pale woods such as satinwood were no longer in vogue. French polish, developed during this period, enhanced such dark timbers. Brazilian rosewood, with its black grain, was introduced—some cheaper woods such as beech were even painted to simulate this fashionable timber. Other popular imports with exotic grains were zebra wood (from Guyana) (272), amboyna (from the East Indies) and calamander (from India and Ceylon).

Sabre legs and turned legs were used throughout the period (273); fluted legs were also popular towards the end of the Regency era. After about 1805, the Trafalgar chair (274) had a rope twist to the back rail. Brass studs for chair upholstery lost favour to gimp, a ribbon that hid the tacks holding the cover in place.

Room arrangements were less formal, and for the first time furniture was arranged in functional groups and in the centre of rooms rather than around the walls (275). Nests of tables on slender turned legs were a new feature, as were narrow sofa tables with drop ends and drawers (276), that stood by the sofa.

Regency chiffoniers often had mirrored backs, beneath a shelf

272 Regency secretaire bookcase veneered with zebra wood, with ormolu Egyptian-style mounts, early 19th century. (Victoria and Albert Museum, London)

271 English marble-top mahogany sideboard, first decade of the 19th century. This shows the Egyptian influence. It is inlaid with ebony and brass. (Victoria and Albert Museum, London)

271

surmounted by a brass gallery, and pleated silk-panelled doors protected by a brass grill.

In the Regency period, chests of drawers often had columns to the sides of the front and *reeded* turned feet. Bow fronts were still fashionable, and drawers usually had a quarter-round moulding to the sides of the baseboard.

Davenport desks were an innovation of the Regency era. The early desks sometimes had a sliding top, which slid forward to provide knee room. Straight whatnots were developed; they were usually made of rosewood and had finer turnings than later Victorian walnut examples. A Canterbury for sheet music or books was in demand from this time, and was immensely popular during the Victorian period.

Regency mirrors were usually convex and often surmounted by an eagle with outstretched wings. Overmantel mirrors were usually in three sections, with moulded or carved classical relief figures as the main decoration.

Duncan Phyfe (1768–1854) was a successful Regency cabinet-maker. At the beginning of the 19th century, when New York was the richest city in the

273 Regency card table and sabre-leg side chair, c. 1815. (The Grafton Galleries, Sydney)

274

274 Trafalgar chair with brass inlay, c. 1805. (The Grafton Galleries. Sydney)

275

275 *Regency rosewood centre table with brass inlay, on platform base. (Christies, London)*

United States, Phyfe was the city's leading cabinet-maker. His well made articles were expensive, yet much in demand. The popular double-pedestal dining table was named after Duncan Phyfe. Dining tables on a single pedestal are relatively common, but original double-pedestal tables are exceptionally rare and valuable.

276 Regency rosewood sofa table, c. 1815. Sofa tables have drop ends, and are of much greater value than Regency side tables that have drop sides. (Christies, London)

276

222

Early Victorian, 1830–1865

This period began with a continuation of the heavier carved designs of the later Regency style—earlier styles were copied and mixed together *(277)*. Less attention was paid to form than to carved details and embellishments. J. C. Loudon published his *Encyclopaedia of Cottage, Farm and Villa Architecture* in 1833—it gave many line drawings of elaborate decorations. Decoration was designed to impress and was not always attractive.

A different style was used for each room. Elizabethan and Greek styles

William IV side chair
c. 1830

Victorian side chair,
c. 1840

Victorian toilet
mirror c. 1850

Victorian cheval
mirror c. 1850

French-style vitrine,
c. 1850

Wellington chest
c. 1835

Victorian Canterbury
c. 1850

Serpentine-fronted
walnut folding top
card table, c. 1855

Sideboard, c. 1850

Gentleman's Armchair
c. 1835

(using oak and mahogany) were favoured for libraries *(278)*, halls and dining rooms, because they were better suited to such large areas and high ceilings. In bedrooms and drawing rooms, walnut, rosewood, mahogany and upholstery predominated.

The neo-rococo style began about 1840 and continued until about 1865. In the beginning of the period, dining chairs had the broad incurved top rail of the Greek *klismos chairs*. This soon gave way to a new style, in which the sole two uprights merged into a curved top rail and the horizontal splat formed the lower part of the oval. This became known as the 'balloon back'. Early balloon-back chairs had turned legs, which were sometimes splayed at the bottom. By 1845, cabriole legs were used, particularly for lighter bedroom

Cabriole leg balloon-back side
chair, c. 1855

223

277

278

279

277 *English rosewood games table, c. 1835. The interior is fitted for chess and backgammon. Note the heavy Grecian style of this period. (Victoria and Albert Museum, London)*

278 *Oak bookcase, c. 1860. (Victoria and Albert Museum, London)*

279 *Right: Victorian cabriole-leg side chair with cameo back, c. 1850. Left: Louis XV-style ebonised lady's writing desk with brass inlay, c. 1850. (The Grafton Galleries, Sydney)*

and drawing room chairs (*279*). The balloon-back chair remained popular throughout the century. Grandfather and grandmother chairs, and settees or chaise-longues (usually with a matching set of side-chairs) were fashionable around the middle of the century. In 1829, coil springs for chair seats were patented, so seat contours were rounded. Until 1850 upholstery was thick, and buttoning emphasised rounded shapes. From the middle of the century, upholstery was surrounded by a wooden framework, which was often carved. *Papier mâché* had been used for boxes and trays during the 18th century, but was now used for chairs and tables. These were usually black and decorated in

Grandmother chair c. 1850

Grandfather chair c. 1850

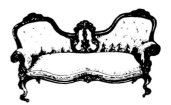

Double ended button-back Victorian chaise longue c. 1850

280

280 Vernis Martin vitrine of the neo-rococo period, c. 1850. (Christies, London)

various colours, sometimes with mother-of-pearl inlay.

After the middle of the century, cast-iron or brass beds were made.

Davenports reached their peak of popularity during the mid-19th century, and those with cabriole legs, serpentine fronts and brass galleries were most in demand. Some Davenports had a 'piano back'—the small drawers at the top could be pushed down into the carcass when not in use. Corner

Cabriole leg
Davenport desk with
brass gallery
c. 1850

Sutherland table—these were not
restricted to the early Victorian
period c. 1850

Work table with
swinging games top
c. 1850

Fold-over table on
platform base, c.
1830

Oval loo table
c. 1850

Credenza with
carved frame mirror
back and white
marble top
c. 1850.

Early Victorian
chiffonier
c. 1830

whatnots were first made in the middle of the century, and were similar in style to the earlier straight whatnots.

In this early Victorian period, Sutherland tables were made. These had narrow tops with deep flaps and gateleg supports, so were useful tea tables as they could be folded away when not in use. Work tables were also typical of this period, and sometimes had chess and backgammon boards on the top and a cloth bag or wooden container beneath. The tables made at the beginning of the period often had a platform base held by a column support with four feet. The later designs without the platform base were lighter in appearance.

Plate glass became less expensive early in the period, so many sideboards and credenzas had mirrored backs. The credenza usually had a marble top and no drawers to the base. Chiffoniers remained popular throughout the century.

Late Victorian, 1865–1900 and early 20th century

There was competition in the Victorian period between the ideals of tradition and reform. This is well illustrated in the furniture of the last half of the century. Fashions had previously alternated between classical and rococo styles, and during the earlier Victorian period many such designs had been copied and embellished, often with a heavy hand. In the late Victorian period there was a swing away from elaborate mixtures towards plainness, originality

Walnut cabinet
c. 1870

Specimen table in
the classical revival
style, c. 1870-1914

Bridge chair in
classical revival style
c. 1870-1914

Revolving bookcase,
c. 1880-1914

Rush-seated chair in
the 'Old English'
Arts and Crafts
style, c. 1860-1914

and lightness, although some of the early Victorian ideas prevailed throughout the century.

There were three distinct new movements. The first was that of the *Arts and Crafts movement* influenced by the architect William Morris, who inspired furniture designs in the years 1861 to 1900. His aim was to defy the machine age and to return to rectilinear uncarved surfaces. The theme of Morris was to 'have nothing in your home that you did not know to be useful, or believe to be beautiful'. He strove to break away from the acceptance of mass-produced goods and ideas. Whilst his styles contrasted with the immediate past, they leaned heavily on much earlier inspirations.

Morris introduced a plain fashion that was a contrast to the earlier rococo style. This period (1865–1890) was sometimes called 'medieval English'. Most furniture was pegged rather than glued, and rush-seated chairs regained popularity. Light-coloured oak, sometimes painted with early English scenes, was characteristic of the period. From about 1870 to 1890, another architect, T. E. Collcutt, used *ebonised wood* that was often partly gilded. His designs often included many balusters and shelves, particularly on overmantels.

In Austria in the 1840s, Michael Thonet began to make bentwood chairs *(281)*. By the end of the century the production of these Austrian chairs had

281 Austrian bentwood chair, by Thonet, production number 13. (Victoria and Albert Museum, London)

Victorian bookcase c. 1880
—similar items were made all
through the Victorian period

China cabinet, c. 1870-1914

Bentwood rocker, c. 1880

Roll-top desk, c. 1880

Large Edwardian library chair,
often covered in hide c. 1880

282 *French armchair in Art
Nouveau style, by Louis Marjdrelle,
c. 1900. (Victoria and Albert
Museum, London)*

282

increased to such an extent that the staff of 6000 at the Thonet factory were turning out 4000 pieces of furniture a day. Over fifty million examples of one style of chair alone have been made since the 1850s. These chairs consisted of six steamed and bent pieces of wood (usually beech). They were exported in pieces packed flat, and then easily assembled just by using ten screws. Their simplicity contrasted with the elaborate styles of 1850. Thonet had sales offices in many European cities (including Moscow, Odessa and St Petersburg) and in America (New York and Chicago). Other Austrian firms made furniture in the Thonet style, and they often marked their products with paper labels.

Morris had encouraged people to decide for themselves. This individuality of thought in the conventional Victorian age led to the fresh style of *Art Nouveau,* which flourished from 1890 to 1910 *(282)*. Art Nouveau was a truly new style, and it influenced all facets of art and manufacture. Sinuous curves were characteristic of the period, but were not always apparent in the actual square form of furniture. The style was, however, used to advantage in applied decoration and metal or cut-out motifs. Besides Morris, two other British architects designed furniture in this new style: Charles Rennie

228

283 Left: Dressing table, designed by Charles Rennie Mackintosh, 1916, showing the beginning of the angular Art Deco style. Right: Three-tiered English table in the Art Deco style, c. 1930. This was designed by R. E. Enthoven and made by A. A. Pegram. (Victoria and Albert Museum, London)

283

Mackintosh (1868–1928) and C. F. A. Voysey (1859–1941).

The traditionalists did not subscribe to these new ideas, and furniture of the early Victorian style was made until the end of the century. There was also a classical Sheraton-type revival, from the time of the Paris Exhibition of 1867 until 1914. The furniture of the Sheraton revival period—such as china cabinets, fall-front bureaus and mahogany bridge-chairs with Sheraton inlay—is often called Edwardian, and was much lighter and more delicate than that of the original Sheraton period. In about 1870, there was a revival of Chippendale and Hepplewhite styles, particularly for chairs, which were very similar to those made in the 18th century. However, the use of timber was not as extravagant as in the 18th century, and *dowels* were usually used instead of mortise and tenon.

Walnut table—this style with inlay was made in the last half of the 19th century

Furniture of the Art Deco period (1920–1940) regained the square look that had preceded the curves of Art Nouveau *(283 left)*. However, Art Deco differed from the Arts and Crafts style in its preference for Aztec shapes and the occasional use of mass-produced materials such as chromium-plated metal. In the 1920s, the square look was joined by more rounded lines *(283 right)*.

Ebonised rectangular fold-over card table, with gilded columns and key pattern feet, c. 1870

Some Important Furniture Dates

Early 17th century	Chairs and dropside tables are made. Main timber is oak.
c. 1660	The wood screw and more reliable glues are produced. The clock pendulum is invented. Lacquer and European japanned ware, twist turnings, chests of drawers more common. Mirrors made in England. Cabinet-makers replace turners and joiners as furniture-makers.
c. 1690	Walnut replaces oak. Veneering is more common. Bracket feet replace bun feet.
c. 1725	Mahogany is the main cabinet-maker's timber. It is dense and dark-coloured at this time. The heavy classical Palladian style begins.
c. 1740	The rococo period begins.
1754	Thomas Chippendale publishes his influential book, *The Gentleman and Cabinet-maker's Director*.
*c.*1765	The neo-classical style, introduced by Robert Adam, replaces rococo.
c. 1780	Hepplewhite's interpretation of Adam is felt.
1788	Hepplewhite's book, *The Cabinet-maker and Upholsterer's Guide*, is published.
c. 1790	Round machine-made nails replace the square hand-made ones.
1791–1794	Sheraton's book, *The Cabinet-maker and Upholsterer's Drawing-book*, is published, and his style is dominant. Satinwood and pale Honduras mahogany are fashionable.
c. 1800	The Regency style, similar to the French Empire styles, emerges. Egyptian motifs, dark French-polished Brazilian rosewood and brass inlays are used.
c. 1830	Heavier, carved Elizabethan and Greek styles are popular. Sprung chair seats have been invented.
c. 1850	The neo-rococo style of curves and cabriole legs is in full vogue. Rooms are crowded with Davenport desks, whatnots, canterburys and loo tables.
c. 1875	The classical-revival style replaces the neo-rococo. Sheraton-style mahogany with satinwood inlay reappears.
c. 1900	The historical styles of the past compete with the classical revival and Art Nouveau.

Appendix

English Monarchs 1485–1910

House of Tudor	Henry VII	1485–1509
	Henry VIII	1509–1547
	Edward VI	1547–1553
	Mary	1553–1558
	Elizabeth I	1558–1603
House of Stuart	James I	1603–1625
	Charles I	1625–1649
	(Commonwealth	1649–1660)
	Charles II	1660–1685
	James II	1685–1688
	William and Mary	1689–1694
	William III	1694–1702
	Anne	1702–1714
House of Hanover	George I	1714–1727
	George II	1727–1760
	George III	1760–1820
	George IV	1820–1830
	William IV	1830–1837
	Victoria	1837–1901
	Edward VII	1901–1910

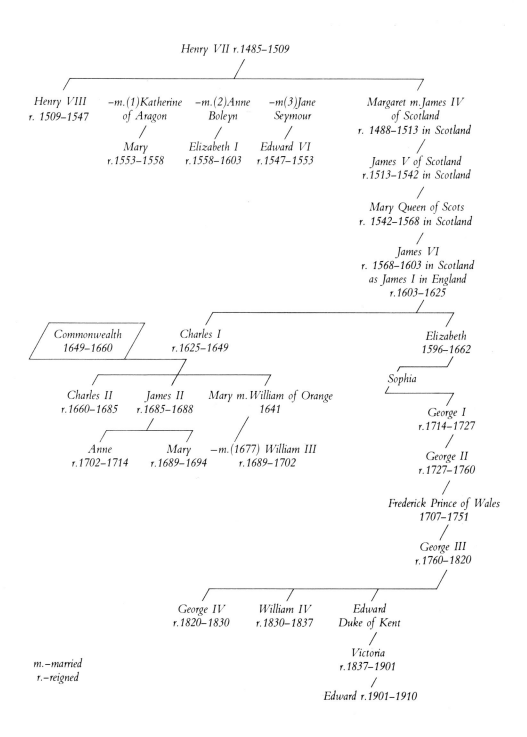

Henry VII r.1485–1509

Henry VIII
r. 1509–1547

–m.(1)Katherine
of Aragon

Mary
r.1553–1558

–m.(2)Anne
Boleyn

Elizabeth I
r.1558–1603

–m(3)Jane
Seymour

Edward VI
r.1547–1553

Margaret m.James IV
of Scotland
r. 1488–1513 in Scotland

James V of Scotland
r.1513–1542 in Scotland

Mary Queen of Scots
r. 1542–1568 in Scotland

James VI
r. 1568–1603 in Scotland
as James I in England
r.1603–1625

Commonwealth
1649–1660

Charles I
r.1625–1649

Elizabeth
1596–1662

Sophia

Charles II
r.1660–1685

James II
r.1685–1688

Mary m.William of Orange
1641

George I
r.1714–1727

Anne
r.1702–1714

Mary
r.1689–1694

–m.(1677) William III
r.1689–1702

George II
r.1727–1760

Frederick Prince of Wales
1707–1751

George III
r.1760–1820

George IV
r.1820–1830

William IV
r.1830–1837

Edward
Duke of Kent

m.–married
r.–reigned

Victoria
r.1837–1901

Edward r.1901–1910

Hallmarks

Hallmarks were introduced in England in 1300, and the hallmarking system has remained basically unchanged since 1478. It can be grasped fairly quickly with a little understanding. Providing the marks are legible, there can be only one correct date for each group of hallmarks.

There are almost always at least four marks—the *assay* mark, the mark of origin, the maker's mark and the date letter—and sometimes a fifth, the duty mark.

ASSAY MARK The lion passant has been used in England since 1544 to indicate silver of sterling standard (925 parts of pure silver in 1000 parts).

MARK OF ORIGIN This differs for each of the eleven main assay offices, but most silver items available today were assayed in London, Sheffield or Birmingham.

 London   *Sheffield*   *Birmingham*

DUTY MARK This is the sovereign's head. It indicated that duty had been paid. This payment was compulsory 1784–1890, therefore the mark was always used in that period. The mark was not used in Dublin until 1807 and in Glasgow until 1819.

MAKER'S MARK This indicates the firm or silversmith who made the article. Sir James Jackson's *English Goldsmiths and Their Marks* lists thousands of such marks.

DATE LETTER This is a letter of the alphabet that gives the year of assay. For each repetition of the alphabet, the style of the letters was changed. Although the style of the letters was repeated over the centuries, the exact date can be determined because the system is devised so that no repeated letter ever accompanies the same combination of other symbols.

For example:

The lion passant indicates English sterling silver. The leopard's head crowned indicates assay in London before 1821. There is no monarch's head, so the piece was not made during the period 1784–1890. The London date tables (over page) show that the small 'a' could mean 1776, 1816 or 1896. If it were 1816, the king's head would be present; if 1896, the leopard's head would not be crowned; therefore the piece can only have been made in 1776.

The lesson here is to use *all* the symbols, not only the date letter. Also, the style of the article should give a clue as to which period is involved when considering the date letter.

A silver assay year was not a calendar year—that of London began in the month of May—and since therefore the assay year ran into two calendar years, the word *circa*, abbreviated to *c.* and meaning 'around', generally prefixes dates for silver. More correctly both years should be included, thus 1829/30.

A most useful guide to hallmarks is *Bradbury's Book of Hallmarks*, published by J. W. Northend Ltd. Several points should be borne in mind when the tables are consulted.

Firstly, between 1696 and 1720 the silver standard was raised from 925 parts of pure silver per thousand to 958; from 1720 the higher standard was optional. The higher standard was indicated by the figure of Britannia (replacing the lion passant) and the lion's head erased (a heraldic phrase which means a profile head, cut off at neck).

Secondly, although Victoria came to the throne in 1837, her head did not appear on London and Birmingham silver until 1838, and on Sheffield silver until 1840.

Thirdly, from 1721 for varying periods, the London leopard's head joined the relevant assay office mark of Exeter, Newcastle and York.

Fourthly, it is useful to look carefully at the lion passant, because from 1821 the lion no longer looked over its left shoulder but faced straight ahead.

A few further points can be noted. Some small items were not fully hallmarked until 1790. Some small Newcastle items in about 1790–1840 often had no date letter mark. *Squeezed marks* on the narrow stem bottom were no longer used for flatware after about 1780, when they were marked on the broader top of such articles. Silver imported to England between 1883 and 1904 was marked 'F' for foreign.

The taxes levied on silver had their effect. A substantial tax of 6d per ounce of manufactured silver was imposed in 1719. 'Duty dodgers' were items marked with a set of hallmarks cut from a small assayed article on which tax had been paid, and transposed to a heavier, non-assayed article on which tax was payable. These pieces were made particularly between 1719 and 1758—in 1758 the death penalty was imposed on those found guilty of 'duty dodging' which had the desired effect of curtailing this practice. The quality and hallmarking of British silver has always been tightly controlled.

	Leopard's Head Crowned	Date Letter	Lion Passant
George II 1736-7		a	
1737-8	...	b	...
1738-9		c	
	...	d	...
1739-40		d	
1740-1			
1741-2		e f	
1742-3		g	
1743-4		h	
1744-5	...	i	
1745-6	...	k	...
1746-7	...	l	...
1747-8	...	m	...
1748-9	...	n	...
1749-50		o	
1750-1	...	p	...
1751-2		q	
1752-3		r	
1753-4	...	s	
1754-5	...	t	...
1755-6	...	u	...

Leopard's Head Crowned	Date Letter	Lion Passant
1756-7		
1757-8		
1758-9		
1759-60 George III		
1760-1		
1761-2		
1762-3		
1763-4		
1764-5		
1765-6		
1766-7		
1767-8		
1768-9		
1769-70		
1770-1		
1771-2		
1772-3		
1773-4		
1774-5		
1775-6		

Leopard's Head Crowned	Date Letter	Lion Passant	King's Head
1776-7			
1777-8			
1778-9			
1779-80			
1780-1			
1780-2			
1782-3			
1783-4			
1784-5			
1785-6			
1786-7			
1787-8			
1788-9			
1789-90			
1790-1			
1791-2			
1792-3			
1793-4			
1794-5			
1795-6			

Leopard's Head Crowned	Date Letter	Lion Passant	King's Head
1796-7			
1797-8			
1798-9			
1799-1800			
1800-1			
1801-2			
1802-3			
1803-4			
1800[4]-5			
1805-6			
1806-7			
1807-8			
1808-9			
1809-10			
1810-1			
1811-2			
1812-3			
1813-4			
1814-5			
1815-6			

Leopard's Head	Date Letter	Lion Passant	King's Head
1816-7			
1817-8			
1818-9			
1819-20 George IV			
1820-1			
1821-2			
1822-3			
1823-4			
1824-5			
1825-6			
1826-7			
1827-8			
1828-9			
1829-30 William IV			
1830-1			
1831-2			
1832-3			
1833-4			
1834-5			
1835-6			

Leopard's Head	Date Letter	Lion Passant	King's Head
1836-7 Victoria			
1837-8			
1838-9			
1839-40			
1840-1			
1841-2			
1842-3			
1843-4			
1844-5			
1845-6			
1846-7			
1847-8			
1848-9			
1849-50			
1850-1			
1851-2			
1852-3			
1853-4			
1854-5			
1855-6			

London hallmarks 1856–1916

Leopard's Head	Date Letter	Lion Passant	Queen's Head	Leopard's Head	Date Letter	Lion Passant	Queen's Head	Leopard's Head	Date Letter	Lion Passant
1856-7	a			1876-7	A			1896-7	a	
1857-8	b			1877-8	B			1897-8	b	
1858-9	c			1878-9	C			1898-9	c	
1859-60	d			1879-80	D			1899-1900	d	
1860-1	e			1880-1	E			1900-1	e	
1861-2	f			1881-2	F			Edward VII 1901-2	f	
1862-3	g			1882-3	G			1902-3	g	
1863-4	h			1883-4	H			1903-4	h	
1864-5	i			1884-5	I			1904-5	i	
1865-6	k			1885-6	K			1905-6	k	
1866-7	l			1886-7	L			1906-7	l	
1867-8	m			1887-8	M			1907-8	m	
1868-9	n			1888-9	N			1908-9	n	
1869-70	o			1889-90	O			1909-10	o	
1870-1	p			1890-1	P			George V 1910-1	p	
1871-2	q			1891-2	Q			1911-2	q	
1872-3	r			1892-3	R			1912-3	r	
1873-4	s			1893-4	S			1913-4	s	
1874-5	t			1894-5	T			1914-5	t	
1875-6	u			1895-6	U			1915-6	u	

Birmingham hallmarks 1773–1849

Lion Passant	Anchor	Date Letter	King's Head	Lion Passant	Anchor	Date Letter	King's Head
George III							
1773-4		A		1798-9		a	
1774-5		B		1799-1800		b	
1775-6		C		1800-1		c	
1776-7		D		1801-2		d	
1777-8		E		1802-3		e	
1778-9		F		1803-4		f	
1779-80		G		1804-5		g	
1780-1		H		1805-6		h	
1781-2		I		1806-7		i	
1782-3		K		1807-8		j	
1783-4		L		1808-9		k	
1784-5		M		1809-10		l	☙
1785-6		N		1810-1		m	
1786-7		O	☙	1811-2		n	☙
1787-8		P		1812-3		o	☙
1788-9		Q		1813-4		p	
1789-90		R		1814-5		q	
1790-1		S		1815-6		r	
1791-2		T		1816-7		s	
1792-3		U		1817-8		t	
1793-4		V		1818-9		u	
1794-5		W		1819-20		v	
1795-6		X		George IV 1820-1		w	
1796-7		Y		1821-2		x	
1797-8		Z		1822-3		y	
				1823-4		z	

Birmingham (earlier dates)

Date	Lion Passant	Anchor	Date Letter	King's Head
1824-5	✓	⚓	A	✓
1825-6			B	
1827-7			C	✓
1827-8			D	
1828-9			E	
1829-30			F	✓
William IV				
1830-1			G	
1831-2			H	✓
1832-3			I	
1833-4			K	
1834-5			L	✓
1835-6			M	
1836-7			N	
Victoria				
1837-8			O	
1838-9			P	✓
1839-40			Q	
1840-1			R	
1841-2			S	
1842-3			T	
1843-4			U	
1844-5			V	
1845-6			W	
1846-7			X	
1847-8			Y	
1848-9			Z	

Birmingham 1849–1925

Date	Lion Passant	Anchor	Date Letter	Queen's Head
1849-50	✓	⚓	A	✓
1850-1			B	
1851-2			C	
1852-3			D	
1853-4			E	
1854-5			F	
1855-6			G	
1856-7			H	
1857-8			I	
1858-9			J	
1859-60			K	
1860-1			L	
1861-2			M	
1862-3			N	
1863-4			O	
1864-5			P	
1865-6			Q	
1866-7			R	
1867-8			S	
1868-9			T	
1869-70			U	
1870-1			V	
1871-2			W	
1872-3			X	
1873-4			Y	
1874-5			Z	

Date	Lion Passant	Anchor	Date Letter	Queen's Head
1875-6	✓	⚓	a	✓
1876-7			b	
1877-8			c	
1878-9			d	
1879-80			e	
1880-1			f	
1881-2			g	
1882-3			h	
1883-4			i	
1884-5			k	
1885-6			l	
1886-7			m	
1887-8			n	
1888-9			o	
1889-90			p	
1890-1			q	
1891-2			r	
1892-3			s	
1893-4			t	
1894-5			u	
1895-6			v	
1896-7			w	
1897-8			x	
1898-9			y	
1899-1900			z	

Date	Anchor	Lion Passant	Date Letter	Queen's Head
1900-1	⚓	✓	a	✓
Edward VII				
1901-2			b	
1902-3			c	
1903-4			d	
1904-5			e	
1905-6			f	
1906-7			g	
1907-8			h	
1908-9			i	
1909-10			k	
George V				
1910-1			l	
1911-2			m	
1912-3			n	
1913-4			o	
1914-5			p	
1915-6			q	
1916-7			r	
1917-8			s	
1918-9			t	
1919-20			u	
1920-1			v	
1921-2			w	
1922-3			x	
1923-4			y	
1924-5			z	

Sheffield 1773–1844

Date	Lion	Crown	Date Letter
George III			
1773-4	✓		E
1774-5			F
1775-6			N
1776-7			R
1777-8			H
1778-9			S
1779-80			A
1780-1			
1781-2			D
1782-3			G
1783-4			B
1784-5			I
1785-6			P
1786-7			K
1787-8			C
1788-9			W
1789-90			D
1790-1			L
1791-2			P
1792-3	✓		U
1793-4			O
1794-5			m
1795-6			Q
1796-7			Z
1797-8			X
1798-9			V

Sheffield hallmarks 1844–1918

Lion Passant	Crown	Date Letter	King's Head	
🦁	👑	E	👤	1824-5
		N		1825-6
		H		1826-7
		M		1827-8
		F		1828-9
		G		1829-30
				William IV
		B		1830-1
		A		1831-2
		S		1832-3
		P		1833-4
		K		1834-5
		L		1835-6
		C		1836-7
				Victoria
		D		1837-8
		R		1838-9
		W		1839-40
		O		1840-1
		T		1841-2
		X		1842-3
		I		1843-4
		V		...20
		V		
		Q		...1
		Y		...2
		Z		...3
		U		...4

Lion	Crown	Date Letter	King's Head	
🦁	👑	a	👤	1844-5
		b		1845-6
		c		1846-7
		d		1847-8
		e		1848-9
		f		1849-50
		g		1850-1
		h		1851-2
		k		1852-3
		l		1853-4
		p		1855-6
		q		1856-7
		r		1857-8
		s		1858-9
		t		1859-60
		u		1860-1
		v		1861-2
		x		1862-3
		z		1863-4

Crown	Date Letter	Lion Passant	Queen's Head	
👑	A	🦁	👤	1844-5
	B			1845-6
	C			1846-7
	D			1847-8
	E			1848-9
	F			1849-50
	G			1850-1
	H			1851-2
	I			1852-3
	K			1853-4
	L			1854-5
	M			1855-6
	N			1856-7
	O			1857-8
	P			1858-9
	R			1859-60
	S			1860-1
	T			1861-2
	U			1862-3
	V			1863-4
	W			1864-5
	X			1865-6
	Y			1866-7
	Z			1867-8

Crown	Date Letter	Lion Passant	Queen's Head	
👑	A	🦁	👤	1868-9
	B			1869-70
	C			1870-1
	D			1871-2
	E			1872-3
	F			1873-4
	G			1874-5
	H			1875-6
	J			1876-7
	K			1877-8
	L			1878-9
	M			1879-80
	N			1880-1
	O			1881-2
	P			1882-3
	Q			1883-4
	R			1884-5
	S			1885-6
	T			1886-7
	U			1887-8
	V			1888-9
	W			1889-90
	X			1890-1
	Y			1891-2
	Z			1892-3

Crown	Lion Passant	Date Letter	
👑	🦁	a	1893-4
		b	1894-5
		c	1895-6
		d	1896-7
		e	1897-8
		f	1898-9
		g	1899-1900
		h	1900-1
			Edward VII
		i	1901-2
		k	1902-3
		l	1903-4
		m	1904-5
		n	1905-6
		o	1906-7
		p	1907-8
		q	1908-9
		r	1909-10
			George V
		s	1910-1
		t	1911-2
		u	1912-3
		v	1913-4
		w	1914-5
		x	1915-6
		y	1916-7
		z	1917-8

Gold and silver weights and fineness

SILVER Because some auction catalogues and price guides record silver weights in Troy ounces, and others use the metric system, it is as well to know how to convert Troy ounces to grammes as a means of comparison.

1 Troy ounce = 20 pennyweights (dwt) = 31.1 grammes.

GOLD Gold is usually alloyed with other metals, generally copper. The purity of the metal (*fineness*) is expressed in carats (ct). There are 24 carats in one Troy ounce. Pure gold is therefore 24 carat, and an alloy of 22 parts of gold with 2 parts of copper is 22 carat. (The gold carat is not to be confused with the metric carat of 200 milligrams, used for weighing gems.)

It is useful to know when various degrees of fineness were used as a means of dating British articles of gold.

In 1575, the standard was raised from 18 ct to 22 ct with the lion passant became the standard for all gold, including coins.

From 1789, 18 ct was reintroduced in addition to 22 ct and a crown was used. Pieces of 22 ct with the lion passant were still made up to 1844.

From 1844, 22 ct with a crown was used.

From 1854, 15 ct, 12 ct and 9 ct pieces were made.

In 1932, 15 ct and 12 ct were discontinued, and a new standard of 14 was substituted.

DECIMAL FINENESS In 1854, a decimal system of specifying fineness was introduced, indicating the number of parts of precious metal (gold or silver) in 1000 parts of alloy. Pure gold is 1000 fine; 12 ct, being 12 parts of gold with 12 parts of copper, is 500 fine; 9 ct, being 9/24ths pure gold, is 375 fine. Non-British silver marked 850 or 900 means those numbers of parts of pure silver in 1000 parts. British sterling silver is 925, and the higher Britannia standard of 958 that was compulsory in 1696–1720 and was used voluntarily on rare occasions after that, is 958.

Some silver marks used outside Britain

Non-British silver marks are complex because there were many centres on the European continent assaying and marking silver. Many of these changed their systems after short intervals. The marks included here show how to identify nationality and date some of the more common items likely to be encountered. These points are by no means comprehensive·

AUSTRIA from 1866 used the fineness numbers 750; 800; 900; 950.

THE AUSTRO-HUNGARIAN EMPIRE between 1806 and 1866 had slight variations of this circle and cross. One of 12 letters represented various assay offices—'A' Vienna, 'B' Prague, etc. The number 13 indicates 13 lots or 812.5/1000 pure; 15 indicates a purity of 937.5/1000's. The date is also included in the mark.

   Former Austro-Hungarian Empire, 1806-1824, for 13 lot silver

   Former Austro-Hungarian Empire, 1825-1866, for 13 lot silver

From 1st January, 1867 four symbols of purity were used instead of above marks. Between 1872–1922 a letter was included to indicate the town of assay. 'A' Vienna

Former Austro-Hungarian Empire, 1 January 1867–1 April 1872, purity 950/1000, purity 900/1000, purity 800/1000, purity 750/1000

Former Austro Hungarian Empire, 1 April 1872–1 May 1922

FRANCE in addition to the makers mark, had a Government Standard as well as an excise mark between 1798–1838. From 1838 the purpose of these two marks was combined in a single mark.

	1798–1809	1809–1819	1819–1838	From 1838
	Paris Provinces	Paris Provinces	Paris Provinces	Paris and Provinces
				Standard and Excise

Standard

Excise

This is the basic French system of this period, however there are additional provincial etc., marks not included here.

Germany, since 1888, minimum purity 800/1000

GERMANY from 1888 had a national system for the first time consisting of a crown, crescent and 800 or higher standard. Earlier German marks were numerous and varied between German States.

Holland 1814–1953, purity 934/1000, purity 833/1000

THE NETHERLANDS between 1814–1953 used a lion rampant as a higher purity symbol for 934/1000, and a lion passant for a lower standard of 833/1000. A guarantee symbol such as a human head, a makers mark and a date letter, similar to the British system, completed the group. From 1953 purities were expressed with numbers .925; .835.

RUSSIA used a zolotnik standard of purity—84 zolotniks = 875/1000; 94 zolotniks = 980/1000. The numbers 84 and 94 are usually included with a woman's head after 1891 when uniform marks were introduced for the whole of Russia.

Russia, 1908–1917, purity 875/1000 (84 zolotniks), for items weighing less than 8.5 g

Russia, 1908–1917, purity 875/1000 (84 zolotniks), for items weighing more than 8.5 g

Russia, 1908–1917, items of sub-standard purity

SCANDINAVIA *Denmark* from 1888. Makers mark fineness number with letter 'S', official mark and date.

Norway from 1891 makers mark; fineness number and 'S'; Norwegian lion and crown.

SWITZERLAND from 1880 used purities of 935, 925, 900, 875 and 800. These uniform marks were introduced from 1882 with the rampant bear whose shield shape altered slightly in 1893.

Switzerland, 1882–1892, purity 875/1000

 larger items, smaller items   Switzerland, 1893–1934, purity 875/1000,

THE UNITED STATES from the middle of the 19th century used the words 'Sterling Silver', and sometimes a fineness number. The words Sterling Silver on an 18th-century item usually indicates Irish origin.

Note other countries with smaller volumes of production also used fineness numbers from the end of the 19th Century.

AUSTRALIA Two good books on Australian silver are those by Kurt Albrecht and John Hawkins (see bibliography).

Chinese reign marks

When read from top to bottom right to left, marks 1 (Great) and 5 and 6 (made in this period) have remained unchanged for 600 years. Mark 2, the dynasty mark, has only changed twice in that period. Concentrate on marks 3 and 4 which are the reign dates of the relevant emperor. Four character marks always omit marks 1 and 2. In Qing dynasty group note the difference in mark 2 which is the dynasty mark. Here the dynasty has changed from Ming to the Manchu or Qing dynasty.

The stylised seal marks sometimes now replace the normal marks. These stylised block marks are written in three columns each of two words. Those referring to the emperor's reign are in the centre column. So concentrate on this column.

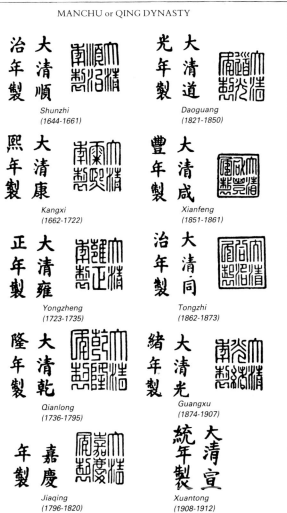

284 Chinese blue-and-white bowl of the Xuande period, 1426-1435. (Victoria and Albert Museum, London)

MING DYNASTY

Hongwu (1368-98)

Yongle (1403-24)

Xuande (1426-35)

Chenghua (1465-87)

Hongzhi (1488-1505)

Zhengde (1506-21)

Jiajing (1522-66)

Longqing (1567-72)

Wanli (1573-1619)

Tianqi (1621-27)

Chongzheng (1628-43)

MANCHU or QING DYNASTY

Shunzhi (1644-1661)

Kangxi (1662-1722)

Yongzheng (1723-1735)

Qianlong (1736-1795)

Jiaqing (1796-1820)

Daoguang (1821-1850)

Xianfeng (1851-1861)

Tongzhi (1862-1873)

Guangxu (1874-1907)

Xuantong (1908-1912)

Useful 19th-century English ceramic marks

'England'   signifies a date of manufacture after 1891, when President McKinley of the United States decreed that any country wishing to export to America must mark on the article the country of origin in English.

'Made in England'   usually indicates a date of manufacture after 1900. However, there are exceptions—for example, for Royal Doulton this mark indicates after 1930; for Royal Crown Derby, after 1921.

'Limited'   usually indicates a date of manufacture after 1875.

'Royal'   when included in the trade mark or manufacturer's title (e.g. Royal Worcester), indicates a date of manufacture after 1850.

The Royal arms   when incorporated in the mark, indicate manufacture in the 19th century—for example, some Mason's ironstone is marked in this way.

'Bone China'   The mark was not used before the 20th century. Although the product was made from the late 18th century.

'Trade Mark'   was not used until 1862.
The diamond-shaped registration mark was used in 1842–1884, when registration numbers were used (351202 was reached by 1900).

Staffordshire   used knot- and garter-shaped marks from about 1845.

Minton   used impressed cyphers for a hundred years from 1842, such as a fighter aircraft in 1941, and V for victory in 1942. The letter 's' was added to the name Minton after 1871, but there are a few exceptions (including marks after 1951).

Wedgwood   used in addition to the factory mark three impressed letters between 1860 and 1906, when a number was incorporated with the letters (see p. 252).

Royal Worcester	used a capital letter beneath the factory mark in 1867–1889. When two numbers appear below the mark, they indicate the year (e.g. 74 = 1874). A series of dots was used from 1892 (see p. 251 for full list of Royal Worcester date marks).
Royal Crown Derby	used year cyphers between 1882 and 1958. Until 1900, these were modified horizontal lines, crescents, ovals or diamonds. The words 'Bone China' were added after 1945.
'S', 'T', 'B', 'H', 'L', 'F'	stood for one of the six main pottery towns (Stoke-on-Trent, Tunstall, Burslem, Hanley, Longton and Fenton)—above which initial some Staffordshire manufacturers used their own initials.
'1790'	or some other 18th-century date incorporated in the mark showed the earliest date that a particular branch of a factory was established. It does not imply the date that the piece was made.

Pattern numbers on English porcelain

Many English porcelain factories marked their wares with a pattern number to enable the customer and retailer to re-order. This system began as early as 1790, but was uncommon until the 19th century. There were two numbering systems:

1. FRACTIONAL When 1000 was reached, the prefix 2/ was placed in front of the second thousand, 3/ in front of the third thousand and so on, e.g. 3/45 for 3045, and 6/2 for 6002.

2. PROGRESSIVE Some factories continued numbering progressively, so the numbers reached several thousand.

The systems used by various factories, and the dates that certain numbers were reached, are listed here. Whilst the pattern number alone will not necessarily identify or date an article, it is a help when considered in conjunction with other characteristics.

There are several useful aspects of this system. For example, Spode never used a fractional system, therefore a piece marked, for example, 2/950 could not be Spode; also, rococo-style porcelain decorated in green and gold resembles Rockingham ware, but if it bears a fractional number above 2/150 it cannot be Rockingham because Rockingham used only a few, low, fractional numbers.

Factories using fractional numbers

COALPORT (*c.* 1797–present day under the name John Rose Factory)

Before 1805, no pattern number.

1805–1824, 1 to 1000.

1824, 2/1 etc. No. 2/783 bears date 27th April, 1832.

1833–1838, 3/1, 3/2 etc. to 3/999.

1839–1843, 4/1, 4/2 etc.

1844–1850, 5/1, 5/2 etc.

After 1850, fractional numbers 6/1 etc., 7/1 etc., 8/1 etc.

Later in the 19th and in the 20th centuries, progressive numbers.

RIDGWAY, various partners (*c.* 1802–1855)

Tea wares (*not* dessert and dinner wares), fractional numbers 2/1, 2/2 etc. to 2/9999, then 5/1, 5/2 etc.

Vases and ornamental objects, fractional numbers 4/1, 4/2 etc.

ROCKINGHAM (*c.* 1825–1842)

Progressive to number 1600.

Fractional numbers were perhaps used, between 2/17 and 2/150.

Factories using progressive numbers

CHAMBERLAIN WORCESTER (*c.* 1786–1852)

Pattern numbers began in 1790. By 1797, 100 was reached, by 1807, 400, by 1817, 790, by 1822, 1000. They climb to 1752, then continue in a broken series, 2000 to 2625, 3000 to 3099, 4000 to 4099, 5000 to 5019.

COALPORT, Arstice, Norton & Rose (*c.* 1800?–1814)

Progressive, 1 to 1419.

COPELAND & GARRETT (*c.* 1833–1847)

Progressive, taking over Spode's system at about 5000.

In 1847, reached 7260.

Continued by Copeland alone until 1852, when 9999 was reached.

DAVENPORT (*c.* 1793–1887)

Progressive numbers to 700 (e.g. 1174 indicates 1856).

DERBY (*c*. 1750–1848)

Between 1780 and 1810, progressive, normally painted below the painted crown, crossed batons and 'D' mark.

1810–1848, pattern numbers rare. They may have small numbers near rims, and painter's or gilder's personal identification marks.

If ware looks like Derby *c*. 1790–1815, and has pattern number without Derby mark and is below 500, it is probably Pinxton.

GRAINGER WORCESTER, various partners (*c*. 1801–1902)

1801–1839, progressive 1 to 2019.

1839–1845, new progressive series 1 to 2000 plus small cross.

After 1845, fractional numbers.

MINTON (*c*. 1797–present day)

Before 1850, progressive.

After 1850, letter prefixes.

Before 1805, prefixed by 'N' or 'No.' in range 1 to 20.

1805–1816, pattern numbers in range 15 to 948 below Sèvres-like cross, 'S' (or 'L') mark.

1816–1824, Minton did not produce porcelain.

After 1824, progressive numbers beginning again from 1, usually without factory mark.

In 1830s, 1300 to 4200.

1840–1845, 4200 to 7500.

In November 1850, letter (A, then B, C, D, E, G, H, M, NP, O, P, PA, S and X) used as prefix to number.

NEWHALL (*c*. 1781–1835—hard-paste, *c*. 1781–1812)

Progressive (large numbers ½ cm high), usually prefixed 'N' or 'No'.

Before 1812, up to about 940.

1812, for bone china, from about 1040.

1812–1835, 1040 to 1800, for larger tea wares, jugs, teapots, sugar basins (usually not on cups and saucers).

Other factories producing wares similar to Newhall used progressive numbers. The Newhall patterns book is necessary for identifying Newhall pieces.

PINXTON (*c*. 1796–1813)

Progressive, 1 to 500.

ROCKINGHAM (c. 1825–1842)

Progressive, 410 to 850 for dessert services and 407 to 1600 for tea services.

SWANSEA (c. 1814–1822)

Usually no pattern numbers. When used, progressive up to 600. If the piece is of Swansea type and with a higher pattern number, could be Coalport.

SPODE (c. 1761–1833)

Spode pattern numbers.

Because of the remarkably constant tempo at the Spode factory there is an easy formula for arriving at an approximate date for pattern introduction:

$$\frac{\text{pattern no.}}{150} + 1800 = \text{approx. 19th-century date of pattern}$$

introduction.

For example, a pattern number of 3000 is:

$$\frac{3000}{150} + 1800 = c.\ 1820.$$

Pattern numbers are a useful guide to the identification of encrusted porcelain, which was popular c. 1820–1840.

The encrusted vase illustrated on p. 184, *(235)* bears a pattern number 1505. This could not be Coalport, as they used fractional numbers. It could be Rockingham, the highest number recorded there was 1600. It is likely to be Minton, because numbers 1300 to 4200 were used in the 1830s.

Pattern numbers are also useful for identifying rococo-style pieces. For example, the plate illustrated middle right on p. 186, *(236)*, bears pattern number 5263. This is too high for Rockingham. It is likely to be Copeland since they used numbers 5000 to 7620 between 1833 and 1847, which agrees with the period style of the plate.

Registration marks used in Britain 1842–1883

Between 1842 and 1883 there was in use a system of registering some British metal, wood, glass and ceramic products. Although the aim at the time was to show that the design was registered, the marks now serve to give an approximate date of manufacture.

Mark used until 1868   *Mark used after 1868*

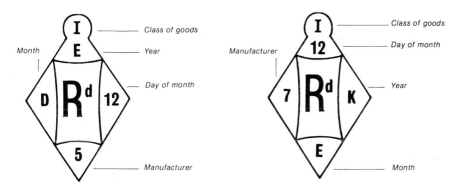

The Roman numeral at the top indicates the material of the article: I—metal, II—wood, III—glass, IV—ceramic.

Year letter

1842	X	1853	Y	1864	N	1875	S
1843	H	1854	J	1865	W	1876	V
1844	C	1855	E	1866	Q	1877	P
1845	A	1856	L	1867	T	1878	D
1846	I	1857	K	1868	X	1879	Y
1847	F	1858	B	1869	H	1880	J
1848	U	1859	M	1870	C	1881	E
1849	S	1860	Z	1871	A	1882	L
1850	V	1861	R	1872	I	1883	K
1851	P	1862	O	1873	F		
1852	D	1863	G	1874	U		

Month letter

January	C	May	E	September	D
February	G	June	M	October	B
March	W	July	I	November	K
April	H	August	R	December	A

Design registration numbers and dates, 1884–1909

Design registration number	was registered in January of
1	1884
19754	1885
40480	1886
64520	1887
90483	1888
116648	1889
141273	1890
163767	1891
185713	1892
205240	1893
224720	1894
246975	1895
268392	1896
291241	1897
311658	1898
331707	1899
351202	1900
368154	1901
385500	1902
402500	1903
420000	1904
447000	1905
471000	1906
494000	1907
519500	1908
550000	1909

Royal Worcester date marks from 1892

1892	One dot added above 'Royal'.
1893	Two dots, one each side of 'Royal Worcester England'.
1894	Three dots.
1895–1915	Four dots, and then one dot added each year until there were 24 dots—some placed below the main mark.
1916	Dots replaced by a star below the main mark.
1917–1927	One dot added to star, and then one dot added each year until there were 11 dots with the star.
1928	Dots and star replaced by a small square.
1929	Small diamond.
1930	Mark like a division symbol.
1931	Two interlinked circles.
1932	Three interlinked circles.
1933–1948	One dot added to the three circles, and then one dot added each year until there were 9 dots (1941), and for the next seven years there was no change in year marks.
1949	'V' placed under main mark.
1950	'W' placed under main mark.
1951–1955	One dot added to 'W', and then one dot added each year until there were 5 dots with 'W'.
1956–1963	Dot series continued but 'W' replaced by a circled 'R'. By 1963 there were 13 dots with the circled 'R'.
1963–present	Year of registration added in full to main mark.

Wedgwood date marks from 1860

From 1860 the Wedgwood factory impressed three letters into the base of their products. The third letter denoted the year of potting, as shown in this table.

O = 1860 or 1886

P = 1861 or 1887

Q = 1862 or 1888

R = 1863 or 1889

S = 1864 or 1890

T = 1865 or 1891*

U = 1866 or 1892*

V = 1867 or 1893*

W = 1868 or 1894*

X = 1869 or 1895*

Y = 1870 or 1896*

Z = 1871 or 1897*

A = 1872 or 1898*

B = 1873 or 1899*

C = 1874 or 1900*

D = 1875 or 1901*

E = 1876 or 1902*

F = 1877 or 1903*

G = 1878 or 1904*

H = 1879 or 1905*

I = 1880 or 1906*

J = 1881

K = 1882

L = 1883

M = 1884

N = 1885

*with 'ENGLAND' added.

From 1907 the alphabetical sequence continued, but a number 3 replaced the first letter. In 1924 a number 4 replaced the 3. After 1930 the month was numbered and the last two numbers of the year were given, so that 1A32 = January 1932, 'A' being the workman's mark. On some later post-war items the last two numbers only were given, i.e. 53 = 1953.

Is it real?

AMBER becomes electrified when rubbed and will pick up scraps of paper when so charged. As several imitations also do this, it is not a positive test, but if the sample does not have this characteristic, it is not amber.

GEMSTONES are colder than glass. As the tongue is more sensitive than the fingers, test with it. Use tongs, as fingering the article will make it warmer. It is useful to have a known piece of glass for comparison.

Glass has a tendency to form conchoidal (curved shell-like) fractures. Examine the object with a lens where the claws of a setting may have caused these fractures. Some gemstones also do this to a lesser extent.

Bubbles are a give-away characteristic of glass. Sometimes they are just below the surface and can only be detected with a lens. Striations like swirl marks are also often found in glass.

GOLD of less than 9 carats will be turned green by nitric acid. To make a nitric acid solution, add acid very slowly to water (*not* water to acid) until they are mixed in equal proportions.

Gold of less than 18 carats will immediately become much paler in colour if aqua regia is applied. Aqua regia is made by adding hydrochloric acid to nitric acid in the proportion of three to one. It can after considerable time dissolve gold, so the solution must be washed off immediately the test is done. Any visible effects can be removed by polishing with jeweller's rouge.

It is a fallacy that the more copper-coloured the gold, the lower the carat—red gold is a gold-copper alloy. Green gold, which is more yellow, has silver added.

JADE cannot be scratched with a piece of hard steel or, better, a piece of quartz, whereas steatite, with which jade can be confused, is very soft and can be cut with the edge of a piece of glass. Steatite will leave a soapy mark on a sheet of glass.

PEARLS if real or cultured have a rough feel when drawn across the teeth. Imitation pearls feel smooth on the teeth.

PHOSPHATE TEST Porcelain containing bone ash in the paste can be verified with a phosphate test. Put one drop of hydrofluoric acid on an unglazed part. (Porcelain glaze can if necessary be removed from an inconspicuous part with a carborundum stone.) Leave for five minutes then wash off the acid with a syringe into a test solution of warm ammonium molybdate in nitric acid. The solution becoming yellow indicates the presence of a phosphate, which means the piece contains bone ash. Wash well to remove the hydrofluoric acid, which has corrosive properties.

The age of porcelain pieces can be determined with a thermo-luminescence test. The principle is that the rate of loss of radio-activity of materials that have been fired is known. Enquiries about thermo-luminescence testing, which may be undertaken for a fee, should be made through a university.

SILVER If silver plate is suspected, clean an inconspicuous spot with a file to be sure of reaching the base metal. Put on a drop of nitric acid solution. Sterling standard will show a light cream-grey deposit, sub-standard will show a dark grey deposit, and base metal a greenish effervescence. Wash off the acid immediately the test is finished.

Repairs and cleaning

BRASS if lacquered should not be cleaned—clear lacquer is applied so that an abrasive cleaner does not have to be used. However, often the lacquer partly wears off, and then it will have to be cleaned off altogether, using a mild abrasive such as Brasso. Lacquer should be applied to as few articles as possible.

BRONZE will lose its patination if an abrasive is used. Merely wash with warm soapy water.

CLOCKS that do not go can sometimes be remedied by ensuring that the pendulum is 'in beat' and swings equally each side of the vertical line. Do not oil—over-oiling attracts dust, and this sort of maintenance is best left to a clock-maker.

DRAWERS if over-filled with objects protruding above the front top rail can usually be opened by using a long knife blade to dislodge the objects. A tight drawer is best lubricated with candle-grease. Worn drawer runners can be improved by this means.

FURNITURE Beeswax and turpentine make a good furniture polish: in a double saucepan gently heat three parts of beeswax with eight parts of turpentine. Keep in a closed tin or it will harden. However, a satisfactory sheen comes from hard polishing, not merely from the material. 'Antiquax' is an excellent commercial furniture polish. Best results are obtained if surfaces are cleaned periodically with 'Antiquax' spirit cleaner every few months.

Ring marks should be avoided by being careful about glasses or plates allowed to stand on surfaces for some time, i.e. overnight. A light wax protection also helps. However, ring marks can sometimes be removed with a mild abrasive such as cigarette ash, Brasso, or very fine steel wool rubbed on very gently.

Borer-infected furniture is best sent to a pest exterminator for treatment in a fumigating chamber. If this is not possible, brush with liquid insecticide; repeat after a few weeks.

Screws that are difficult to loosen should not be attempted with a screwdriver that is too small. Do not persist if the slot is becoming damaged. Try placing the screwdriver in the slot and hitting the end with a mallet. A poker brought to red heat and held in contact with the head of the screw will cause it to expand—when it cools and contracts it will usually be freed. A brace fitted with a screwdriver instead of a bit is helpful. A screw coated with tallow or soap is easier to insert and withdraw.

GLASS Small chips can be removed by gently grinding with emery paper or an oil stone (a knife sharpener).

To remove a stuck decanter stopper, mix 2 teaspoonfuls of alcohol with 1 teaspoonful of glycerine and 1 teaspoonful of common salt. Let the mixture remain in contact with the stopper for some hours, then tap gently and the stopper should be able to be removed.

Often a stopper is so tight that it is necessary to heat the neck of the decanter first in hot water then under a flame so that the neck expands slightly. This requires extreme care or the glass will crack.

GOLD, SILVER AND JEWELLERY may be cleaned with an ammonia solution, which dissolves grease. Scrubb's Cloudy Ammonia is a 10 per cent solution of ammonia in water, and is suitable. It should not be used on bronze as it attacks the metal.

IVORY should not be soaked in water, as it can disintegrate into layers. Clean with a damp cloth.

KNIFE HANDLES should not be immersed for lengthy periods in hot water during washing up as this will damage the fixative and the handles will become loose. It is for this reason that old knives in their original condition are almost non-existent.

LEATHER is an organic material and requires the application of a good dressing from time to time. 'Antiquax' leather cream is recommended.

KEYS If a drawer key is lost, a substitute can often be found from a bunch of old keys as many are interchangeable. However, the dust board at the back of a chest of drawers can usually be easily removed, and the lock may be unscrewed from the inside.

PEWTER may be cleaned with a very mild abrasive such as whiting.

PORCELAIN cracks can be made less obvious by removing dirt. Cover the crack with cotton wool dampened with bleach and keep the cotton wool damp with bleach for a few days. English soft-paste porcelain, which is slightly porous and so absorbs dirt, does not respond much to this treatment.

PRINTS affected by foxing or mildew can be treated with a mixture of approximately equal parts of hydrogen peroxide and absolute alcohol applied with a fine brush to bleach out the brown spots. (Hydrogen peroxide should be stored in a dark place.) Two corks fixed between the framed print and the wall will allow air to circulate and lessen the risk of foxing.

Values

The following section is intended to give some idea of the market value of a few of the items discussed earlier in the book. They were auctioned by Christies at Hilborough Hall.

A picture of the house is included so that surroundings and atmosphere may be imagined. The time has come when choice items for choice homes have become much harder to obtain than was so a few years ago.

An English sale was selected because the greater volume of antiques available in England than elsewhere, forms a base for international values . This does not imply that all antiques are necessarily cheaper in England. In fact, the higher the quality the less this is true.

Test your knowledge by dating and valuing items before reading the captions. Look for date indicators and note how the items are listed in a catalogue description. This can, with experience, give a picture of the object without sighting it. The 10% buyer's premium charged by most London auction rooms and the government value added tax has not been added to their prices.

Except within certain limits, an antique cannot be valued precisely.

A loaf of bread has a value based upon the cost of ingredients, baking, distribution and a margin of profit, related to the price of thousands of identical loaves sold on an identical market. More significantly a baker knows fairly accurately how many loaves he can sell in 24 hours, 7 days or 6 months.

The prediction of the value of an antique is based upon the judgement of a valuer experienced in a particular field, from which he should not depart. He bases his value on his experience of seeing similar items sold recently. Judgement is necessary to assess the quality, condition, rarity and age of the item under consideration, against the average of a number of similar, but not identical items. Saleability has a very strong impact on the assessment of value.

There are two broad purposes for which such valuations may be made. These very logically and legitimately have a different value. The first is what the item would cost to replace with a reasonable equivalent, without too much delay. The second purpose is the estate value, when it is legitimate to estimate what certain items might fetch at a forced sale, again without undue delay. There is obviously a considerable difference in these two values, and usually the rarer or more costly the item, the greater the variance. This is largely due to the time factor inherent in the replacement or sale, in the respective circumstances.

An inexpensive, or common functional item is often easier to find or to sell than a rare or expensive item that fewer people can identify, desire or afford.

A layman, wishing to dispose of an item, seldom realises the delay in selling even a good antique at its correct value, either privately or from a suitable antique shop or auction room.

The original cost, unless recent, has only a limited relevance to current value. Fashion affects value and not all antiques have appreciated uniformly in value, whether one looks at records over the last hundred, or last twenty years.

Inflation alone does not show the current value when added to the purchase price. One item may have been wisely or fortunately purchased, another may have always been a 'bad buy'. Good quality has appreciated more than mediocrity, and a good item, which may have seemed expensive when purchased, is usually a better investment than a poor item bought as a bargain. Some readers may better understand the thoughts expressed in the last two paragraphs if related to real estate values.

Previous ownership by an interesting personality does not necessarily affect value, particularly when this is not authenticated in writing by a relevant authority.

A plain simple item may be of more value than a complex item, which would be prohibitively expensive to reproduce today, but for which there is no current demand.

Items of quality which are currently fashionable are often more valuable than certain older items for which there is less demand. Age alone does not necessarily add to value.

A valuation must be made by someone conversant with particular items. This may necessitate one person valuing pictures, another antiques, within his ken. It should be in writing and must state the purpose of the valuation. It must be dated and show the particulars of owner and a location. It must show sufficient detail for a third party to identify the objects, without the presence of the owner or the valuer, perhaps later when located in a different building. Damage or deficiencies to particular items should be mentioned when of significance.

286 A mahogany writing table with baize-lined moulded rectangular top with two frieze drawers, the sides carved with trelliswork, the channelled square legs with trelliswork. 105 cm (41½") wide. (Christies) £2.300

287 A fine and unusual regency mahogany Canterbury with rounded rectangular divided body and ormolu carrying-handles above two drawers on ribbed tapering legs. 73.5 cm (29") wide. (Christies) £3,500

288 A fine George I walnut
bureau-cabinet with moulded
stepped cornice above a
shaped bevelled glazed door
flanked by Corinthian pilas-
ters, the interior with adjust-
able shelves and three drawers, the base with a
crossbanded leather-lined
fall-flap enclosing a fitted
interior above two short and
three graduated long drawers
on bracket feet. 77.5 cm
(30½") wide; 198 cm (78")
high; 49.5 cm (19½") deep.
(Christies) £20,500

289 A George III mahogany bureau-cabinet, the moulded key pattern cornice with blind fretwork pediment centre above a pair of geometrically-glazed cupboard doors, the fall-flap enclosing a fitted interior above four graduated long drawers on ogee bracket feet. 108 cm (42½") wide; 213.5 cm (84") high. (Christies) £5,200

290 An Edwardian mahogany Carlton House desk, the shaped superstructure with ormolu balustraded gallery, eight drawers and two cupboards with three frieze drawers on square tapering legs. 137 cm (54")wide. (Christies) £2,600

291 A fine George III mahogany card-table with baize-lined crossbanded serpentine top, the moulded legs headed by fruitwood paterae and filled with descending husks and splayed feet. 107 cm (42") wide; 74 cm (29") high; 44.5 cm (17½") deep. (Christies) £7,000

292 *A pair of famille rose tapering oviform vases and domed covers painted with figures at discussion outside pavilions and with river landscapes and flowers within blue foliage cartouches, reserved on an iron-red cell-pattern ground, the domed covers with Buddhistic lion finials (one vase extensively repaired, one cover with slight chip), Qianlong 49.5 cm (19½"). (Christies) £1,700*

293 A George II plain
baluster tankard, the
body with moulded rib,
with scroll handle, domed
cover and open-work
scroll thumbpiece,
engraved with a coat-of-
arms within scroll and
foliage cartouche, by
Thomas Whipham, *1745.
19.7 cm (7¾")* high.
(Christies) £1,200

294 A George IV shaped-
rectangular two-handled
tray, engraved with a
band of scrolls and
foliage on a matted
ground, with shell, foliage
and gadroon border and
reeded and foliage hand-
les, engraved with a coat-
of-arms within foliage
surround, by William
Elliot, 1822. *66.2 cm
(24½")* long.
(Christies) £2,000

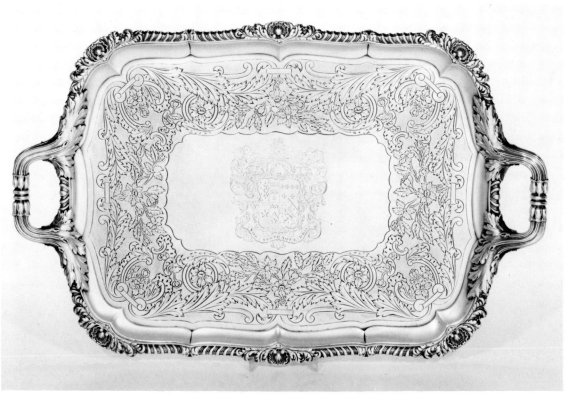

295 A George III mahogany chest with rectangular top, the frieze inlaid with fruit-wood paterae and flutes above four graduated long drawers with waved apron and splayed feet. 96.5 cm (38″) wide. (Christies) £3,500

296 A George III mahogany open armchair, the arched back carved with husks, the pierced interlaced splats with rosettes and husks, the serpentine padded seat upholstered in patterned cotton, the moulded tapering legs filled with husks. (Christies) £980

297 A fine set of sixteen George III mahogany dining-chairs, including an armchair, the pierced oval backs carved with husks and halved flowerheads, the bowed seats variously upholstered on moulded square tapering legs joined by plain stretchers. (Christies) £28,000

298 *A giltwood mirror of George III style with shaped bevelled plate, the pierced naturalistic frame with a fishing Chinaman beneath a baldacchino cresting flanked by ho-ho birds, the conforming base with a squirrel. 153.5 x 58.6 cm (60 x 27"). (Christies) £9,700*

300 *A Scandinavian silver-gilt cylindrical tankard on three pomegranate feet, with scroll handle, flat hinged cover and pomegranate thumbpiece, engraved with a coat-of-arms within scroll mantling, maker's mark P.K.I., possibly for Peder Knudsen of Oslo, circa 1660. (Christies) £5,400*

299 *A George III mahogany tripod table, the waved circular piecrust top possibly later, with spreading partly fluted shaft, the legs carved with flowerheads and scrolling foliate with claw feet. 71 cm (28") diam.* Christies) £4,300

301 *A George III mahogany card-table, the crossbanded D-shaped baize-lined top painted with a border of ribbon-tied summer flowers on square tapering legs and splayed feet. 93.5 cm (36¾") wide. (Christies) £3,500*

302 A fine George III ormolu-mounted yew-wood and marquetry commode attributed to William Ince and John Mayhew, the shaped serpentine top inlaid with scrolling flowerheads and etched foliate spandrels with gadrooned border, the front with a pair of cupboard doors inlaid with a ribbon-tied floral spray and conforming etched foliate banding, the angles mounted with scrolling foliate clasps, the sides with similar inlay on bracket feet. 156 cm (61½") wide; 83 cm (32¾") high; 62 cm (24½") deep. (Christies) £4,300

Glossary

(Illustration numbers are in bold type)

ACID-CUT-BACK GLASS
Type of CAMEO art glass consisting of layers of CASED GLASS of contrasting colours cut by acid rather than by a wheel. (See p.52, **64**.)

ACID-ETCHED GLASS
Glass decorated on the surface using hydrofluoric acid. (See p.18, **14**.)

AGATE GLASS
Type of decorative opaque glass made by mixing METAL of various colours before shaping the object, resulting in colour patterns similar to those of natural semi-precious stones such as agate. (See p.41, **51**.)

ALEXANDRITE
Type of art glass first produced around 1900, made in one layer but with three blending colour shadings towards the rim of amber, blue and fuchsia, obtained by successive reheating of different parts of the object.

AMBERINA GLASS
Lustrous pale amber glass tinged with ruby. First made by the New England Glass Company (of America).

ANTIQUE
During the last century, the meaning has changed. It once meant a work of art made in ancient Greece or Rome. It now means a work of good quality, usually decorative in interest, made with hand tools over a century ago. The interpretation of the word is not precise, and tends to be governed by the fact that items over a hundred years of age are admitted duty-free to most countries.

APPLIED
Decoration in relief, attached to the surface of an object after it has been formed rather than being an integral part of the object.

ARITA PORCELAIN
Product of the Arita kilns on the western Japanese island of Kyushu. IMARI and KAKIEMON are the most typical. The style was much copied in Europe in the 18th century particularly. In about 1760 the Sèvres influence challenged this style. (See further, pp.150, 151, 152, 154, 155.)

ARMORIAL
Heraldic coat of arms. (See p.66, **73**.)

ART DECO
Universal style *c.* 1920–1940, with sharp square lines and bright eye-catching colour and movement. It was less angular in the 1920s than in the 1930s. It followed, and was in strong contrast to, ART NOUVEAU. (See pp.56, 180, 229, **67, 68, 69, 227, 229, 283**.)

ART GLASS
Decorative glassware made from about 1870 in newly developed and sometimes patented surface textures and shades of colour. Products were ornamental rather than utilitarian. Art glass was a result of advances in manufacturing techniques—where glass-makers previously had obtained effects by APPLIED decoration and by CUTTING, the makers of art glass were able to give varying chemical treatments to the metal itself, thus obtaining their tints, swirls and colouring. (See p.47, **58**.)

ART NOUVEAU
Universal style *c.* 1880–1910, characterised by soft flowing lines, pastel colours and languidness. (See pp. 49, 50, 175, 227, **59, 60**.)

ART POTTERY
English ceramics made from around 1870 under the influence of the ARTS AND CRAFTS MOVEMENT, in a deliberate attempt at original artistic creation. (See p.137, **178**.)

ARTIFICIAL PORCELAIN
See SOFT-PASTE PORCELAIN.

ARTS AND CRAFTS MOVEMENT
Revival of interest in decorative art in England around 1875. The theme was a return to the standards of personal craftsmanship in England in the Middle Ages. A deliberately amateur quality was produced, glorifying hand work in the face of industrialisation. (See p.137, 227.)

ASSAYING
System of testing silver or gold items for their correct content of precious metal. (See pp.234, 235, 240.)

ASTRAGAL
Small half-round or convex bead moulding; moulding on overlapping doors.

BACCARAT
Glass factory founded in 1764 in France. Now the most important maker of lead glass in that country.

BAIL HANDLE
Plain type of LOOP HANDLE, most popular during the last half of the 18th century.

BALLOON-BACK CHAIR
Design originated *c.* 1827 in which the top rail and the bottom rail of the back are united with the uprights in the form of an oval. (See p.223, line drawing.)

BALUSTER
Form of stem or leg of furniture, as in a staircase baluster. (See pp.27, 67, **30 right, 73, 242**.)

BANDING
Veneered borders on furniture.

BAROQUE
Style in the period *c.* 1600–1730 that developed from the straight renaissance style, and was characterised by lively curved exuberant forms. It was based on classical sources and was symmetrical (whereas the subsequent ROCOCO style was asymmetrical). (See pp.66, 205, **72, 255**.)

BEAD BORDER
Series of small half balls used as border on English

silver mainly 1775–1790. (See pp.78, 100, **89, 133**.)

BIEDERMEIER STYLE
German style of the first half of the 19th century, based on a plainer version of the French Empire style.

BISCUIT
Porcelain or earthenware that has been fired but not glazed; sometimes erroneously called *bisque*. This first firing is the BISCUIT FIRING; it is usually followed by glazing and decoration. (See p.159, **202**.)

BLANC DE CHINE
Highly translucent Chinese porcelain made from the end of the Ming period (mid-17th century) until the present time. During the 17th and 18th centuries it was left unpainted, hence the name. The colour ranges from ivory to chalk-white.

BLEEDING BOWL
Shallow bowl with a single, flat handle, perhaps used for letting the blood, a common form of medical treatment. First made during the first quarter of the 17th century. (See p.67, **73**.)

BOCAGE
Grove or thicket—stylised leafy background to porcelain figures of the period 1758–1770. Bocage belonged to the ROCOCO period and almost ceased with NEO-CLASSICAL styles. However, it was used on Staffordshire earthenware figures *c.* 1810–1820. (See p.148, **190**.)

BODY
Composite material from which earthenware, stoneware or porcelain is made. In the case of porcelain the term paste is more generally used. (See p.116, **152**.)

BOMBE
Furniture or hollow ware body with swelling outline near the base. (**119**.)

BONE-ASH
Powdered bones used as an ingredient of some porcelain paste, used by Bow and Lowestoft factories and a few others in the last half of the 18th century. It can be detected by a phosphate test (see Appendix, p.253).

BONE CHINA
Type of fine white hybrid hard-paste porcelain containing BONE-ASH, invented in England at the end of the 18th century. It became the standard 19th-century English paste. Softer than hard-paste porcelain, it was not used outside England except by Sweden in the mid-19th century. (See further, p.165.)

BOULLE
Usually called BUHL WORK—19th-century term for the technique of decorating furniture with a veneer of brass and tortoiseshell in the manner of A.-C. Boulle (1642–1732), a Swiss furniture-maker who worked in France. (**255**.)

BOW-FRONT
Convex curved front on furniture, chiefly chests of drawers, made in the late 18th and early 19th centuries. (See p.215, line drawing.)

BRACKET FOOT
One consisting of two flat pieces mitred together. Used on bureaux and chests in the late 17th century and throughout the 18th century. (See p.204, **253**.)

BREAK-FRONT or BROKEN-FRONT
(Sideboards and bookcases) in which the front is on two or more planes divided by vertical breaks. (See p.212, **264**.)

BRIGHT-CUT ENGRAVING
Form of silver engraving popular *c.* 1785–1815. Broad facets were cut, resulting in 'brightness'. (See pp.81, 83, **95, 97**.)

BRITANNIA STANDARD SILVER
Silver consisting of 958 parts of pure silver in every 1000 parts of alloy (more than in sterling silver, which has 925 out of 1000). Compulsory in 1697–1720 and voluntary thereafter. Distinguished by a hallmark of Britannia which is close to the Irish Hibernia mark. (See p.235.)

BRITANNIA METAL
Cheap alloy of antimony, tin and copper, used as base for some items that were silver-ELECTROPLATED.

BROKEN-FRONT
See BREAK-FRONT

BUN FOOT
Flattened form of ball foot introduced *c.* 1660; largely used on oak and walnut furniture. (See p.204, **254**.) Replaced by bracket foot *c.* 1690.

BURMESE GLASS
Opaque ART GLASS shading from greenish yellow to light rose at the top. The surface is usually dull and sometimes glossy. Patented by the Mount Washington Glass Company in 1885. A licence was granted to Thomas Webb & Sons in England who patented this glass in England in 1886. Their colours shaded from lemon yellow to pink, and painted flowers or birds were added as decoration. Some pieces are marked with a moulded mark on the base. (See p.47, **58**.)

CABRIOLE LEG
Furniture leg with an outward bulge in the upper part, and a slight inward bend meeting the foot. (See p.224, **279**.)

CAMEL-BACK CHAIR
Design associated with Hepplewhite, from about 1780, in which the back has a hump at the top. (See p.215, line drawing.)

CAMEO
Originally a stone or shell carved in low relief, the raised design in contrast to the background. The method used for jewellery, glassware and ceramic decoration. (See p.35, **46, 47**.)

CAMEO GLASS
Object formed of CASED GLASS of two colours, often opaque white forming an OVERLAY on coloured glass. The outer layer was carved on a wheel so as to leave a design in relief on the coloured background. The process was known to the ancient Egyptians and Romans, also used during the 18th century in China. It was revived in Bohemia, France and England in the 19th century. (See p.35, **46, 47.**)

CAMPAIGN FURNITURE
Folding chairs and tables, and chests dividing into two pieces, for transport by sailors, soldiers and settlers during the 19th century. Usually fitted with recessed drawer pulls and protective brass-bound corners. (See p.218, line drawing.)

CANDELABRUM (plural CANDELABRA)
Ornamental table candle holder with at least two branches. Usually made in pairs.

CANEWARE
Unglazed STONEWARE coloured tan, developed by Wedgwood *c.* 1770.

CANTERBURY
Stand with partitions for such items as books and music, dating from the late 18th century, but Victorian examples are most common. (See p.218, line drawings.)

CARD FRET
Fretwork cut in low relief on a solid ground, characteristic of CHINESE CHIPPENDALE manner. (See p.208, **260.**)

CARLTON HOUSE DESK
Late 18th-century flat-top desk with small drawers across the back and curving around the sides. First made for the Prince of Wales (later George IV) when he was living at Carlton House. (See p.215, line drawing.)

CARNIVAL GLASSWARE
Cheap and garish pressed glass with iridescence, usually gold. Offered as prizes at country fairs and carnivals during the period 1895–1924. (See p.40, **50.**)

CARTOUCHE
Scrolled ornamentation, often enclosing a coat of arms.

CASE FURNITURE
The box-like structure forming the shell of a chest of drawers or cabinet is a case. Therefore case furniture is enclosed furniture of this type rather than open items such as chairs or tables.

CASED GLASS
Glassware made of two or more layers of different coloured glass. With cased glass an article is blown, one end is opened, and the resulting cup placed in a mould. The second colour is blown inside the original piece. The article is removed from the mould and reheated to fuse the two layers. If more than two colours are required, the process is repeated. Differs from FLASHED glass in that the cased glass outer layer is thicker, being blown, whereas the flashed glass outer layer is thin, having been applied by dipping into molten glass. (See p.35, **45.**)

CAST BORDER
Moulded silver border on waiters and salvers. (See p.68, **76.**)

CAST GLASS
Made by fusing powdered glass in a mould or by the *CIRE PERDUE* process. The method was known before the time of Christ. (See p.42, **52.**)

CELADON
Glaze used on Chinese stoneware, ranging in colour from putty to sea green. Decoration is usually incised or carved beneath the glaze. Early specimens sometimes have a brown rim. (See further, p.118.)

CHAISE LONGUE
Couch or day-bed, of which the most common examples today are Victorian. Often part of a suite of grandfather, grandmother and side chairs. (See p.225, line drawing.)

CHAMFER
To bevel off an angled corner.

CHASING
Silversmith's term for decoration indented from the front rather than embossed from the rear. Also now applied, by extension of the term, to gilding on porcelain that is worked into patterns of depth.

CHEVAL GLASS
Long dressing mirror mounted between two posts. Introduced to England late 18th century. The name derived from the mechanism regulating the position of the mirror, which was known as a 'horse'. (See p.223, line drawing.)

CHIFFONIER
Small sideboard with two-door cupboard underneath a cutlery drawer, and generally a little shelf attached to the back. (See p.218, line drawing.)

CHINESE CHIPPENDALE
Mid-18th-century English furniture in the Chinese taste. The fashion declined with the introduction of the NEO-CLASSICAL style. (See p.210, **261.**)

CHINESE SOFT-PASTE
White fine-grained Chinese porcelain with an undulating CRAZED surface. Usually painted in finest quality cobalt blue. Made from the Kang Hsi to Chi'en Lung reigns; rare.

CHINOISERIE
European decoration in the Chinese manner with a certain element of fantasy.

CHIP CARVING
Shallow faceting executed with chisel and gouge on early chests of the 13th–15th centuries.

CIRCA or C.
Latin: approximately. In connection with silver, used with hallmarks because a silver assay year was not a calendar year, for example that of London begins in May. Therefore as the date letter encompasses two calendar years, the prefix *c.* is sometimes used, whereas more accurately the two years should be given in full, for example, 1773/74.

CIRE PERDUE
Literally 'lost wax'. Glass-making process originally used for casting bronze. The model was carved in wax then encased in a mould; heat was applied and the molten wax ran out, after which the cavity of the mould was filled with molten glass.

CLASSICAL STYLE
Plain symmetrical style of classical Rome and Greece, popular in England particularly during part of the 18th century. (See p.212.)

CLOISONNE
Adjective often mistakenly used as a noun, describing a type of ENAMEL in which brass or bronze wires divide the different enamel colours. The wires appear as little lines on the finished article.

CLUB FOOT
Plain circular foot used to terminate early 18th-century legs. (See p.207, line drawing.)

CLUTHA GLASS
Glass, usually greenish, with embedded bubbles and streaks of pink and white. Patented in the 1890s in Glasgow. It was an early form of ART NOUVEAU glass.

COASTER
Holder for decanters or bottles for sliding or coasting these along a table. (See p.97, line drawing.)

COCKBEADING
Small projecting moulding applied around edges of drawer fronts on furniture from about 1730.

COLLET FOOT
Single central pedestal support used on mid-18th-century sauce boats. (See p.92, **121**.)

COMMODE
Similar to a chest of drawers but more highly decorated with gilt bronze mounts. Often decorated with marquetry, usually BOW or BOMBE shaped with a marble top. (See p.205, **255**.)

COMMONWEALTH PERIOD
Years of Puritan government under Cromwell, 1649–1660.

COMPORT
Form of dish on a stem base.

CONSOLE TABLE
Table fixed at the back against a wall and supported at the front by one or two, often scroll-shaped, legs. (See p.207, **259**.)

CONTINENTAL SILVER
Silver made on the European continent rather than in Britain. (See p.240.)

CORNUCOPIA
Vase or fruit holder in the form of a 'horn of plenty'.

COROMANDEL SCREEN
Folding lacquered Chinese screen named after the Indian south-west coast on which they were transshipped en route to Europe.

COURT CUPBOARD
From the French *court*, short. A 17th-century stand with open shelves and no doors, sometimes with a drawer enclosed in the frieze. (See p.194, **242**.)

CRACKLE GLAZE
Numerous minute surface cracks in a glaze, deliberately produced for decorative purposes.

CRANBERRY GLASSWARE
Transparent reddish-pink glass made in England and America from the mid-19th century. Sometimes called RUBY GLASS, but different to the ruby FLASHED Bohemian glass. (See p.43, **53**.)

CRAZING
Tiny surface cracks on porcelain caused by glaze and paste shrinking at different rates.

CREAMWARE
Cream-coloured earthenware with a transparent lead glaze. Developed *c.*1740–1760 mainly by Wedgwood from earlier wares to compete with porcelain. The result quite seriously affected the sales of tin-glazed enamels and exports to Europe affected sales of *FAIENCE*. Also made in Europe from *c.*1775 but not in great quantities until after 1800. Popular until about 1830. Painted decoration was both underglaze and overglaze. (See p.135, **173 back**.)

CREDENZA
Victorian chiffonier, usually with a marble top and mirrored back but seldom fitted with a drawer. The term originally referred to an early Italian marble-top sideboard. (See p.226, line drawing.)

CREST
Small motif above a coat of arms, shared by a number of families not necessarily related. May be used independently of the coat of arms on small items such as candlesticks. (See p.69, **75**.)

CRICKET TABLE
Circular table, usually oak, with tripod legs resembling cricket stumps. Originated in the 17th century, common during the 18th century.

CRISTALLO
Type of Venetian SODA GLASS made colourless with manganese, so thin it was unsuitable for cutting or carving except by diamond point originating in the 14th century. It became the standard Venetian METAL by the mid-16th century. It was decorated with gilt, enamel and *FILIGRANA*. (See p.11, **3**.)

CRIZZLING
Deterioration on the surface of glass resulting in a network of fine cracks. (See p.14, **7**.)

CROSS-BANDING
Border of veneer in which the grain runs across the band.

CUP-AND-COVER
Bulbous shape resembling a large cup with a cover, used for late 16th-century and early 17th-century table legs, bedposts and supports. (See p.193, line drawing.)

CUT-CARD FRET
Low relief fretted ornament used on mid-18th-century furniture.

CUT-CARD WORK
Decoration with a sheet of silver cut and pierced with a design, generally foliage, which was soldered to the object. Popular in the late 17th and early 18th centuries. (See p.95, line drawing.)

CUTTING
Process of cutting glass in geometric patterns to make FACETS, grooves and depressions. Glass was cut as early as the 8th century BC. (Cutting differs from ENGRAVING in that it produces regular patterns whereas engraving is generally used for inscriptions or sculpted designs.) (See p.10, 17.)

DAMASK
Heavy silk fabric with figures woven into it, largely used for hangings and upholstery. The name is derived from Damascus, which as early as the 12th century produced such material.

DAVENPORT
Small lady's desk with a lift lid and drawers fitted to the right side. Originated early in the 19th century, but most popular in Victorian times. (See p.226, line drawing.)

DECANTER
Decorative bottle into which wine was decanted, to leave the dregs, and used for serving wine at the table. Later used for spirits, cordials and even ale. Appeared in present form from the mid-18th century. (See further, p.22.)

DELFTWARE
Tin-glazed earthenware made in Holland, particularly at Delft, also in England. The English product should be referred to as English delftware. The best period in both countries was about 1640–1740. (See further, p.128, **168**.)

DENTELS
Series of small rectangular blocks with spaces between, generally placed in a cornice moulding.

DIAMOND-POINT ENGRAVING
Technique of engraving glass with a diamond point to scratch the surface. Used on Islamic glass. Superseded in the 18th century by the finer wheel-engraving and STIPPLING techniques. (See p.17,**11**.)

DIAPER
Repetitive pattern with the units of design being similar and usually connected to each other. The unit is normally diamond- or lozenge-shaped.

DIE-STAMPING
Method of pressing metal in a mould.

DOVETAILING
Method of joining wood by cutting wedge- or fan-shaped projections in one piece and correspondingly shaped slots in the other.

DOWEL
Round wooden peg used to join two pieces together.

DRAWN STEM
Drinking glass stem produced by drawing the METAL from the bowl. (See p.27, **31**.)

DROP HANDLE
Strip of metal, usually brass, suspended as a handle from a single fixing. Introduced in the second half of the 17th century and remained in favour until the early Georgian period. (See p.199, **248, 288**.)

DROP-IN SEAT
Seat consisting of a separate upholstered frame fitting into the seat rail.

DROPSIDE TABLE
Table that can be reduced in surface area by dropping the sides, which may be supported either by gatelegs or brackets. (See pp.193, 226, line drawings.)

DUMP
Solid glass of ovoid shape with a flat bottom, used as a doorstop. Made of green glass usually decorated with bubbles. Late 19th century; mostly from Yorkshire.

EBONISED WOOD
Wood blackened to look like ebony. (See p.229, line drawing.)

ELECTROPLATE
Deposition of a metal such as silver on to a base metal such as copper by electrolysis. Invented *c*. 1840. (See further, p.110.)

EMBOSSING
Relief decoration worked from the back. The detail is sometimes further refined by being *repoussé* (literally, pushed back) from the front. (See p.84, **102**.)

ENAMEL
Pigment of vitreous nature applied to glassware and porcelain as surface decoration by low-temperature FIRING. FLUX such as borax is used to lower the fusing point. The enamel firing takes place at a slightly lower temperature than the GLOST FIRING and is intended just to remelt the surface of the GLAZE. Sometimes several firings are necessary for different colours. (See further, p.120.)

ENAMEL COLOURS
See LOW-TEMPERATURE COLOURS.

ENCRUSTED

Ceramic ware with applied relief decoration, particularly popular *c.* 1820–1840. (See p.169, **212.**)

ENGRAVING

Processing of decorating (glass) by cutting the design into the surface by a diamond or other sharp instrument or by a rotating wheel. Wheel-engraving was more successful on the heavier lead crystal. (See pp.12, 16, **4, 9.**)

EPBM

ELECTROPLATE on BRITANNIA METAL. (See p.110.)

EPNS

ELECTROPLATE on NICKEL SILVER. (See p.110.)

EPERGNE

Recent term for a table centrepiece. Usually a silver frame holding a series of glass dishes or vases.

ETCHED GLASS

Glass surface decorated by using hydrofluoric acid. The glass is covered with an acid-resistant wax or varnish, through which the design is scratched with a sharp point. Acid is applied to corrode, or etch, the exposed design. Although hydrofluoric acid was discovered in 1771, it was not generally used for this purpose until the mid-19th century. (See p.18, **14.**)

FACETED GLASS

Glass that has been cut with a wheel to produce a partially flat surface. This form of decoration did not appear on English glass until the mid-18th century. It was well developed in Germany by that time and had been used earlier on Islamic and Roman glass. p.29, **36.**

FACON DE VENISE, A LA

In the style of Venice. High-quality thin SODA GLASS made throughout Europe, often by emigrant Venetians, was so called. Began in the mid-16th century and flourished throughout the 17th century. (See p.11, **3.**)

FAIENCE

Tin-glazed earthenware made in France, Germany and Scandinavia. The French term is derived from Faenza, an Italian town that exported similar wares known as *maiolica.* (See further p.128, **169.**)

FAIRINGS

Small porcelain groups made in Saxony *c.* 1860–1890 for sale at fairgrounds particularly in England. The subject is often a couple in or about to get into bed, but many other subjects were used.

FAIRYLAND LUSTRE

Type of decoration made by Wedgwood between 1915 and 1941, depicting fairyland figures. (See p.182, **231.**)

FALL-FRONT BUREAU

Writing desk with sloping front, late 17th and 18th centuries. When open, the front forms a horizontal writing surface. (See p.214, line drawing.)

FAVRILE GLASS

Developed by Tiffany *c.* 1892 in ART NOUVEAU style. It has an iridescent surface. The name 'Favrile' was registered as a trade name by Tiffany in 1894. (See p.50, **61.**)

FEATHER-BANDING

Banding of two strips, each with the grain running at an angle of 45 degrees to the edge but at a right angle to each other in the manner of a herringbone or feather. (See p.204, **253.**)

FELDSPAR (adjective FELDSPATHIC)

Essential component of almost all crystalline rocks, which fuses under a high temperature (about 1450°C) into a kind of natural glass. It is an essential constituent of most TRUE PORCELAINS, although it was sometimes replaced by SOAPSTONE (SOAPROCK). It was used for glazing Chinese and Japanese porcelain and it also formed part of some European glazes. It is also called *petuntse.*

FERN ASH GLASS

Glassware made with potash FLUX obtained by burning bracken. Mainly produced in France particularly during the 14th century where it was called *verre de fougère.*

FILIGRANA

Thread-grained, a term applied to glassware. The coloured threads inside drinking-glass stems and glass bodies are sometimes erroneously called *LATTICINO* (white threads). Filigrana originated with the Venetians in the 16th century. Filigree is the English word for filigrana.

FINIAL

Architectural term for a decorative terminal and used particularly on the cover of a pot, bowl or other receptacle. Sometimes termed a knop.

FIRE CRACK

Crack caused during firing when porcelain shrinks by as much as one-sixth in volume. Inherent in much English soft-paste porcelain, particularly when thickness varies. Common near outer edges and more often at the extreme edge. English soft-paste specimens should not be rejected because of fire cracks.

FIRING

Process of heating the ingredients of earthenware, stoneware porcelain or glass in a kiln. The temperatures vary but, broadly, for earthenware it is from 800°C; for porcelain and stoneware as much as 1450°C; and for glass 1300–1500°C.

FLAMBE

Usually deep crimson glazes often streaked with blue. Introduced during the Sung dynasty (960–1280) but far more common during the late 17th and in the 18th centuries in China. Not produced in Europe until the end of the 19th century. (See pp.118, 180, **155, 225**.)

FLASHED GLASS
Glassware in which one thin layer of coloured glass has been superimposed on to the body of the object, by dipping the object into molten glass. The outer layer is thinner than with CASED GLASS. (See p.34, **27**.)

FLAT-BACK FIGURES
Staffordshire earthenware figures made in the 19th century for cottage mantelpieces. So called because the back is flat to facilitate quantity mould production. (See p.149, **191**.)

FLAT-CHASING
Surface decoration in low fine relief. Sometimes looks like ENGRAVING, with which it can be confused. The work to be chased is rested on a bed of pitch for softness and the pattern is hammered from the front. (See further, p.73.)

FLATWARE
Term for cutlery.

FLINT GLASS
Term often used for LEAD GLASS. The name came about because the invention of lead glass by George Ravenscroft in England in the late 17th century occurred at a time when ground flint was substituted for Venetian pebbles as a source of SILICA for making the glass. Sand later replaced flint with this production but the name flint glass persisted. A modern name for flint glass is lead crystal. Crystal is a non-definitive commercial term, and the best name for the result of Ravenscroft's development is LEAD GLASS. (See p.15.)

FLUTING
Series of parallel grooves (the converse of REEDING).

FLUX
Substance added to lower a fusion point during FIRING; it is soda or potash for glass, and borax for ENAMEL.

FOLDED FOOT
Glass foot with the rim slightly turned under, making a double layer of glass to reduce the risk of chipping. Its use was rare in England after the Excise Act of 1745 imposed a tax on glass by weight, but its use never completely ceased. On objects other than drinking glasses it persisted well into the 19th century. (See p.26, line drawing.)

FOOT RIM
Rim on which ceramic holloware stands. Not found on Chinese plates. (See p.163, **207**).

FOREST GLASS
See WALDGLAS.

FRANKISH GLASS
SODA GLASS wares made in Central Europe *c.* 400–700.

FRENCH FOOT
Slender outward-curving BRACKET FOOT used on late 18th-century furniture. (See p.215, line drawing chest of drawers.)

FRIGGER
Decorative item made by a glass-worker in his own time from left-over materials. Friggers include such items as glass walking sticks, bells and rolling pins. (See p.20, **17**.)

FRIT
Vitrifiable (i.e. that will fuse and become glassy) material mixed with clay in making SOFT-PASTE (ARTIFICIAL) PORCELAIN.

GADGET
Metal rod used from the late 18th century, which has a circular spring clip to grip the foot while the GAFFER trims its rim with the shears, thereby avoiding the use of a PONTIL ROD that leaves a mark. Pontil rods were used contemporaneously with the gadget.

GADROONED
(Edge) decorated with alternative grooves and convex sections. (See pp.70, 79, **78, 90**.) Popular late 17th century; *c.* 1760–1775 and from *c.* 1800.

GAFFER
Master-worker of a team of glass-makers.

GATELEG TABLE
Table in which one or more drop leaves are supported by a leg or gate that swings away from a central fixed structure. Began during the 17th century. (See p.193, line drawing.)

GERMAN SILVER
Alloy of nickel, copper and zinc. Thought to have been brought from China in 1820, but proved too brittle for use until 1830 when Englishman Samuel Roberts, working in Berlin, produced it commercially, and by about 1836 it had been perfected as a basis for SHEFFIELD PLATE as well as copper.

GESSO
Finely ground chalk worked into a paste, used as a foundation for painted and gilded decoration.

GIBBONS GRINLING
(1648–1721) Designer and wood carver who came to England from Holland at the age of 19. He was employed by Christopher Wren. Fruit and flowers were favourite subjects. He influenced a group of carvers who worked in churches, colleges and country houses.

GILDING
The method of gilding is a useful means of dating ceramics and, to a lesser extent, glass. The main processes were: *oil- or size-gilding*, in which gold leaf was affixed with a mixture including linseed oil. It was not fired, could not be burnished, and was easily rubbed off. It was used in Europe prior to about 1755. *Honey-gilding* was used from that date; this was fired

and was fairly permanent. It can be chased and burnished, and the tone is rich. *Mercury-gilding* began around 1780, perhaps at the Derby porcelain factory. An amalgam of gold and mercury was fired with a permanent result. The colour was more brassy and not as rich as the honey-gilding that it replaced. *Unfired or oil-gilding* was continued on cheaper items during the 19th century.

GIRANDOLE
Large, branched, candelabrum. (See p.31, **37**.)

GLAZE
Finish applied to porous earthenware bodies to seal them against the penetration of liquid, and to porcelain and stoneware for decoration. True porcelain has a FELDSPATHIC glaze fired at a high temperature (up to 1450°C) to fuse the glaze. One firing only takes place for body and glaze on hard-paste porcelain. For SOFT-PASTE or ARTIFICIAL PORCELAIN, the glassy glazes are made by heating together the ingredients of glaze which are then ground to a fine powder, and either dusted on to the body or applied with water. The glaze is then fired, at a lower temperature than the first (BISCUIT) firing, thus melting the powder that spreads over the surface in a liquid form. As a result glazes on soft-paste porcelain are thick and soft. Enamel colours sink into them due to partial remelting of the glaze in the enamelling kiln. In the case of the thin, hard, feldspathic glaze, the enamel appears in high relief. There are five major types of glaze: *feldspathic; siliceous;* (similar to SODA GLASS); LEAD; TIN; and SALT. (See pp.116, 118, 126, 137, **152, 168, 175**.)

GLOST FIRING
Second firing of ceramic ware for the purpose of fusing the glaze, which is applied after the BISCUIT firing. In the case of HARD-PASTE PORCELAIN, biscuit and glaze are usually fired simultaneously.

GRANDFATHER and GRANDMOTHER CHAIRS
Victorian drawing-room chairs, the former with arms that may be open or closed in. Often in suites with a CHAISE LONGUE and side chairs. (See p.225, line drawings.)

GRAND FEU
High-temperature range (1100–1450°C) used for firing items decorated in the HIGH-TEMPERA-TURE COLOURS.

HARD-PASTE or TRUE PORCELAIN
Ceramic incorporating a fusible rock (PETUNTSE) with clay (KAOLIN) and fired at a higher temperature than SOFT-PASTE or ARTIFICIAL PORCELAIN. Most oriental and continental European porcelain is hard-paste; most 18th-century English porcelain is soft-paste.

HIGH-TEMPERATURE COLOURS
Limited range of colours of the GRAND FEU—blue, green, purple, yellow and red, obtained from cobalt, copper, manganese, antimony and iron respectively, that can withstand a temperature of between 1100–1450°C. They are used underglaze on porcelain. All red colours gave trouble and were usually used overglaze, painted after the first firing. These high-temperature colours were also the colours used to paint TIN-GLAZED earthenware. (See pp.122, 131, **160, 169**.)

HOLLOW WARE
Term for articles of hollow form such as teapots, sugar basins and cream jugs.

IMARI
Japanese porcelain made in the ARITA district from the beginning of the 18th century. Underglaze-blue and a strong overglaze-red are the predominant colours. (See further p.150, **193**.)

IMITATION DE LA BOHEME, A L'
Coloured glassware made *c.* 1840 in various countries in the popular Bohemian styles, particularly OVERLAY. Some English glass-houses employed Bohemian artisans to assist in the production of such wares. (See p.35, **45**.)

INTAGLIO
Style of decoration cut into the surface. (It is opposite to the relief decoration of CAMEO.) (See p.35, **45**.)

IRONSTONE
Type of opaque STONE CHINA, patented by Mason in 1813.

JACOBITE GLASSES
Glasses engraved with inscriptions or motifs supporting the two Jacobite pretenders to the English throne in the 18th century. (Similar *Williamite* glasses were made *c.* 1720 in memory of William III, supporting the Protestant cause.)

JAPANNING
European lacquering in imitation of the oriental. In the late 18th century the term came to be used for any type of overall painted decoration. (See p.198, **246**.)

JARDINIERE
Stand or container for flowers or plants.

JASPERWARE
Name given by Wedgwood to the hard fine-grained STONEWARE that he introduced in 1775. It is still manufactured, and the designs available include many 18th-century ones. (See further, p.134.)

JUGENDSTIL
German version of ART NOUVEAU *c.* 1895–1912.

KAGA WARE
See KUTANI.

KAKIEMON STYLE
That of the first Japanese potter (17th century) of that name. Asymmetrical designs painted in an overglaze POLYCHROME palelle of iron-red, bluish green, light blue and yellow. There is a characteristic large

area of open undecorated space in the design. (See p.150, **192**.)

KAOLIN
White clay essential to the manufacture of TRUE PORCELAIN. The other essential ingredient is FELDSPATHIC ROCK (PETUNTSE).

KINGWOOD
Sometimes confused with some cuts of ROSE-WOOD. Used in the 17th century and revived, particularly as CROSSBANDING, from 1770. The name was apparently not used before about 1850. It is a Brazilian wood related to rosewood and was originally called *violetwood*.

KLISMOS CHAIR
Ancient Greek chair widely copied in the early 19th century with a broad, curved top rail and curved legs.

KNIFE CASE or BOX
Late 18th-century cutlery container that stood on the first sideboards, which did not have cutlery drawers. (See p.213, **266**.)

KNOP
Component usually spherical or oblate. In the stem of a drinking glass, made in many styles that may be used singly or in groups. The term is also used for a FINIAL. (See p.27, **33**.)

KUTANI
Porcelain made in the remote KAGA kilns in the province of Kutani in Japan. Most examples are late 19th century or 20th century in date and are reddish-brown, often gilded. Production began in the late 17th century. (See p.152, **194**.)

KWAART
Dutch word for ware with a lead glaze added after the decoration and firing of TIN GLAZE to enhance the appearance and give a smooth glassy finish that distinguishes it from English and German wares. In England some Bristol DELFTWARE was given this lead overglaze in the first half of the 18th century. The same procedure in Italy was termed *coperta*.

LACQUER
Sap of the *lac* tree grown in China, Japan and Malaya, which was originally applied to furniture in many thin coats. It becomes extremely hard after exposure to the air. It is coloured before hardening with a variety of pigments, of which scarlet and green are the most sought-after.

LATTICINO
From the Italian *latte*, milk. Describes glass with embedded threads of white glass. It is often used where the term *FILIGRANA* would be more accurate to describe coloured threads.

LEAD GLASS
Type of glass containing a high percentage of lead, developed by George Ravenscroft *c.* 1676. The METAL is soft; it has light-reflecting qualities,

especially when FACETED. A more accurate term than FLINT GLASS or crystal. (See p.15.)

LEAD GLAZE
Transparent glaze containing lead oxide. Its use dates from pre-Roman times and is widespread.

LINENFOLD
Type of carved decoration suggestive of the folds into which hanging textiles fall, used on panels, mainly in the 16th century. (See p.193, **240, 241**.)

LOADED
(Candlestick) made of sheet-metal and filled with resin to give it weight for stability.

LOO TABLE
Oval drawing-room table, usually Victorian, used for the playing of a card game called loo. (See p.226, line drawing.)

LOOP HANDLE
Curved grip handle suspended from two points, introduced during Queen Anne's reign.

LOST WAX PROCESS
See *CIRE PERDUE.*

LOVE SEAT
Chair wide enough for two people to sit side by side. Victorian versions are usually shaped like the letter 'S'.

LOW-TEMPERATURE COLOURS or ENAMEL COLOURS
Colours of the *PETIT FEU*, fired at a lower temperature than the fusion point of the glaze. They do not need to be applied at the factory that made the article. A wide range of colours is available because many pigments are stable at low temperatures. (See p.120, **156**.)

LUSTRE
1. Candlestick decorated with prismatic cut glass pendants. The term also refers to the pendant or drop itself. Vases were also so decorated (vase lustres). Usually made of FLASHED glass made in Bohemia during the Victorian period and often OIL-GILDED. (See p.31, **38, 39**.) 2. An iridescent or metallic decoration on earthenware and occasionally on porcelain. (See p.146, **187, 188**.)

MAIOLICA
Tin-glazed earthenware made in Italy and Spain or more loosely, made in the Italian style. The name is derived from Spanish examples made in Valencia and exported via the island of Maiolica (now Majorca). The technique is the same as that of DELFTWARE and *FAIENCE*. (See pp.128, 166–169.)

MAJOLICA
Sometimes used as an anglicised version of the word *MAIOLICA,* but more correctly a trade name introduced by Minton in the last half of the 19th century for a type of earthenware covered with coloured lead glaze. Numerous other potters, including Wedgwood, made majolica, which does not

closely resemble MAIOLICA. (See p.147, **188**.)

MANDARIN PORCELAIN
Late 18th-century Chinese export porcelain. With elaborate figure subjects, mainly in rose pink, red and gold set in panels framed in underglaze-blue. (See p.120, **156**, mug.)

MANTLING
Flowing drapery around and behind a coat of arms. (See p.67, **73**.)

MARBLED GLASS
Glass with coloured streaks, resembling marble. The colours are mixed haphazardly when the glass is in liquid form. (See p.41, **51**.)

MARQUETRY
Surface ornamentation in which patterns are formed from sheets of veneer or such materials as brass, tortoiseshell or ivory, clamped together and fret-cut in one operation. (See p.197, **245**.)

MARVER
Polished iron or marble table upon which molten glass is rolled. The process is marvering.

MATTING
Type of CHASING of fine punched dots covering a silver surface to give a matt texture.

MEISSEN
Most important 18th-century European porcelain factory, and the first to make HARD-PASTE or TRUE PORCELAIN from about 1710. The town of Meissen is some 16 kilometres from the larger city of Dresden, by which name the product is sometimes known in England and Australia. (See further, p.154.)

METAL
Final product of the mixing and melting of the ingredients of glass.

MIDDLE AGES
The period between the fall of the Roman Empire (476 AD) and the RENAISSANCE. Europe had a common religious system yet culture was at a low ebb.

MILK GLASS (*MILCHGLAS* in Germany)
OPAQUE WHITE GLASS with the appearance of white porcelain. Popular during the late 17th and early 18th centuries in Venice, France, Germany, England and China. It had been made in a small way in earlier times in Venice. It had a revival in the late 19th century. It is often confused with OPALINE GLASS. (See pp.21, 44, **16**, **56**.)

MONOCHROME
(Ceramics) painted or otherwise decorated employing a single colour or coloured glaze.

MORTISE
Slot in wood to take the tongue or tenon—a method of joining.

MORTISE AND TENON
Recess (mortise) made in one piece of wood to receive a projection (tenon) in the other.

MOTHER-OF-PEARL GLASS
Type of ART GLASS *c*. 1870-1900 with a double FLASHING. The inner opaque layer is blown into a patterned mould and then covered with a flashing of clear or coloured glass. Air bubbles are trapped in the moulded spaces that form the internal pattern. The object is again covered with clear glass flashing, which is acid-dipped to produce a matt surface. (See p.47, **57**.)

MOULD-BLOWN GLASS
Made by blowing the molten glass *paraison* (bubble) into a mould. The glass can be removed from the mould, reheated and enlarged by blowing. The process was used in Egypt in the 2nd-4th centuries AD. It was adapted for machinery at the end of the 19th century, for making bottles and electric light globes.

MOULD-PRESSED GLASS
Glass made by machine process developed in America *c*. 1827 to produce cheap copies of cut glass. Also used in England from about 1830. There are usually seam marks where sections have been joined, also by machine.

MUFFLE
Inner chamber of a kiln into which ceramic objects are placed to keep them from the flames and smoke during firing in the PETIT FEU, especially during the firing of ENAMEL decoration.

MULE CHEST
Chest having small drawers to the bottom so that small items could be made accessible without disturbing the main contents. Made from the end of the 16th century.

NEO-CLASSICAL
New classical style introduced by Adam at the end of the 18th century. Excavations at Pompeii and Herculaneum in the middle of the 18th century were an influence that shaped the light and graceful neo-classical lines, which followed the heavier classical forms of the Palladian period. (See pp.212, **269**.)

OGEE FEET
Used on CASE FURNITURE during the ROCOCO period. (See p. 208, **260**.)

OIL-GILDING
See GILDING.

OPALINE GLASS
Slightly translucent type of glass, opacified with the ashes of calcined bones. It is less dense and has more sheen than OPAQUE WHITE GLASS. The name originated at the Baccarat factory *c*. 1823, however the process was thought to have been made first at Murano (Venice) in the 17th century. The best French pieces were made *c*. 1840-1870. Made in various hues such as pale green, turquoise, pink, coral, yellow and

red. It has been MOULD BLOWN and MOULD PRESSED. (See p.44, **56**.)

OPAQUE WHITE GLASS

Type of tin oxide opacified white glass having the appearance of white porcelain. Often decorated with enamel, the surface has a greater density than, and without the sheen of, OPALINE GLASS. Made from the 15th century in Venice and in the late 17th and in the 18th centuries in France, Germany, and England. (See p.21, **16**.)

ORMOLU

Gilding with gold paste. Gilding bronze with an amalgam of mercury and gold. Often used in a generic, imprecise, manner. (See p.205, **255**.)

OVERLAY

Outer layer on CASED GLASS.

PAD FOOT

Similar to a club foot (plain circular foot used to terminate early 18th-century legs) but resting on a disc or pad. (See p.205, line drawing.)

PAKTONG

Alloy of copper, nickel and zinc, imported into England from China c. 1750–1800. Used in the manufacture of candlesticks, grates and fenders.

PALLADIAN STYLE

Severe version of the architectural styles of ancient Rome and Greece based on the designs of Italian architect Andrea Palladio (1518–1580). In vogue in England from about 1730, it was not completely replaced there by the ROCOCO style that was fashionable from around 1740. (See p.206, **257**.)

PAP BOAT

Small sauce boat made between about 1710 and 1830, used for feeding infants or invalids. Without feet or handle.

PAPIER MACHE

Material made from paper pulp, glue, chalk and sometimes sand. Originated in Persia and introduced to England from France. In 1772 Henry Clay of Birmingham patented a form of this material and it was used for furniture and other items.

PARIAN

Type of porcelain extensively used for figure-modelling in the last half of the 19th century. Similar to a hard BISCUIT porcelain and resembling marble, from which the name is derived. (Marble for ancient Greek statues came from the island of Paros.) (See further, p.173, **214**.)

PARQUETRY

Design of wood block floors laid in such a way as to contrast the grain. The term now also used to describe furniture veneers applied on the same principle.

PASTE

Composite material from which porcelain is made (excluding glaze).

PASTILLE-BURNER

Ornamental object in which may be placed a smouldering scented substance. In the 19th century many were made in the form of cottages.

PATCH MARK

Patch bare of glaze on the under side of the base of some figures due to the object having stood on clay pads in the kiln during GLOST FIRING. Usually an indication of 18th-century Derby. (See p.159, **201**.)

PATE DE VERRE

Literally, glass paste. Produced by grinding glass to a powder, coloured then fused by firing in a mould. Mainly from the late 19th century. (See p.42, **52**.)

PATERA (plural PATERAE)

Round flat ornament usually in low relief on such items as friezes—often a rosette. May also be painted or inlaid. (See p.69, **77**.)

PATINA

The surface changes occuring as the result of the passage of time are referred to as patination. Good patination enhances value. Usually tops of tables are lighter in colour than the bases because they are subject to more light. There is nothing more valuable to a collector than a knowledge of the effects of time on the things in which he is interested.

PEACHBLOW GLASS

American ART GLASS intended to resemble the peach-bloom glaze of Chinese porcelain. A typical version was that made by the New England Glass Company from 1885. This was uncased glass and shaded from an opaque cream to deep rose.

PEARLWARE

Improved CREAMWARE introduced by Wedgwood c. 1779. It is more bluish-white than creamware. Continued in use beyond the middle of the 19th century.

PEMBROKE TABLE

Small table with two flaps supported by hinged brackets. Introduced third quarter of the 18th century. (See p.215, line drawing.)

PETIT FEU

Low-temperature (700-900°C) or MUFFLE kiln used to fix the LOW-TEMPERATURE COLOURS used in overglaze enamel decoration.

PETUNTSE

Fusible rock, forms the essential part of TRUE PORCELAIN. Gives porcelain its hardness and translucency. (See FELDSPAR.)

PIER GLASS

Looking-glass designed to go on a pier between two windows.

PIERCED WORK

Silver and Sheffield plate decorated during the last half of the 18th century, either with a small fret-saw or, particularly in the case of Sheffield plate, by stamping. The fashion was extended to CREAM-WARE and porcelain. Pierced covers and necks to vases mean they were intended for POT POURRI. More recently, George Owen (died 1917) made elaborately pierced or reticulated porcelain for the Worcester Porcelain Company. This was derived from Japanese ideas introduced to Worcester in 1872. (See pp.91, 176, **120, 219**.)

PINCHBECK
Alloy resembling gold, containing about five parts of copper and two of zinc. Named after its inventor, Christopher Pinchbeck, an English watch-maker who died in 1732.

PLATE
From the Spanish *plata*, silver. It came to mean wares made of either gold or silver, and now sometimes implies imitations of such wares. It is a term to be avoided even when implying plated wares—Old Sheffield plate or electroplate being more definitive.

POLYCHROME
Several-coloured decoration. In the case of ceramics, also used for ware in only two colours, in contrast to MONOCHROME.

PONTIL (sometimes PUNTY)
Iron rod to which a partly made object of molten glass is transferred from the blow-pipe on which the metal has been gathered from the melting pot and MARVER, and tentatively shaped by blowing. The final shaping, shearing and attachment of handles are done when the piece is on the pontil. The rough mark on the bottom of a glass where the pontil was attached was sometimes ground smooth (between about 1780 and 1820) or star-cut. The mark almost ceased by about 1850 and does not appear on some glass made from the late 18th century, due to the use of the GADGET.

PORCELAIN
Most recently introduced type of ceramic ware. Made in China from the 8th century AD although not in its more familiar form until the Yuan Dynasty (1280–1368). Made in Europe from the 18th century. The European definition requires some degree of translucency. The essential Chinese requirement was one of resonance. (See p.117, **153**.)

PORRINGER
Two-handled vessel that in most cases originally had a lid. The use is to some extent doubtful—it may have been to serve a kind of porridge. In silver form popular in the late 17th and early 18th centuries, although some were made later. (See p.96, **128**.)

PORTLAND VASE
Originally known as the Barberini vase because it was originally owned by Matteo Barberini, Pope Urban VIII (1623–1644). CAMEO GLASS, its origin and early history are unknown but it is thought to be Roman glass of the 1st century AD. It was smashed in 1845 whilst on display in the British Museum, where it still resides in a restored form. Two accurate detailed copies were made—a Wedgwood JASPER series in 1790, of which sixteen remain, and a CAMEO glass example made in 1873 by John Northwood of Stourbridge. Thousands of jasper copies have been made subsequently. (See p.134, **172**.)

POTASH GLASS
Glassware made with potash, an alkali FLUX alternative to soda. Becomes rigid more quickly on cooling, is harder and more suitable for cutting and engraving.

POT POURRI
PIERCED vessel made to contain herbs that emit aromatic perfumes.

POTTERY
Generic term for all ceramic wares, but in normal use it more accurately describes wares that are not porcelain.

POUNCE BOX
Pierced box fitted to the ink stand for shaking pounce over writing paper. Pounce was the powder of gum sandarach, a Moroccan tree, used to prepare unsized paper for writing. The word sandarach became confused with 'sand', and hence arose the fallacy that sand was used in lieu of blotting paper.

PRATTWARE
Lead-glazed earthenware 1790–1820 with a light-weight body. Decorated with relief-moulded decoration in conjunction with under-glaze colours, mainly brown ochre, dull blue and green. (See further, p.144, **185**.) Also describes mid-19th-century polychrome printed ware such as pot lids. (See further p.144, **186**.)

PRESS-MOULDED
(Pottery and porcelain) made by pressing clay into a mould and removing it for firing after it becomes cheese hard. (See p.160, **203**.)

PRUNTS
Blobs of glass applied to a drinking vessel as decoration and also to afford a firm grip. (See p.12, **5**.)

PUNCHED EDGE
(Silver) rim decorated with a punch, in lieu of BEADING or REEDING; less valuable than the latter edges.

QUAICH
Scottish word for a cup—a low, two-handled bowl made in the 17th century. (See p.96, line drawing.)

QUEENSWARE
Cream-coloured lead-glazed earthenware developed by Wedgwood *c*. 1765, named after Queen Charlotte—an improved CREAMWARE. He used less lead and more clay in the glaze than on the earlier creamware. This glaze had a transparent lustrous finish.

RAISING
Hammering from ingot or sheet into items such as sauce boat.

REEDING
Series of raised parallel mouldings, the converse of FLUTING.

REFORMATION
Religious revolution against the Catholic Church by the Protestants in the 16th century.

REGENCY STYLE
English style in the period *c.* 1800-1825, which followed the French Empire style. Egyptian and Grecian motifs were fashionable. Dark woods with exotic grains, highly polished surfaces, brass inlay and metal mounts are characteristic. (See further p.218.)

RENAISSANCE
Literally rebirth—of interest in classical cultures of Rome and Greece, at the end of the MIDDLE AGES. At its height in 15th-century Italy; spread to France and England in the 16th century.

REPOUSSE
See EMBOSSING.

RESTORATION
Period beginning in 1660 when the monarchy (in the person of Charles II) was reinstated in England after the Puritan COMMONWEALTH.

RETICULATED
Decorated with interlaced or PIERCED WORK. (See p.176, **219.**)

ROCK CRYSTAL
Natural quartz almost colourless and nearly translucent. Very nearly pure SILICA. It has been carved since ancient times and early glass-makers sought to imitate it.

ROCOCO
Style in the period 1735-1767 in England, beginning and ending earlier in France. It developed from the BAROQUE. In addition to flowing lines, an essential characteristic is asymmetry, which is the main difference between it and baroque. The asymmetrical fashion was encouraged by the imported Japanese porcelains of KAKIEMON. There was a rococo revival *c.* 1830-1865. (See pp.69, 151, **79, 192.**) (See p.69, **79.**)

ROEMER or ROMER
Type of wine glass, usually green, made principally in the Rhineland and the Netherlands from the 16th century. (See p.12, **5.**)

ROLLED GOLD
Analagous to Sheffield plate. A layer of gold is applied by bonding to one or both sides of a sheet of metal, which may then be rolled to any desired thickness.

ROMAN GLASS
Glass made throughout the period of the Roman Empire, *c.* 100 BC-400 AD. Includes glass made in Alexandria and Syria, and in Italy, Gaul, the Rhineland and possibly England. (See p.9, **1.**)

ROSEWOOD
Dense timber with a dark purplish black grain, almost all imported from Brazil, very popular during the Regency period although it was used to a small extent during the last half of the 18th century. (See p.222, **277.**)

ROUNDEL
Round decorative motif found on chests during the 13th to 15th centuries.

RUBY GLASS
Strictly speaking, thin red FLASHING over colourless glass. However, in England and Australia the term is used for CRANBERRY GLASS. As custom is unlikely to change, it is probably better to regard it as an alternative name for cranberry glass. (See p.43, **53.**)

SABRE LEG
Leg curving in the manner of a sabre, widely used on the front legs of early 19th-century chairs. (See p.221, **273.**)

SALT-GLAZED STONEWARE
STONEWARE glazed with salt, of which the earliest European ware was made in the Rhineland from the 14th century and in England from the late 17th century until the present time. Made by throwing common salt into the kiln. (See pp.124, 137, **163, 175.**)

SALVER
Silver serving article of more than 20 centimetres diameter with small feet and without handles. Smaller items are WAITERS; larger ones with handles are trays. (Trays may or may not have feet.) (See p.70, **78.**)

SAMSON COPIES
Porcelain copies of Chinese, European and English porcelain made in hard-paste porcelain by the firm Edmé Samson & Cie Paris from *c.* 1840. Usually fake marks such as Chelsea anchors are too large and colours too bright. The firm claimed that they were marked with the letter 'S' (in addition to the mark of the factory that produced the original). However, today that 'S' letter is rarely seen.

SATIN GLASS
Satin-finished glass, the effect produced with hydrofluoric acid. The design is protected and the acid attacks the background to the design, leaving a matt smooth surface. Late 19th century. (See p.47, **57.**)

SATSUMA
Fine CRACKLED glazed Japanese pottery decorated with ENAMEL COLOURS and gilding. (See p.152, **195, 196.**)

SCALE GROUND
Background pattern on ceramics simulating overlapping fish scales. Popular at Worcester 1760-1785. Usually underglaze-blue but other colours were also

used. (See p.163, **206**.)

SCONCE

Branched light-holder attached to the wall.

SECESSION MOVEMENT

Viennese interpretation of ART NOUVEAU that began in the last years of the 19th century. It had a 'whiplash' effect and more geometric characteristics than the earlier flowing plant forms of ART NOUVEAU.

SERPENTINE

Double-curved surface (often the front of a chest), with the centre slightly projecting.

SETTEE

Seat about twice the width of a chair sometimes with low arms and back.

SETTLE

All-wood settee with solid wood arms. Usually large, sometimes with a lift seat for storage. Originated in Tudor times.

SEVRES

Porcelain factory established at Sèvres between Paris and Versailles in 1753, when the older Vincennes factory was moved to Sèvres. Royal support was necessary to keep the factory solvent during its early years. SOFT-PASTE was made until about 1772 when HARD-PASTE was made in quantity. Soft-paste was abandoned by about 1800. Sèvres replaced MEISSEN as the European style-setter from the Seven Years War (1756–1763), which isolated Germany. (See p.155, **198**.)

SGRAFFITO

Cutting through outer layer of SLIP. (See p.127.)

SHAGREEN

Sort of untanned leather from the Middle East, from the hide of horse or wild ass, with a granular surface produced by pressing small seeds into the skins when wet. Later made from shark skin. Used particularly in the 18th century for covering boxes, fan cases, parasol handles and many other such items.

SHEFFIELD PLATE

Silver fused on to a base metal, usually copper, by heat and pressure, and the resultant sheet then rolled. Main period c. 1760–1860. (See p. 108, **147**.)

SIDEBOARD

Originally in Elizabethan times a table or, literally, a side board. Developed by Adam and others in the last half of the 18th century into its present form. (See p.213, **266**.)

SILICA

Mineral essential for glass-making. The most common form is sand. Pure silica can now be melted to form glass but such a high temperature is required that the process is impractical, and for glass-making a FLUX is necessary.

SILVER-ELECTROPLATED GLASS

Type of art glass with an electroplated deposit of silver on the surface. Patented in England in 1889. The style was popular c. 1890–1920.

SINGLE-STRUCK

(Flatware) decorated on one side only, for example Scottish King pattern.

SLAG GLASS

Glass that is streaky like marble due to the inclusion of waste slag. Usually formed by PRESS MOULDING. Main period c. 1875–1890. (See p.41, **51**.)

SLIP

Potter's clay mixed with water to a semi-liquid, creamy consistency. (See p.126, **165**.)

SLIP-CAST

Pottery and porcelain models made by pouring slip into plaster of Paris moulds. Intricately modelled ware can be cast by this method, much finer than PRESS-MOULDED figures. Slip-casting was introduced in England c. 1745 and was used in the Chelsea and Derby factories. (See p.158, **200**.)

SLIPWARE

General term for pottery decorated predominantly with SLIP. (See further, p.126.)

SOAPSTONE or SOAPROCK

Fusible rock used as an alternative to the normal FELDSPATHIC rock used in the manufacture of TRUE PORCELAIN, resulting in thin, precise BODIES. Used in England c. 1748–1820 by Lund's Bristol, Worcester, Caughley and Liverpool. (See p.161, **205**.)

SODA GLASS

Glass of which the alkali FLUX consists of soda rather than potash. Light in weight, non-resonant. It is slow to set and lends itself to plastic shaping rather than cutting. (See p.11, **3**.)

SOFT-PASTE or ARTIFICIAL PORCELAIN

Made of clay with powdered glass instead of the fusible FELDSPATHIC rock (which is used with HARD-PASTE or TRUE PORCELAIN). Fired at a lower temperature than hard-paste. Made in the early stages of porcelain production in Italy, France and England.

SPADE FOOT

Tapered square block foot, much used in the late 18th century. (See p.217, **269**.)

SPANGLED GLASS

ART GLASS with an OVERLAY of glass of various tints, covering an inner layer of clear glass embedded with flakes of mica. Originated in America c. 1883. (See p.44, **56**.)

SPATTER GLASS

ART GLASS of OVERLAY GLASS encasing small multicoloured pieces of glass. (See p.44, **56**.)

SPLAT
Vertical piece of wood forming the centre strut of a chair back. (See p.206, line drawing.)

SPLIT BALUSTER
Wooden baluster split in half longitudinally and applied decoratively to 17th-century furniture.

SPOON TRAY
Narrow tray to hold a hot or wet spoon.

SPRIGGING
Ceramics term for the process of attaching separately made parts to the main body with thin SLIP.

SPRING TOOL
Used for holding molten glass during manufacture. The mark left by the tool on the edge of the bowl is a major way of distinguishing an old glass from a reproduction.

SPUR MARKS
Found under some ceramics where the article was rested on small supports during firing. Chelsea plates are good examples.

SQUEEZED MARKS
Hallmarks placed on the bottom of stems of FLATWARE before completion and stretched or squeezed during manufacture. The practice had ceased by about 1780.

STILE
Vertical member of a piece of furniture such as the uprights of a panelled chest. (See p.193.)

STIPPLE ENGRAVING
Method of decorating glass by building up the design with minute dots marked with a diamond point. (See p.18, **12**.)

STONE CHINA
Type of fine white porcelaineous STONEWARE sometimes slightly translucent. First developed c. 1800 by John Turner of Staffordshire. (See p.138, **176**.)

STONEWARE
Non-porous pottery close to porcelain but without porcelain's translucency. First made in China in 1100–400 BC and in Europe in the 14th century. (See further, p.124.

STOURBRIDGE
Worcestershire town that has been an important glass-making place since the 16th century.

STRETCHER
Horizontal member used to brace the legs of such items as chairs and tables.

STRINGING
Narrow band or line of wood or other substance used as inlay to contrast with surrounding veneer. (See p.202, **252**.)

STUDIO ART
Objects made by artist-craftsmen rather than workers in factories. The ware is designed, modelled and decorated by the designer or under the designer's immediate supervision. Many pieces are signed. From c. 1860. (See p.159, **178**.)

STUFFED-OVER SEAT
Completely covered with upholstery, in contrast to a DROP-IN SEAT.

SULPHIDE
Silvery opaque medallion enclosed in transparent glass. Originated last half of the 18th century, later used in paperweights.

SUNG GLAZE
Term used by Doulton to designate a glaze used by that firm in the early 20th century. The glaze is similar to some mottled FLAMBE glazes.

SUTHERLAND TABLE
Victorian gateleg tea table with a narrow top and deep drops. (See p.226, line drawing.)

SWAG
NEO-CLASSICAL motif in the form of a suspended festoon of foliage or drapery. (See p.206, **258**.)

TALLBOY
Alternative name for a chest on chest, the top above eye level and not veneered or polished. (See p.210, line drawing.)

TANTALUS
Two or more decanters held in a case or stand, named after the mythological figure who was chained in water in such a way that he could not drink. (See p.25, **29**.)

TAPERSTICK
Taper holder made in small candlestick shape until about 1780 when coiled tapers came into use. Much less common than candlesticks, therefore of about the same value despite the smaller size.

TAZZA
Late 17th- and early 18th-century salver supported on a cylindrical centre column. (See p.72, **80**.)

TENON
Wooden tongue that fits into a slot or mortise. It may or may not be secured with a wooden pin.

THERMO-LUMINESCENCE TEST
Objects that have been fired in a kiln can be dated scientifically. All materials receive and emit luminescence over a lengthy period. When ceramics are fired at a temperature over several hundred degrees, there is no luminescence at all. The amount of luminescence absorbed for a known type of material can be measured, and the time span since firing calculated. Accuracy is within 10 per cent, and the newest object dated by this method is as recent as 70 years of age.

THREAD BORDER
Finely REEDED border used on English silver, mainly between about 1785 and 1800. (See pp.68, 83, **74**, **97**.)

TIGER WARE
Term used in Elizabethan England for Rhenish STONEWARE with a mottled brown glaze over a greyish body. (See p.125, **163**.)

TIN GLAZE
Glaze rendered white and opaque by the addition of tin oxide.

TOBY JUG
Earthenware drinking jug usually in the form of a seated man holding a mug and pipe and wearing a tricorn hat. Other models were also made. The original period was 1748–1795 but Toby jugs have been reproduced extensively since that period.

TODDY LIFTER
Late 18th-century and early 19th-century decanter-shaped object for lifting toddy or punch from a bowl to a glass. There was a hole in the base which was placed in the punch bowl. A thumb was put over the neck end, and the air pressure kept the liquid in the base while it was lifted to the glass.

TRAFALGAR CHAIR
Dining chair with a rope twist back rail. First made in the year of the battle of Trafalgar, 1805. The rope perhaps symbolised the Royal Navy. (See p.221, **274**.)

TURKEY COFFEE POT
Coffee pot with a pouring lip rather than a spout, the purpose originally being to take the less dense coffee at the top—the thick Turkish coffee being much heavier at the bottom. Mostly last half of the 18th century. (See p.78, **87**, **88**.)

TURKEY WORK
Imitation of carpets woven with knotted pile, found on some 17th-century chairs. (See p.195, **244**.)

TURNING
Woodworking process dating to Egyptian times. Produced by the application of cutting tools to a rotating surface. The device for turning the wood is a lathe.

VASELINE GLASS
Glass made with the addition of a small amount of uranium, producing a yellowish green, greasy-looking surface. Late 19th century. (See p.47, **57**.)

VENEER
Slices of figured wood glued to a backing timber. The method was used from the RESTORATION. Veneers of the 19th century are more thinly cut by machine. There is a fallacy that veneered timber is secondary to solid timber.

VERNIS MARTIN
(French) Martin's varnish. Painted, varnished scenes on furniture. Began *c.* 1730, most examples are from the 19th-century.

VERRE DE FOUGERE
See FERN ASH GLASS.

VITRIFIED
Fused at high temperature into a glassy form which is waterproof, i.e. porcelain and stoneware as opposed to earthenware.

VITRINE
Cabinet with clear glass door for displaying such items as pieces of porcelain. (See p.225, **280**.)

WAINSCOT
Panelling of a room or CASE FURNITURE. Up to the 17th century it also meant oak. (See p.199, **248**.)

WAITER
Small salver less than 20 centimetres in diameter.

WALDGLAS
Literally, forest glass. Produced in glass-houses in the forests of Europe in the Middle Ages. Usually green, yellow or brown. In Germany Potash replaced soda as the flux from *c.* 1000 AD. Similar glass was made elsewhere in Europe, particularly in France and Holland.

WELLINGTON CHEST
Narrow chest of drawers made from the early 19th century. (See p.223, line drawing.)

WHATNOT
Tier of shelves supported by turned posts. Mostly Victorian, although a few were made earlier. (See p.218, line drawing.)

WHIELDON WARE
Mid-18th-century English pottery by Thomas Whieldon and later by others. A cream-coloured earthenware body covered with a coloured surface. The colour was sponged on and covered with a clear glaze, which when fired intermingled the colours. (See p.133, **170**.)

WILLIAMITE GLASSES
See JACOBITE GLASSES.

WINE COOLER
Lead-lined box for keeping wine bottles cool, sometimes on legs. In the Regency period, often made in the form of a sarcophagus (ancient stone coffin). Mostly made in the last half of the 18th century. (See p.215, line drawing.)

WINE-GLASS COOLER
Bowl to hold iced water in which wine glasses could be washed and cooled, with a pouring spout at one or both ends, which was used to support the foot of the glass as it rested flat in the bowl.

WINE TASTER
Small shallow bowl of silver with a domed centre against which the colour of wine could be seen. Made up to the end of the 18th century. (See p.96, line drawing.)

WING CHAIR
Comfortable large upholstered chair with side pieces at head level.

Bibliography

Art Nouveau and Art Deco

BATTERSBY, Martin. *The Decorative Twenties.* London, 1969.

—— *The Decorative Thirties.* London, 1971.

RHEIMS, Maurice. *The Age of Art Nouveau.* London, 1966.

Ceramics

EYLES, Desmond. *Royal Doulton 1815–1915.* London, 1965.

GODDEN, Geoffrey. *Encyclopaedia of British Pottery and Porcelain Marks.* London, 1964.

—— *Godden's Guide to English Porcelain.* London, 1978.

—— *Illustrated Encyclopaedia of British Pottery and Porcelain.* London, 1966.

—— *Oriental Export Market Porcelain.* London, 1979.

HODGKIN, J. E. and E. *English Delftware.* London, 1948.

HOWARD, David. *Chinese Armorial Porcelain.* London, 1974.

IMBER, D. *Collecting European Delft and Faience.* London, 1968.

PAYTON, M. & G. *Observer's Book of Pottery and Porcelain.* London, 1973.

SAVAGE, George. *18th-century English Porcelain.* London, 1964.

—— *Illustrated Dictionary of Ceramics.* London, 1976.

SANDON, Henry. *Illustrated Guide to Worcester Porcelain,* 1751 to 1793. London, 1969.

—— *Royal Worcester Porcelain from 1862 to the Present Day.* London, 1973.

WILLS, Geoffrey. *English Pottery and Porcelain.* London, 1969.

Furniture

ANDREWS, John. *The New Price Guide to Antique Furniture.* Woodbridge, Suffolk, 1978.

EDWARDS, Ralph and JOURDAIN, Margaret. *Georgian Cabinet Makers 1700–1800.* London, 1955.

JOY, Edward T. *English Furniture 1800–1851.* London, 1977.

HONOUR, Hugh. *Cabinet Makers and Furniture Designers.* London, 1969.

JOURDAIN, Margaret and FASTNEDGE, Ralph. *Regency Furniture 1795–1820.* London 1948, rev. by Ralph Fastnedge 1965.

MACQUOID, Percy, and EDWARDS, Ralph. *The Dictionary of English Furniture,* 2nd edn. 3 vols. rev. Ralph Edwards. London, 1960.

TOMLIN, Maurice. *English Furniture.* London, 1972.

WILLS, Geoffrey. *English Furniture 1550–1760.* London.

—— *English Furniture 1760–1900.* London.

286

Glass

GARNER, Phillipe. *Emile Galle.* London, 1976.

DAVIS, Cecil. *English Drinking glasses of the 18th Century.* London.

GROVE, Lee and TUTTLE, Charles. *Carved and Decorated European Glass.* Vermont, USA.

HAYNES, E. B. *Glass Through the Ages.* London, 1948.

LALIQUE, Claude. *Lalique Par Lalique.* Lausanne, 1977.

NEWMAN, Harold. *Illustrated Dictionary of Glass.* London, 1977.

SAVAGE, George. *Art Glass.* London, 1965.

WILLS, Geoffrey. *Victorian Glass.* London, 1977.

Silver

ALBRECHT, Kurt. *Australian Gold and Silversmiths.* Melbourne, 1969.

BRADBURY, F. *Guide to Marks of Origin on British and Irish Silver Plate.* London, various editions.

—— *History of Old Sheffield Plate.* London, 1912.

GRIMWADE, Arthur. *London Goldsmiths, 1697-1837. Their marks and Lives.* London, 1976.

HARRIS, Ian. *The Price Guide to Antique Silver.* Woodbridge, Suffolk 1969.

HAWKINS, J. B. *Australian Silver 1800-1900.* Sydney, 1973.

HONOUR, Hugh. *Goldsmiths and Silversmiths.* London, 1971.

HUGHES, B. and T. *Three Centuries of English Domestic Silver 1500-1820.* London.

JACKSON, C. J. *English Goldsmiths and Their Marks.* London, 1949.

More specialised bibliographies may be obtained by reference to some of the above books. For example, *Godden's Guide to English Porcelain* leads one to a detailed list of books relating to individual porcelain factories.

Index Numbers shown in bold type indicate an illustration on that page.

Glass

Silver

Ceramics

Furniture